UFOs - WICKED THIS WAY COMES
The Dark Side Of The Ultra-Terrestrials!

By Timothy Green Beckley
With Sean Casteel, Scott Corrales,
Peter Robbins, Brad Steiger and Tim R. Swartz

UFOS – WICKED THIS WAY COMES: THE DARK SIDE OF THE ULTRA-TERRESTRIALS

**Dedicated To My Good Friend
William Kern**

POST OFFICE BOX 753
NEW BRUNSWICK, NJ 08903

UFOS - WICKED THIS WAY COMES
THE DARK SIDE OF THE ULTRA-TERRESTRIALS

GLOBAL COMMUNICATIONS

UFOs - Wicked This Way Comes
The DARK SIDE Of The Ultra-Terrestrials!

By Timothy Green Beckley

With: Sean Casteel, Scott Corrales, Peter Robbins, Brad Steiger and Tim R. Swartz

Copyright © 2013 - Global Communications
All Rights Reserved

ISBN-10: 160611-158-2

ISBN-13: 978-1-60611-158-1

Printed in the United States of America

No part of this book may be reproduced, stored in retrieval system or transmitted in any form by any means, electronic, mechanical, photocopying, recording or otherwise without the express permission of the publisher. Please address any questions about this book to: mrufo8@hotmail.com

Timothy Green Beckley: Editorial Director

Carol Ann Rodriguez: Publishers Assistant

Tim R. Swartz: Editor

Sean Casteel: Associate Editor

William Kern: Associate Editor

Illustrations by: Carol Ann Rodriguez and Gene Duplantier

Cover Graphic: www.dreamstime.com

For Free Subscription To The Conspiracy Journal Write:

Tim Beckley/Global Communications

Box 753, New Brunswick, NJ 08903

Sign Up On Line: MRUFO8@hotmail.com

www.ConspiracyJournal.Com

www.TeslasSecretLab.Com

UFOS – WICKED THIS WAY COMES: THE DARK SIDE OF THE ULTRA-TERRESTRIALS

CONTENTS

EXPOSING THE FEAR FACTOR	6
STRANGE EFFECTS OF FLYING SAUCERS	15
THE STRANGEST UFO ENCOUNTER EVER	41
UFO BEINGS DIRECT MY LIFE	49
FLYING SAUCER BASE IN FOOTHILLS	57
PROBING THE MYSTERY OF THE UNEXPLAINABLE RADIO TRANSMISSIONS	61
THE NIGHT ET RETURNED HOME	75
A NIGHT OF TERROR ABOARD A MOTHERSHIP	85
MAN'S LIFE DRAMATICALLY ALTERED AFTER CLOSE ENCOUNTER	95
PROVEN BEYOND A DOUBT!	99
SECRET MILITARY BASES AND UFOs	106
THE CRAWLING LIGHTS	111
BOB SHORT IS THE MAN WHO TALKS WITH SPACE BEINGS	117
"VEGETABLE MAN"—A SEMI-ABDUCTEE	125
UNDERSEA SAUCER ATTACK!	133
A WIDE—AND WILD—VARIETY OF ALIENS	141
AUTHOR BIOGRAPHIES FOR ADDITIONAL MATERIAL	154
KARLA TURNER REVEALS WHY THE ALIENS ARE WICKED	159
AN EXCERPT FROM KARLA TURNER'S "TAKEN"	169
AN EXCERPT FROM KARLA TURNER'S "MASQUERADE OF ANGELS"	187
ENTERING THE DARK REALMS OF THE ULTRA-TERRESTRIALS	203
EXTRATERRESTRIALS, ULTRA-TERRESTRIALS, OR DEMONS?	215
CONTROVERSIAL DEATHS OF UFO INVESTIGATORS, RESEARCHERS AND AUTHORS	225
CALLING DOWN THE ULTRA-TERRESTRIAL SPIRITS	255

EXPOSING THE FEAR FACTOR
By Timothy Green Beckley

ALL is not as rosy in UFOland as it might appear on the surface!

Stories of encounters with the supposedly friendly "all-too-cute" ETs are NOT always the norm, and represent only one side of the coin (or disc since we are referring to flying saucers). Little Elliot may have befriended Steven Spielberg's cozy, cuddly alien, but all too often our almond eyed visitors have their own agenda, which frequently puts them at odds with our earthly plans and aspirations. They have been known to abduct, dice and slice and put us through a world of utter discontent.

Not only can the Ultra-Terrestrials—my favorite term for any entity that comes out of or is associated with a UFO, since we cannot really determine their origin, be it interplanetary or more close to home, perhaps from a parallel universe—be damned ornery, but they have the power to interfere with both our physical and mental states and put fear into our hearts. Thus the term "Fear Factor." Even the peace-loving contactees of the early days of UFOlogy were made aware of the Ultra-Terrestrials' shenanigans.

In our previously published book, "**Round Trip To Hell In A Flying Saucer**," we documented the many instances of shape-shifting, levitation and the presence of transparent or translucent entities that can oftentimes wreak havoc on an entire household following what might seem like a benign close encounter but which ends up going well beyond a one night cosmic stand. Likewise, in the book "**Evil Empire Of The ETs and Ultra-Terrestrials**," I pointed out how the occupants of the craft we have come to identify as Unidentified Flying Objects—UFOs! —have some of the same characteristics as spirits from the dark corridors of demonology and have been known to produce the same sort of phenomena at landing sites as you would find in a haunted house or at a séance.

I've chatted for hours with Coast to Coast Am host George Noory about such eerie matters and most of the conversation has been preserved on You Tube, where you can find the interviews by simply typing in my name and Coast to Coast and all manner of links will pop up in a matter of mere seconds.

There are numerous aspects of this dark side of UFOs that we must examine closely, to include:

+ The connection between UFOs, demons and possibly Satan himself.

+ The fascination for and the link between Nazism, occultism and German-made flying saucers.

+ The ghastly exercise of blood draining and human sacrifice throughout antiquity and their relationship to animal and human mutilations and bloodletting in modern times, which align closely to the appearance of UFOs in specific theaters of operation on our planet.

+ The weird claims of John Lear that aliens are coming here to kidnap humans and not return them. That people are being used for food, and how "they" are experimenting with us—sadistic experimentations—and attempting to suck out our souls and place them in containers for their own use.

+ The Islamic belief in the normally invisible elementals identified in the Koran as the Jinn and how these malevolent spirits are able to misrepresent themselves by camouflaging their true identity and traveling around at fantastic speeds.

+ Shape-shifters who can turn into human-looking beings, animals, orbs, fireballs or manifest themselves even as physical "hardware" to fool us into believing they are mechanical devices.

+ The casting of magical spells, occult rituals and the ability to conjure up spirits and beings often mistaken for UFOnauts but more closely aligned with the elemental kingdom.

Their ongoing plans for us, which include rape, pillage and plunder both of humans as well as of the entire planet? Witnesses tell tales of unbelievable aggression...

"The creatures were hostile and went into attack modes several times, putting up dense fogs. One time when they stopped, it was like a backwards tornado coming from the mouth of the leader of the ships. It was like a ray that he was sending down a funnel. He did it five times, then he left..."

One Navy Commander with strong CIA ties has stated: "Much if not all of the phenomenon is nefarious. . .a monstrous evil with occasional good."

According to Dr. Karla Turner, whose work Sean Casteel examines later on, there is evidence that the intelligence behind the mysterious discs can control what we think we see. They can appear to us in any number of guises and shapes. They can alter our perception of our surroundings. They can take over our consciousness, disable our control of our bodies, install one of their own entities, and use our bodies as vehicles for their own activities.

WHAT BECAME OF THE MYSTERIOUS "NEW AGE" FIGURE KNOWN AS MICHAEL X?

If you have been following what is roughly known as the UFO/New Age communities, you would probably have heard of the mysterious figure known as "Michael X," one of the great avatars of the early Flying Saucer-Contactee movement of the 1950s. He spoke articulately and sincerely at many of the well-attended outdoor conventions held annually at Giant Rock, a private landing strip just outside Joshua Tree in the hot Mojave Desert of Southern California. He was calm and collected as he spoke about the arrival of the silvery spaceships, dubbed flying saucers, explaining how they were piloted by friendly space beings from this solar system and way beyond.

Did Hitler's SS corps Manage to tap into some outside force to build their own Flying Saucers based upon Ultra-Terrestrial Technology?

On a mission of peace and harmony, Michael hailed the arrival of the Space Brotherhood, whom he believed were materializing here to offer assistance in any way possible in the hope of elevating our consciousness to a more harmonious one. Their ultimate goal? Allowing us to join the cosmic league of nations, a federation of spiritually advanced worlds that exist all around us in this and other dimensions, whether we believe it or not!

I guess you could call Michael X a guru of sorts, though he didn't head a religious cult nor was he looking to attract a fanatical following in the manner of other more self-absorbed "masters" of universal wisdom. No! Michael X was an avatar in the true sense of the word – an advocate for all of humanity. So that he didn't become part of a cult of personality, Michael refused to reveal his last name but added the "X" after his first name as sort of a symbol that represented all of the mysteries of our world and the space and time we inhabit, even if we had not officially acknowledged the legitimacy of others hobnobbing among the stars.

If one owned a complete collection of Michael X's monographs, which I estimate number around 25 and were self-published by his Futura Press from roughly 1956 through the late 60s or early 70s, one might be able to put together some incomplete biographical notes.

We know that Michael Barton was residing in Los Angeles when he found his life changed after his best friend Jim became very ill with a condition that baffled the best doctors. While meditating over his buddy's deteriorating health, Michael found he was able to receive telepathic communications beamed to him from more advanced cosmic souls.

Not wanting to alienate his business clients, but desperate to get the information he had collected out to a growing number of adherents to UFO and New Age philosophy, he began to self-publish courses and monographs under the pseudonym of Michael X. His work was read and distributed widely as believers and skeptics alike instinctively took to what he had to say and recognized the importance of its content.

You see, Michael X didn't just write about lights in the sky—or about close encounters for that matter. No, Michael X got his information firsthand via telepathy from his extraterrestrial "guides." And they taught him much; everything from health secrets to how the Space Brother's understanding of science, philosophy and religion could possibly propel us forward into a New Age of reason and enlightenment.

Above all else, Michael X shared what he learned from the "Venusians"—whom he said were his closest acquaintances—in a series of very concise study guides which he sold mainly at UFO and metaphysical meetings but were also advertised in publications like "Fate" and Ray Palmer's "Flying Saucers From Outer Space" magazine. In fact, truth be told, I was selling Michael X's books when I was 15. We would advertise them in our little mimeographed publications and Michael would drop ship them to our readers. He had books on cosmic telepathy, how to initiate contact with the UFOnauts, health secrets, visions at Fatima, Nazi UFO secrets and so forth. Before he vanished from the scene, he sold most of his books to Gray Barker of Saucerian Press. When Barker passed away, I purchased all the remaining copies and had them lying around in various cubbyholes for years but now I feel it is important for these monographs to be brought back into circulation.

I do not know if Michael X is still with us or not. If he is, I know he will not be resentful of the fact that we have decided to compile and reissue some of his most vital writings for an entirely new generation to consume and gain knowledge from. We have already reprinted his work "***Flying Saucer Revelations***" as a bonus section in the book "***Vi Venus: Starchild***," now obtainable directly through us, or on Amazon.com, of course.

Inside Information

But, as it turns out, Michael X's career was not involved with only the sweetness and light aspects of the New Age movement. He had also stumbled upon the darker side of UFOlogy, which so frightened him that he eventually left behind the work he loved so much. This is a little known "secret" about Michael X that I don't believe has ever been presented before.

I got this information from a buddy, Dr. Frank E. Stranges, author of the book "***Stranger at the Pentagon***" and a fairly good friend of Michael's. For years they crossed paths, speaking at the same venues, mainly California-based metaphysical centers and Spiritualist churches that were open to ideas involving extraterrestrials, doubtlessly because of their highly evolved secular appeal.

Michael X eventually came to not rule out the negative aspects of what he was involved in, although I don't believe he ever felt his life would be placed in great jeopardy, as it subsequently turned out to be.

Michael spoke about Nazi UFOs years before anyone else dared touch the theory that German scientists had stumbled upon a revolutionary form of propulsion and had constructed disc-shaped devices that they had hoped would help them win the war. Michael also received a warning from the space people to get our tail off the moon and never return— OR ELSE! And if you think David Icke was the first to write about reptilians roaming the Earth, guess again. Michael had earlier told about the existence of a race of serpents running around inside Rainbow City as part of an inner earth contingent. Apparently, he went TOO FAR somewhere along the line in releasing this information and "they" went out of their way to get him!

Call it the Psychic Mafia if you want, whatever, it doesn't make much difference. The threat turned out to be real and VERY DEADLY.

During one of his meditations, a "voice" came to Michael and gave a specific place and time to meet for a face-to-face encounter with his supposed alien friends. They promised to reveal some information that had not been disclosed before that would be helpful in the dissemination of his work.

Michael was sent to an out-of-the-way place in the Mojave Desert where they could be secluded from others who might see their landed ship and "turn them in."

When Michael first got to the desolate spot he saw nothing, so he sat in his car and waited. Suddenly he saw the glint of something in the sunlight. Thinking it was their glittering craft, he got out of his vehicle and began to walk in the direction of where he had seen the reflection. The next moment, he felt something was just not right. He heard an inner voice telling him to get out of there RIGHT AWAY or he would be in big trouble. At the point of sliding back into his automobile, he looked back over his shoulder and saw the men he had intended to meet putting down their rifles, which they had been pointing in his direction. One of the rifles was the object that he had actually seen glittering in the sunlight.

Michael quickly realized he had every reason to be concerned – frightened might be a better term. He had his family to think of. He had second thoughts about continuing with this work, especially if it was going to put him and his loved ones in danger. And so Michael X quickly retreated from the field, never to be heard from again. A great loss for everyone—especially for humanity, who could certainly have gained from his teachings, be they from extraterrestrials or not.

I did manage to get Michael on the phone by using a contact number Dr. Stranges had given me. He refused to talk about what had happened, feeling it was better to leave well enough alone. But he did confirm the basic facts of the account I have just revealed, and so we should take him at his word and leave him alone and be content with reading the work he left behind for all of us to learn from.

UFOS – WICKED THIS WAY COMES: THE DARK SIDE OF THE ULTRA-TERRESTRIALS

* * * * * *

As far back as the 1960s, when I first started with this Ultra-Terrestrial business, I heavily promoted the works of Michael X. I still stand behind them as they contain some very excellent spiritual counseling and advice. Two of his works we have combined together into one volume. *"**Venusian Health Magic/Venusian Secret Science**"* is a workbook and study guide of monumental brilliance and was aimed at a New Age audience back when the term New Age was not even widely in use.

*"**Trilogy Of The Unknown - A Conspiracy Reader: Exposing The Dark Side Of UFO Research!**"* contains three of Michael's investigations which tend to lean toward the fear factor element.

The first is a warning by the "aliens" to keep off the moon, a warning that might have some substance since we haven't been back since Michael was told we should "stay away."

The second deals with the mysterious Nazi UFO Connection. Did Hitler's SS corps manage to tap into some outside force to build their own flying saucers based upon Ultra-Terrestrial technology?

And finally, the secret of the Serpent Race, a bunch of underground thugs who cooperate with aliens to make our live as miserable as they possibly can.

These titles are available directly through Timothy Beckley, Box 753, New Brunswick, NJ 08903 or from Amazon.com, of course.

But now let us dally no further and get on with some of the most puzzling high strangeness cases that I have had the opportunity to investigate and report on over the years, followed by contributions from my fellow highly esteemed associates.

UFOS – WICKED THIS WAY COMES: THE DARK SIDE OF THE ULTRA-TERRESTRIALS

STRANGE EFFECTS OF FLYING SAUCERS
By Timothy Green Beckley

Disks And Glowing Hair

AS an explanation of the current epidemic of flying saucer sightings and encounters, I offer the following account involving my five-year-old daughter:

At the time of her birth, her doctor reported that he had seen a gleaming silvery object in the sky, traveling at great speed. He attributed the sensation to one of these two things: an after image, common to everyone; or an electrical phenomenon that could not be explained. Several times since, usually near their birthday, bright objects, round in shape and traveling at great speed, have been seen by members of my immediate family.

Little weight was attached to seeing these circular objects until after her first birthday, when her hair began to turn snow white. It has remained white and now gives off a peculiar random glow. Disinterested persons have called attention to the fact that they have noticed this emanation as her birthday approaches.

We are willing to submit to questioning or examination of the child's hair in an effort to explain the current outburst of discs which seem certainly to have focused on my little girl.

[Letter to the Editor from Raymond Barcklow of Philadelphia—*Philadelphia Evening Bulletin*, July 14, 1947]

There are theoreticians who maintain that the presence of UFOs over the half century has given us the necessary inspiration and motivation to forge ahead with our attempt to conquer the universe. Their theory is that we would, as a unified planet, feel more comfortable on a more equal footing.

If such a hypothesis is valid, then without a doubt this wide-reaching effect—probably an unconscious one on the part of those behind the UFOs—will have a tremendous impact in the years ahead. It could even result in far-reaching changes and advancements in our culture.

But what have been the visible effects, if any, on those individuals involved in a personal sense with beings whose existence is still generally denied? How have they been "touched" by such interstellar vehicles and their occupants?

Unrecognized by most researchers is the fact that over the ensuing years, flying saucers have made themselves "known" in a variety of awesome and thought-provoking ways.

Well established are the instances in which unidentified airborne objects have been accused of causing blackouts and power failures. Lights in entire communities, down to the most modest single dwellings, have flickered out due to the approach of a "foreign" apparatus of unknown origin. Ample exposure has also been given to cases in which UFOs have brought to a complete halt automobiles and other mechanical devices. Several well-seasoned UFO researcher-writers have penned lengthy papers on this so-called EM (electromagnetic) effect. What of other, even more bizarre, irrational side effects, traceable to disturbingly close confrontations with UFOs and their many-faceted crew members?

The news story reprinted as a lead to this article appeared more than 40 years ago, buried away on the inside pages of a widely circulated daily newspaper.

The mere thought that UFO activity might cause a young girl's hair to glow in the dark and change colors is staggering. Of course, it is impossible to check on the validity of this episode at this late date, but we do have other equally unusual tales which lead us to speculate that this experience was indeed not a hoax, a fabrication or a coincidence.

Doubtless this case must be placed in a category by itself—there are no others precisely like it on record. Yet, from the bulging files of clippings and personal eyewitness testimony I have amassed over the years, this particular incident by no means misrepresents the many strange after-and side effects which can be directly attributed to flying saucer activity.

Despite a new respectability about this topic, there remain many factors deeply ingrained as part of the UFO puzzle which have not been openly publicized. Nor has adequate research been done to explain them. It is a documented, well-established fact that UFOs have affected or been able to alter in some way:

- The growth of plant life, insects and humans;
- The forces of gravity;
- The passing of time and anything remotely connected with it;
- The placement of physical objects; and

Strange Growth Patterns

Scientific evaluation of the Bikini atom bomb experiments some years ago established the fact that existing life forms on and near this closely-guarded South Pacific coral reef had undergone drastic transformation following the testing of two atomic warheads there in June of 1946. For years after these top secret blasts (whose mushroom clouds rose 30,000 feet), sea creatures—from the most microscopic to larger varieties—were found washed ashore, their bodies mutated in any number of ways. Marine navigators in the area even reported seeing a monstrous 66 foot shark, much larger than any ever previously seen. On the island itself, insects were reported to have grown to tremendous proportions, six and seven times their normal size. Often they were found to have additional limbs and tentacles.

Of course the causes of these abnormalities are easily traced, scientifically. We know, for instance, that excessive radiation, especially "close-control" radiation, where atoms and molecules undergo initial changes, causes mutations to occur in nature. And certainly the radiation swept into the atmosphere by these two tremendous atomic weapons were among the most deadly ever.

However, what of instances where radioactivity cannot be pinpointed as having set off the phenomenal and rapid growth of plant life, insects—and yes, even human beings? Let us consider cases in which UFOs can be associated with such mutations.

Several years ago a story was brought to my attention which, at the time, seemed incredible. So unusual was it that I neatly creased the report—which had come to me in the form of two personal letters—down the middle and placed them in the back of an unmarked file folder out of sight and for a long time out of memory. It was not until recently, with the reporting of several similar cases, that I vaguely recalled the rejected episodes and retrieved them from their resting place. During the summer of 1967, 18-year-old Jerry James, his father, mother and younger sister were driving toward California and a long-cherished vacation from their Colorado home. It was during the first night of their trip that a series of peculiar events began to transpire.

Jerry, scheduled to enter college in the fall, had taken turns with the driving chores. Finally, after being on the road for more than 18 continuous hours, the family pulled their new Chevrolet pickup, behind which they towed a house trailer, onto a service station lot to refresh themselves.

As they proceeded to stretch their limbs and catch a breath of fresh desert air, their eyes were attracted to a peculiar-looking object moving about overhead. Later, Jerry was to give me the following description of what the family had witnessed. "The object—a definite aircraft of a completely unknown type—was shaped similar to a child's top—round at the top and pointed at the bottom. It was encircled by a ring of brightly-colored lights, and from out of the lower portion of the 'ship' came a beacon similar to a searchlight. This light beam passed over the area as if in search of something. We became quite shaken, moments later, when it shone directly on our trailer."

Jerry states that the object appeared to be about the size of an automobile. "Before disappearing from our view, the UFO hovered only a few feet above the top of our truck and then quite noiselessly zoomed off into the distance, and went out of sight." None of those present found it easy to believe what they had seen.

The next day the James' camped off the main highway, miles from where their observation of the previous evening had taken place.

"We thought we were once again going crazy when we saw a silver-looking vessel floating in from over a nearby mountain peak." This time, Jerry revealed, "The UFO got so close—within 75 feet—that we could even see rivets visible in the metallic gray structure. At one point, as the orb made a direct pass at us, my mom fainted dead away. We had to use smelling salts to revive her!"

Entering the back of the trailer they immediately noticed that something truly strange—well beyond their mysterious traveling companion—had come about. "Everything inside the trailer compartment was in perfect order, although when we left it the bunks had been unmade and the sink area strewn with silverware and unwashed dishes and utensils. Our beds had been put together and everything was as neat as it could be—though not as my Mom would have done it." It was then, looking around them, that Jerry noticed the most unusual feature.

"On the kitchen cabinet we found a small dish with a sprouting carrot which had been placed there sometime during the last 24 hours. But something drastic and truly puzzling had happened to it, for the carrot did not resemble a carrot any longer. It had spread out, as if having grown for weeks in a tempered, professional hot house. Roots were everywhere, running outside the dish and reaching almost to the floor."

Examining the vegetable closely, Jerry and his parents and sister noticed a slimy green-colored substance on the cabinet and dish. "It was a vile smelling substance," Jerry observed, "and other than that I can't tell you much about it. One thing strange, though. When I touched it with a pencil it 'ate up' the wood and lead in a matter of seconds."

Soon after this Jerry telephoned the police, who they hoped would investigate the series of phenomena. En route, their truck began to accelerate against the will of its driver. "Only a fractional depressing of the accelerator was enough to send the vehicle—truck and trailer—speeding along at 40 miles per hour."

But this was not all, as Jerry later confirmed. Upon arriving at the nearest gas station, the attendant proceeded to remove the gas cap. As he did, out rushed an odorous and gaseous material, causing a hissing noise and bringing with it a strong smell like that of sulfur dioxide, or rotten eggs.

Even later, they discovered that the part of the truck seat where the driver sat had rotted out and the ignition key itself now glowed in the dark and had gotten soft and rubbery.

UFOS – WICKED THIS WAY COMES: THE DARK SIDE OF THE ULTRA-TERRESTRIALS

While the law enforcement officials they contacted refused to believe that the James family had actually encountered a strange visitor from the depths of the universe, their insurance company was remarkably less skeptical. "They bought us a brand new truck to replace the one that had been wrecked so badly," Jerry reported. "They informed us that they had never seen anything quite like it before. What happened really had them stumped—almost as much as it had us frightened."

Jerry remarked in a later communication that he was well aware that a good portion of what transpired could have been caused by a harmful dose of radioactivity. Yet, he also added that no one in his family showed the slightest symptoms of radiation poisoning. "None of us became ill afterwards. Even if the amount of radioactivity had been negligible, we should have become sick In addition, it seems very probable that if the UFOs which passed directly overhead had carried with them some sort of contamination—enough to make the carrot root grow so wildly, or the ignition key to glow and turn soft—surely it would have made us ill enough to need medical treatment. Probably we would have been quarantined in a hospital for observation. Thus I have my doubts that radioactivity was what caused these peculiar things to happen."

But if radiation wasn't the cause of this family's problems, what was? It seems more than coincidental that two UFOs were seen while all this was taking place. A careful examination of other close sightings reveals numerous instances of a similar rapid "growth pattern."

A good deal of excitement and tension was generated in the out-of-the-way community of Gait, Ontario, Canada, where in July, 1957, a group of frightened teenagers came within inches of a "spaceship," as they readily referred to the object on the ground in front of them.

Jack Stephens, truly among the trustworthy, according to parents and teachers, said the party of five had accidentally stumbled upon the object, complete with portholes, as it rested on two ball-shaped "landing gear" in a field outside town.

Additional credibility came after an analysis was made of the scorched black earth discovered on the spot. Paul Hartman, a stringer for the "Gait Reporter," says the change in soil composition at this location was incredible. Top-soil dug up from the site glowed in the dark. Also, when grain samples from the burnt-out region were studied under a microscope, it was found that they were healthier and sturdier than the grain samples taken from elsewhere in the field. Finally, the insects here had undergone a certain instability and peculiarity in character. Ants where the saucer had touched down were larger and stronger-looking than their exact counterparts located in untouched areas. The ant hills themselves, according to Mr. Hartman, were much higher than ordinary and a spider which had by chance found its way into a jar containing soil from the Gait UFO landing site had grown to about ten times the usual size for this particular species.

Strange? Unexplainable? All a coincidence? During the summer of 1973, a mysterious encompassing "ooze," dubbed the "blob," began sprouting up nightmarishly in yards throughout Texas. Although never directly related to UFO activity, speculation that the fungus was an extraterrestrial manifestation remained on the tip of everyone's tongue. While news of the "blob" spread far and wide, other mutations in the world of biology and botany have not been publicly discussed, let alone explained.

In Corvallis, Oregon, on November 12th, 1973, a woman telephoned the "Gazette Times" after having located a hillside where a large unidentified object allegedly crash-landed. Police at the site confirmed that there was a sizable burned area and that here—and only here—a strange wild-growing fungus seemed to be thriving in the charred soil. Investigation determined they weren't any species of toadstool or mushroom known to the area—because they were much too large!

Similarly, from Argentina, Guillermo Aldunati, President of the Association de Observadores de los Astros, a private UFO investigating body in Rosario, confirmed that mushrooms of enormous size had been found in the provinces of Santa Fe and Necochea (north and south of Buenos Aires). The latter was discovered on a supposed UFO landing strip and the soil around the mushrooms was scorched for a radius of 25 feet.

In the previous instances we have seen how UFOs apparently are able—either accidentally or for some unknown purpose—to influence the growth of plants, and insects. But what of humans? Have they had such a devastating impact on unsuspecting observers?

Back in the spring of 1964, one of the biggest, most productive UFO flaps of that decade took place in the Southwest corner of the United States. Literally thousands of individuals in New Mexico, Texas, Oklahoma, Missouri and Nevada huddled in groups nightly as an Armageddon of whirling discs and penetrating lights cascaded across a starry backdrop.

Without a doubt, the major highlight of this majestic wave of sightings came when Lonnie Zamora, a Socorro, New Mexico, police officer came to within 50 feet of a landed UFO and its small-sized occupants.

While this flap was well publicized, one sighting did not receive the attention it rightfully deserved.

On April 29th of that year, 10-year-old Sharon Stull stood outside the Lowell school yard where she was attending the fourth grade. With her on the day in question was her sister Robin, age eight, and another classmate.

As they went about their recess games, they noticed an egg-shaped "thing" high in the sky hovering above their elementary school. No one paid much attention to it, though Sharon kept looking up at it from time to time for roughly 30 minutes.

After their noon break, the children returned to class. A half hour later, Sharon asked to be excused so she could wash out her eyes, which had gotten red and were causing her considerable discomfort. Noting that the irritation did not disappear after a while, Sharon's teacher told her to see the school doctor. He in turn called Sharon's mother, Mrs. Max Stull, and recommended that the child be taken at once to the Batton Hospital for a thorough examination.

Sharon was treated at the infirmary and was told not to allow any sunlight to touch upon her face, which had turned a blue-red color. "They instructed me to keep her blinds drawn and to protect her inflamed eyes and eyelids from light," Mrs. Stull told newsmen. "Part of my daughter's face and nose appeared to be puffy and red. She continued to complain of burning pains."

Seeking an explanation, Sharon told the attending physician what she had seen in the clear, blue noonday sky. "The doctor seemed interested," her mother revealed, "and I remember him remarking about how such a short exposure to the sun, even at the brightest time of day, would under normal circumstances be insufficient to cause such burns and inflammation."

UFOS – WICKED THIS WAY COMES: THE DARK SIDE OF THE ULTRA-TERRESTRIALS

Subsequent newspaper coverage revealed that Sharon was getting better, although it was reported that she would have to wear dark glasses for a while, in order to protect her sensitive eyes.

Nothing more was to be heard about Sharon's unfortunate luck until four months later, when a brief update appeared in the "Albuquerque Tribune." What had been a major front page story only weeks before was now only worthy of two paragraphs, and these were neatly tucked away somewhere between the comic section and the sports pages. Yet, despite the apparent lack of interest on the part of the "Tribune's" editorial staff, Sharon had undergone a continuing series of traumatic changes, all of which had a near-disastrous effect upon her emotional and physical well-being.

According to Mrs. Stull, her little girl had grown 5 and a half inches and gained 25 pounds in the month following the sighting of the mysterious egg-shaped craft which had hung over the school yard. "A while ago she was just a child who liked to play with dolls and paper cut-outs," Sharon's mother said. "Now she is suddenly mature and grown-up, cooks meals by herself, cleans house and takes care of the younger children."

At the time she saw the strange object in the sky Mrs. Stull confirmed that Sharon had been 4 feet, 8 inches tall and weighed about 85 pounds. "Now Sharon is 5 feet, 2 inches tall and weighs 110 pounds—and is still growing. My daughter had outgrown all her clothes and quickly outgrows new garments and shoes. I'm so confused I don't know what to believe," she sadly observed. "I just feel funny' was all Sharon herself would say when questioned about her UFO experience.

"I know she definitely saw something in the sky that day, but I don't know what," Mrs. Stull said. "It has been a nightmare ever since. I wish I had let her play hooky that day."

While this is the only case of phenomenal human growth attributable to the close approach of a flying saucer, there remains a strong possibility that similar effects have transpired—and may be taking place at this very moment.

After all, how many persons would report such a peculiar change in their physical stature to authorities? Also, it is an established fact that once they have been stricken from the pages of newspapers, most UFO observers return to a life of anonymity. Researcher John Keel has stated that UFO percipients who have established a seeming rapport with these phantoms by way of a close sighting frequently undergo a series of physical and emotional changes.

Levitation

One episode fraught with emotional effects took place in a Southern state in the 1970s. The mere thought of confronting an alien ship and its not-so-human crew is enough to give the strongest man a heart seizure. In this case, the two men involved managed to escape with their lives, but their psyches were seriously shaken. One of the weird effects they experienced was a period of weightlessness, when their bodies were apparently levitated through the air.

It was October when these men, Charles Hickson and Calvin Parker, were seized and forcibly taken aboard a UFO in Pascagoula, Mississippi. What transpired—a physical examination administered by a king-sized, revolving eye—is now a matter of history. Hundreds, if not thousands, of pages of hot copy flashed across newspaper pages the world over calling attention to this weird encounter. Overwhelmed by the enormity of the abduction itself, no one yet seems to realize that, on top of the unusual nature of the kidnapping, a mighty blow had been dealt to a well-established scientific principle—the law of gravity. For Hickson and Parker had been rendered weightless by their captors. Grabbed on all sides by the "web-footed creatures" before them, they were levitated out to a circular ship waiting for them silently in the night's pitch blackness.

Such a suspension of the earth's gravitational field is impossible to contemplate even in terms of modem-day physics. The technology needed to produce such an effect—if at all possible—is definitely well beyond our limited space-age understanding.

Several days after the excitement died down in Pascagoula, a 47-year-old Columbia County, Pennsylvania, man found himself tangling with an identical "force" rendering the car which he was driving totally weightless.

Edward Deutsch, who commutes daily to the Mack Truck Plant in Allentown, 70 miles from his home, was proceeding on a mountainous, rural road outside of Hazleton. "I was traveling alone and thinking how nice the weather was turning, when suddenly this object the size of a tractor-trailer tire came from over the mountains. At first I didn't have any idea what it was," Deutsch stated, "but realized quickly enough that it was flying very low—about the level of the treetops."

As it approached his automobile, Deutsch said he rapidly accelerated. "No matter how fast I went, the object kept pace with me. It was right above the car, going around and around." The somewhat shaken percipient in this UFO encounter recalls that it was at this precise point that gravity ceased to exist for him and his vehicle. "Before I knew what hit me, the front seat got red-hot and lifted straight up in the air—hovering, with me holding onto the steering wheel for dear life. In a matter of seconds, which I assure you seemed like endless minutes, the car was turned around in midair, heading me back in the direction from which I had originally come."

Deutsch was visibly upset, according to a reporter from the Harrisburg, Pennsylvania, "Times Leader," who interviewed him within hours of his dramatic encounter. The professional trucker subsequently told of a meeting with a hunter who saw the unidentified flying object hover over two deer, lift them ten feet off the ground and place the animals gently down, but again facing in the opposite direction.

Serious consideration should be given as to why these reports—sightings of such an important magnitude—dealing with these side and after-effects of UFOs, seldom, if ever, see the light of day in the printed media. In several instances, newspaper editors deliberately omitted references to such peculiar behavior on the part of UFOs because they knew such aspects would throw a great deal of doubt into the legitimacy of the case itself. "It's hard enough for us to present a saucer sighting in a credible format," one columnist told me. "And, since I'm a believer in these things myself, I want the public to feel that observers are not just a bunch of crackpots. So if we have to 'leave out' or eliminate specific 'hard-to-believe' facts, it's for the best!"

Despite this attitude on the part of the journalistic community who are seeking a certain amount of respectability for UFOs, many of the effects we are dealing with eventually do leak out after qualified investigators appear upon the scene.

Wilton Eater and his wife, Rosalin, of the Blackfoot Indian Reserve near

Gleichen, Ontario, Canada, told W.K. Allen, a serious and long-time student of UFOlogy, about the time their automobile, a 1962 Pontiac, rose up seemingly of its own volition while a bright light maneuvered nearby. Writing in the prestigious—but long defunct— "Canadian UFO Report," Allan quoted Mr. Eater as giving the following account:

"It was on the evening of May 14, 1971. As we went up a hill, returning home from town, we saw this bright light. It hit us on the right side of the car just like lightning. We went on a short distance and I didn't notice anything for a few seconds, until my wife remarked, 'The car's off the ground.' Well, I kept steering and managed to stay on the right side of the road. We went for a quarter of a mile. I had the lights on. Then all of a sudden the car hit the ground. I could feel the wheels when we landed."

As can be seen, instances of cars floating into the air are not unusual. Nor do they happen only occasionally. My own files list a good two dozen cases, all very similar—all very monumental,

Taken By Force

Fewer cases seem to exist of individuals being drawn skyward by UFOs, This, however, we might well speculate, is because of the anxiety on the part of participants to report such events after they occur. Of course there are numerous stories, well-worn and often told, about individuals vanishing into thin air without a trace. Many of these cases, such as the Christmas Eve, 1898, disappearance of young Oliver Larch, have been attributed to wayward alien beings. Oliver's cries for help were audible in the frosty air. His footprints in the snow abruptly came to a halt near the well on his family's Midwest farm. Although armchair UFOlogists have often tried to associate this disappearance with the presence of otherworldly astronauts, proof is flimsy.

At least some persons living in Thompson, Manitoba, Canada, however, do not suspect, but know, who the culprit was in an unsuccessful attempt to "take away by force" a lovely 8-year-old girl. The near-tragic incident occurred in June of 1967 to Nancy LeMarquands, and was promptly investigated by the Canadian Aerial Phenomena Research Organization.

According to their completed report, the horrifying encounter began at around 6:00 PM, when Nancy's mother heard a loud "beeping" noise coming from the yard in which her daughter was playing with some neighborhood friends. Looking out the window to see what was causing the disturbance, Mrs. LeMarquands saw only dirt and debris moving rapidly around the house in a circular motion. Upon going outside, she saw that along with five neighborhood children, her husband, who had just driven into the driveway, was staring up into the sky.

At first, only dust and soil moving in a vortex could be seen, but then Mrs. LeMarquands was able to perceive the cause of the disturbance. There, immobile in the air, at an altitude of 30 feet, was a rectangular object of considerable size, the under carriage of which was revolving counterclockwise. It had no apparent openings and remained silent.

As she stood transfixed watching the object along with her husband and other credible witnesses, a jet stream of wind emanating from the ship began whipping up around her. Suddenly Nancy began to scream, as her skirt and blouse were yanked off her fragile frame and up. This was immediately preceded by the actual physical lifting of her body. In a moment of desperation, a 13-year-old boy from across the street threw himself at Nancy, pinning her legs against his chest.

With this, the wind died and the object began moving off at a 45-degree angle, eventually shooting towards the southeast. When asked if she could remember anything of her harrowing experience, Nancy replied that she could recall absolutely nothing from the instant the whirlwind filled with dirt, leaves, grass and garbage had started in the yard where she was playing.

Though seasoned investigators, dispatched from the headquarters of CAPRO, spent weeks trying to find any flaws in the witnesses' story, none could be found. Whether the levitation was deliberate—done with hostile motivation—or whether it was simply an unavoidable side-effect of the UFOs presence, is, of course, impossible to ascertain.

Though Nancy's experience certainly has to be considered traumatic to both her and her family, it by no means constitutes the only instance where an innocent bystander was pulled toward the waiting portals of some cosmic power.

A highly sensational episode concerning a Greenhill, Australia, businessman—identified only as Mr. X—who claims that he had been sucked or drawn through a window pane in the kitchen of his home, recently captured my undivided attention. The account, published in the conservative "Mackay Argus" (a daily paper from Kemposey, Australia), stated that the man had reportedly seen a strange, small "saucer-shaped face" at the window before he was lifted through the glass by unseen "hands."

The incident, coming on the heels of numerous sightings of a bright light in the early evening hours, was verified by Mr. X's 26-year-old wife:

"We came home from the neighbors' at about 10:00 o'clock after watching television. My husband went to bed and was playing with the baby. He got up and went into the kitchen to have a drink of water. He didn't turn on the light, but he said afterwards he tipped his head back and saw this little face pressed up against the window. It had no hair and it looked like a small saucer. It had humanoid features, although he could not describe them."

The woman went on to say that her husband didn't remember much about going through the window, except that he was certain that he was "sucked out" by some powerful force.

"He screamed, and I came running out of the inside room just in time to see him busting through the glass and going up and out the window in a horizontal position. He was not struggling or thrashing about—just going through like that, straight out. He plummeted down immediately, and thank God it wasn't from too high up or he might have been seriously injured or even killed. I ran outside. I thought he would be stunned, but he wasn't. He wasn't even winded. He jumped up and ran like hell down to a stockpile in back of our home. I ran after him and he was crying and shaking. I thought he had the horrors, and told him so. I went to go back to the house and he asked me not to leave him alone, he was so frightened."

Telephoning the police, who came half an hour later, the man kept insisting, "You think I'm mad. I'm not. I saw something." Highly disturbed, the authorities took him to the local "lockup" for what they believed was his own safety. An examination of the scene showed that the window frame he went through was 4 feet, 6 inches from the ground. His leap, which shattered the glass but did not break the frame, would be impossible from a standing position.

An interesting highlight pointing out a remarkable similarity between the case of Nancy LeMarquands and Mr. X focuses attention on the fact that in both instances, each percipient had what might be termed a "time lapse," not being able to recollect the exact nature of what had transpired.

In the case of Nancy, she had undergone temporary amnesia, and as for Mr. X, he had a clear recollection of the incident that night, but his wife said the following day he thought—his mind in a state of total disorientation—"that he had put a fist through a neighbor's window and wanted to go and mend it."

The Warping of Time

This effect of "warping time" has been noted in many instances where UFOs and human beings collide. These time distortions have been known to last for several seconds to several hours. Also, in a number of contact cases, time itself, as we know it, is extended or compacted way out of proportion.

It is almost as though UFOs and earth time are incompatible.

Following my appearance on a local radio talk show, the engineer beckoned to me to come into his control booth, signaling that I had a telephone call.

Not knowing what to expect, I picked up the receiver, and Frank Hoffman (a Wall Street executive who heads a well-established stock brokerage house and whose name has been changed for obvious reasons) introduced himself, explaining he wanted to relate an incident which had been disturbing him greatly since its inception back during the summer of 1973. It was an incident where time had really played havoc on his senses.

Returning to New York via Pan Am from a Hawaii business convention, Hoffman related to me that no one else on board, not even his female aisle companion with whom he was becoming acquainted, had seen the UFO which had been following the giant 747.

The sighting, which was instantaneous on Hoffman's part—it took less than five seconds—occurred while over the Pacific, not 45 minutes out of

Honolulu's International Airport. Hoffman said that the craft gave off a pulsating red light, which blinded him for a fraction of a second afterward, "like when you look directly into a light-bulb, then turn away..."

When Hoffman looked again, it was gone. Although startled, to say the least, he mentioned nothing to the young woman about his sighting, especially since nobody else seemed to glimpse it. The time distortion occurred later, 48 hours later to be exact, when he was to pick up the young lady at her East End Avenue apartment for a dinner date. When he arrived, she informed him that their date had been scheduled for the evening before, and when he failed to show up, she'd been quite upset.

Hoffman, telling her she was wrong, even pulled out the slip of paper with her address and the time he was to be there. She was right, showing him the front page of a newspaper with the day's date on it. He was a full 24 hours late. What's more, to this day Hoffman cannot account for the missing time period. Neither could his coworkers, who spent hours on the telephone trying to contact him, without success, "It was as though I did not exist for a day," he told me.

Another peculiar incident involving UFOs and time displacement was reported by John Keel in the May, 1969, issue of "Flying Saucer Review." The account concerned an Adelphi, Maryland, university student who experienced a time distortion while aboard a flying saucer.

According to the young man, a psychology major, he had first encountered the UFO at approximately 1:00 AM on the morning of December 10th, 1967, while driving his car outside of Washington, DC.

A normal-looking man dressed in coveralls approached him from out of a hovering disc and asked simple, routine questions. The man had identified himself as "Vadig."

The student had worked evenings in a Washington restaurant as a waiter. The fact was not mentioned to "Vadig." Nevertheless, two months later, the UFOnaut appeared at the restaurant, told the young man he was an interplanetary visitor and invited him to visit his craft. The youth was taken by automobile to an isolated farm area some 30 minutes outside of the capitol.

Waiting there was a large, egg-shaped vehicle on tripod legs. The young man was ushered aboard and seated alone within a compartment. He was taken for a "ride," which he estimated took approximately four to five hours,

Then he was carried back to the same spot and driven to his home. Entering his apartment and confronted by his roommates, he was amazed to learn that little over an hour had actually passed from the time his interplanetary friend had picked him up at the restaurant.

Researcher Keel reported that the young man described four different meetings with "Vadig," and each time the "spaceman" ended the conversation with the phrase, "I'll see you in time." What was "Vadig's" concept of time? We can't rightfully say. No doubt it is different from our own.

Journalist Arthur Shuttlewood is convinced that the perplexing timepiece stopping phenomena in England is a direct result of UFO activity over his hometown of Warminster—yet another strange effect we must contend with. On the night of September 9, 1969, a dozen residents of Potten End (a suburb near Warminster) had the singular and disturbing experience of having their timepieces remain motionless for about an hour. All the stories seem to coincide, although there was no direct relationship between the witnesses, nor did they know of anyone outside their own dwelling having the same experience.

One of those who found himself faced with such a situation is Norman Gilbert, an engineer who said, "I set my watch as usual and placed it on the nightstand before retiring. Upon awakening the next morning and seeing that it was still early, I dozed again, thinking I still had yet an hour more of sleep coming to me before getting ready for work. Arriving at my job, at what I thought was 7: 00 AM, I was jokingly browbeaten by my fellow employees for being late." Gilbert then discovered that his watch was an hour slow.

Similarly, Mr. E.W. Rayment, a Potten End builder, had the unusual experience of having both his watch and bedside clock lose one hour on the same night. Another one of those who had the puzzling experience was Mr. John Booth of Dunbar Cottage. He described how his wife Kathleen's watch had stopped altogether on that same Saturday night. "We fiddled about with it for around an hour trying to get it to go again, but without success.

The following morning, Booth observed that the watch had started to work again without anyone touching it, and his wife has had no trouble with it since. Each watch-stopping individual could offer no explanation why watches stopped on Saturday night and precisely at 8 PM. They were thoroughly convinced that it was not due to lack of winding.

A spokesman for the Science Research Council based at the Ministry of Defense, Navy Department's observatory at Hurstmonceux, near Eastbourne, said: "Nothing like this has ever been reported before."

However, Arthur Shuttlewood, author and UFO investigator, was told that at the instant the watches and clocks stopped working, a number of Berkhamsted people heard "odd humming sounds" and saw a peculiar shape in the sky—which experts determined to be an extraterrestrial ship.

Shuttlewood himself was involved in an episode where he had a 45-minute time disorientation while atop Cradle Hill watching a pair of UFOs through binoculars. The incident, which transpired in November of 1970, had Shuttlewood—who described in detail his multitude of experiences with flying saucers over this tiny English town in the Summer Issue of "Saga's UFO Report"—observing the celestial multi-hued lights, resembling a string of burning beads. Shuttlewood immediately noted the time on the luminous hands of his wrist watch, marking down the time of the sighting as 11:31 PM. At this point he attempted to signal one of the UFOs, which had descended to a point approximately 30 feet from where he stood. As the beam of this flash pierced the solemn darkness, he was able to distinguish the metallic gray outline of the ship's hull, straddled on top by a spherical dome.

"At this point, something odd and unworldly happened to me. To be honest, I cannot recall with any degree of clarity what transpired next. In short, I cannot remember if the object disappeared or if it continued to hover, or if indeed I walked away from Cradle Hill at all. What I do know is that an awful numbing sensation affected my limbs. I shut my dazzled eyes and felt desperately tired all of a sudden. The next thing I knew—I don't know how I got there—I was standing by a wooden fence at the bottom of Cradle Hill. Glancing at my watch, I was horror-struck. The time was now 12:35 AM. Despite the fact that it was a deadly-cold night and I was well wrapped against the bitter winter chill, my body was bathed in sweat. Moreover, tears were cascading down my face, and I could taste the salt in my mouth."

Shuttlewood says that he was upset because "my son was to have picked me up in my car at midnight at a nearby rendezvous point." Reaching the waiting auto, Shuttlewood apologized for being 40 minutes late. The editor's son, looking at his watch, remarked "You're not late, you're bang on time."

At this point, Shuttlewood realized that he had been the pawn of a bizarre time-distortion game. Checking his timepiece once again, he discovered that time had once more jostled, this time backward. It was now 12:07!

As odd as it may seem, scientific research has actually been conducted at laboratories throughout the world to penetrate the mystery of this perplexing distortion. They have used as their "guinea pig" a direct link to the sky intelligences by the name of Uri Geller. This amazing Israeli-born psychic has astounded the world by being able to bend metal and teleport objects. Among his other skills is the uncanny gift of manipulating the hands of a wristwatch backward and forward. Geller boldly states that he is the earthly representative of extraterrestrials aboard spaceships hovering in our atmosphere.

Why is this manipulation of time taking place? Geller says that the forces behind these effects are trying to warn the world about some impending catastrophe, and since they operate on another vibrational level and from another dimension, this is the only means they have at their disposal. Explaining further, Geller related that to the UFOnauts, time is NOT proportioned the same as it is here. In other words, where they exist—in another time-space continuum—the passing of time is in no way related to what it is here on earth. To them, the moment is to us what might be construed as an hour.

Mysterious Vanishing Acts

In many instances, UFO witnesses have testified that personal property—usually items of relatively little consequence—have simply vanished only to show up later in a different place.

The "Missoulian-Sentinel" (of Missoula, Montana) reported that a local couple, Mr. and Mrs. Allen Lund, who live on the side of a mountain in east Rattlesnake, have been visited several times by what Mrs. Lund described as a "ship definitely not of this world." Mrs. Lund thinks the occupants of the craft were trying to see what human life looks like.

Not only had Mrs. Lund reported television reception on Channel 7 completely disrupted when the ship is near, but also said various personal articles of clothing have "just vanished, to show up again later, somewhere else." Neighbors verified that sunglasses, combs, brushes, toilet articles, stationery supplies, even house keys have vanished, and turned up elsewhere—each instance occurring when the UFO was in sight.

New York City syndicated columnist Brandon Blackman testified that on Sunday, July 8, 1974, at precisely 10:15 PM, an unidentified flying object appeared over the parade grounds of Brooklyn's Prospect Park. Blackman, while sitting on the grass at the park's northeastern end, talking with his fiancee, Claudia Monteleone, a prominent financial magazine editor, glanced up to observe a glow hovering over an apartment building on Caton Avenue. "I saw this glow," Blackman told this reporter, "wobbling in a falling leaf motion. Stopping at a particular level, it would hover and rise again several times. Claudia grabbed hold of me and pulled me toward Caton Avenue for a better look."

Blackman described the object as being very much like a vehicle, with an illuminated compartment underneath. The couple, along with several other people who were playing Frisbee under the arc lights, observed the object, which came closer. It was near enough for the knowledgeable writer, who has a long-time interest in the subject— although this was his first sighting—to realize what he and Ms. Monteleone were witnessing to be unworldly.

Even though the sighting in itself was perplexing and awe-inspiring enough, it was by no means the clincher of the evening. For later, after returning home, Blackman suddenly realized that he had somehow lost or mislaid his key ring. "I knew when I left the house earlier I had my keys with me, since I had double-locked the door," he said, and further related that the building's superintendent had to admit him with a spare set. "I was dumbfounded to find the set of keys lying smack in the middle of the bed after entering the apartment."

By what miracle had Brandon's keys gotten from inside his pocket to within his apartment? Furthermore, Brandon had slashed his finger earlier that day, enough to warrant wrapping it in a bandage. However, before retiring that night, the bandage was removed in order for a fresh dressing to be placed on the wound. "When I removed the wrapping, I discovered much to my amazement that the wound was completely healed, as though absolutely nothing at all had happened!"

Healings From Above

Brandon is not the only percipient of a UFO encounter to report this rapid healing effect. Gordon Creighton, European entrepreneur of UFOlogy, reported a spontaneous healing case to Ralph and Judy Blum, authors of ***"Beyond Earth: Man's Contact with UFOs."*** The case in point concerned Ventura Maceiras, a 73-year-old night watchman from Argentina. Maceiras' entanglement occurred on December 30th, 1972, while at his shack in Tres Arroyas listening to his radio. The radio suddenly went dead. When he tried to get it going, without result, he shut it off.

At that instant, Maceiras heard a loud humming. Then he saw it: directly above a nearby eucalyptus grove was a powerful object whose color changed from orange to purple. Staring further, Maceiras saw a round cabin with windows, and through the windows two figures. As the craft tilted toward him, he could see that the "men wore helmets and what looked like diver's outfits. Both figures had slanted eyes, their mouths a thin line." Macerias was also able to distinguish in the cabin in which the figures stood an "instrument board" complete with dials.

Under the most grueling interrogation, Maceiras' story remained remarkably unchanged. Each time specific details were asked for, they were supplied, never changing or wavering.

Examining physicians verified that the witness had extreme difficulty in speaking and his eyes watered continuously. The Blums maintained that Macerias suffered from "unbearable headaches, violent nausea, diarrhea, abnormal loss of hair and swollen red pustules on his neck"

But the eeriest of all phenomena in this case was the fact that the elderly witness had grown a new set of sturdy teeth—his third!

The authors of this best-selling book describe many other cases of this nature. I had already published a preliminary report on one of them some years earlier, detailing yet other remarkable case histories of miraculous and spontaneous remission. One in particular which is still foremost in mind concerns a report investigated by Philip J. Human, researcher for the Tyneside UFO Society of England.

Human reports in detail the Fred White episode, which had its inception in March of 1961. While night-fishing at Paterson's Groyne, North Beach, Durban, White, together with friend Henry O'Dank, spotted a light high above, traveling in a southerly direction. It was 3:00 AM, and the light had suddenly changed its direction, heading toward the pair. It stopped abruptly at a spot 25 yards away.

Suddenly the light took on the form of a brilliantly glowing craft, which illuminated the entire area while pulsating with a slow, steady whine. It hovered there momentarily and then, just as suddenly as it appeared, it rose, moved off in a westward direction and vanished. The fisherman decided to keep the sighting to themselves.

It was the following spring that Fred was to have a second encounter with a UFO; this time, however, the experience was to be more than just a mere eyeball-to-eyeball confrontation.

It was March of 1962 to be exact. Fred had embarked on another fishing outing, this time to Richard's Bay, situated some 150 miles from Durban, to the north. One evening, after having an outdoor dinner, Fred decided to take a brief walk along the beach before retiring. A sudden, high-pitched sound pierced his ears. He looked up and saw a very bright light, about the size of the moon, traveling due south over the sea at some 200 feet.

Following the identical pattern of his first experience of a year earlier, the light changed direction and came directly towards him, stopping 100 feet away. As it stopped, so did the sound which accompanied it.

It was a spaceship, and Fred could see directly into it, through a large porthole, one of several along its frontal portion. It was then that he saw an occupant, fair-complexioned and quite muscular, wearing what looked like a metallic crash helmet.

Waiting and watching, Fred suddenly noticed a pulsating green light on the ship's dome as the sound—the humming which he heard vibrating from the ship's hull during his former sighting—sounded again, this time somewhat louder. The craft, in a terrific downdraft which sent the sand around it spiraling crazily into the air in all directions, suddenly took off, rising, circling and then vanishing completely.

The following years passed without incident. Then, in September, 1966, Fred had to be hospitalized. His ailment was diagnosed medically as a collapsed lung.

One morning during visiting hours, Fred recalls, "a man walked into my room, pulled up a chair and repeated my name, as if asking for verification. When he told me how well I looked, I thought he was one of the doctors making his rounds. But then, as he extended his hands toward me, as if preparing to begin some sort of physical examination, I noticed that he wore a strange-looking wristwatch. It glowed and gleamed, almost pulsated. It was like no timepiece I had ever seen."

Fred recalls being asked what had happened and telling about the chest pains and the choking sensation preceding them. The visitor smiled and told Fred there was no cause for alarm. "Next, when he asked about my work, I mentioned my interest in shortwave radio radionics and a powerful receiver a friend and I had been working on. I also mentioned a series of signals we had picked up, emanating from an unknown source."

Before he left, Fred's visitor told him to be prepared for beneficial changes and "more contacts." He did not elaborate.

What is even more perplexing than having received a visit from an extraterrestrial craft is that after the visitor left, Fred reported that his chest was pain-free and he was able to breathe without the slightest difficulty. What is more, new X-rays revealed Fred's lung to be completely inflated, with the hole he had there before now totally healed. The doctor treating Fred remarked: "I have never seen anything like it..."

Strange as it seems, Fred's case, and the episodes of Blackman, Mr. Maceiras, and countless others, although unique, are far from singular. Many such miraculous healings have been—and are now—being reported, and in each case UFO activity is common; in some episodes, actual contact is made.

No doubt we are dealing with an alien intelligence whose scientific methodology delves much deeper than our present-day technology can come close to duplicating. Because of what we have observed transpiring on the ground and in the air in connection with UFOs, we must place these celestial ships and their occupants on a level far superior to mortal earthmen and our own limited capacities.

It is only common sense that we here on earth should endeavor to unravel the complex mysteries UFOs are constantly confronting us with. If we can learn the reasoning and the practical know-how behind what they are able to accomplish, then, no doubt, we can push ourselves years, perhaps centuries, ahead in life-saving areas. Some day perhaps these strange effects of UFOs will not be so strange any longer. An understanding of the knowledge behind such aspects of the flying saucer enigma may lead us, as a planet, on to great achievements in science and medicine.

What marvelous wonders we may one day find on our doorsteps, thanks to these remarkable visitors from the stars.

UFOS - WICKED THIS WAY COMES: THE DARK SIDE OF THE ULTRA-TERRESTRIALS

Carol Rodriguez depicts The Case of Micki Eckert and Kathy Erhard.

THE STRANGEST UFO ENCOUNTER EVER

SOME UFO reports just don't seem to fit into any existing mold and, thus do not even correspond with other existing reports...no matter how strange or bizarre.

The hallucination or "Oz Effect" (a term coined by British UFOlogist Jenny Randles) is well illustrated in this account, which I personally investigated, meeting with the witnesses several times.

Mickie Eckert's experience is totally unique in the annals of flying saucerdom. Her story does not seem to fit in with any existing pattern and yet the sincerity shows on her pretty face as she relates a bizarre tale that defies explanation.

Looking at me with bewildered eyes, it was obvious that Mickie, a young woman in her mid-twenties, was seeking answers. She was confused about what had happened and was anxious to find out the reasons she was selected to have a close encounter that goes beyond anything previously recorded.

It was July 22, 1978. Mickie, along with her best friend, Kathy Echard, was driving along Interstate 80 East. They were headed towards Nebraska, near the Wyoming border, when they saw what they thought was an accident on the side of the road.

"We turned to get a better look and saw these white lights bobbing up and down. In order to get a better look, we pulled over to the shoulder of the road and aimed our car headlights in the direction of the crash."

It was apparent that Mickie wanted to talk about what transpired that night. We were seated around a large table, in a private conference room at the Royal Quality Inn in San Diego, California. Mickie had come to the privately-sponsored UFO conference (promoted by veteran newsman Hal Starr) mainly because she wanted desperately to talk with some of the top names in the field who are supposed to be trained in the handling of such matters. In attendance on the podium that day were such leading UFO luminaries as Jim and Coral Lorenzen from APRO (since deceased), Walter Andrus, director of the Mutual UFO Network, and Dr. James A. Harder, Associate Professor of Engineering at the University of California (Berkeley).

Maybe it was because of their tight speaking schedule, but none of those present seemed to be able to find the necessary time to speak with Mickie Eckert. It was only after she was introduced to me by John DeHerrera (a practicing hypnotist who has been involved in the investigation of several contactee cases, most notably that of Brian Scott) that Mickie found someone who would listen intelligently to what she had to offer.

Going back to the evening in question, Mickie maintains that the sun had just set as they drove on a desolate and very isolated stretch of road eighty miles north of Whelock, Nebraska. "Our headlights were trained on what we thought to be a mishap, but all we could see was three round circles hovering a few feet above the ground."

At the time neither of the two young women realized that they were headed for a journey to a Twilight Zone more real than any TV program about the supernatural could ever hope to be. "In front of our eyes these lights turned into two sports cars that were coming toward us." One moment they had been confronted by the mysterious presence of airborne lights and the next thing they were aware of were two automobiles speeding in their direction. To say the least, they didn't know what to make of this transformation.

"We wanted no part of what was happening so we took off in the opposite direction. As we turned the car around to leave, in back of us we saw this whole bunch of lights. We backed up on the Interstate and now there were two trucks that had appeared out of thin air. On the trucks were teeny little lights. The trucks were following us, of this I'm sure."

The two tractor-trailers kept a steady pace on the highway in back of the girls. It was as if unseen eyes were watching their every movement, perhaps seeking an ideal spot to overtake them for some fiendish purpose.

"For some reason, Kathy asked me to stop and she got out of the auto and stood in front of the car. It was then that we saw all these other cars parked along the side of the road. They were just stopped there. When Kathy got back into our vehicle she wanted to drive and so I let her take the steering wheel. To her it felt as if something—some force—were trying to take control of our car. She got scared and eventually turned the driving back over to me and I too felt this strange pulling."

Putting as many miles behind them as possible, the two girls sped on through the night anxious to get back to their home in California. "As we were passing through Salt Lake City, we stopped off at a Safeway store to get some gum and cigarettes." Mickie makes no bones about the fact that they were still shaken but says they were trying to pull themselves back together again, not having seen anything unusual on the road for quite some time now.

"As we were about to leave the Safeway supermarket, I noticed a reflection on one of the large windows coming from either inside or outside. Initially, I just assumed the reflection was caused by either the store lights themselves or from some street light nearby.

"Out in the parking area I discovered this was not at all the case, for directly across the lot was this little light about the size of a basketball just sitting near the ground."

There seemed to be so much that Mickie had to say that the words wouldn't come out fast enough. Several times I had to slow her down so as not to miss any part of her narrative.

Totally freaked out by what was transpiring all around them, Mickie's friend was anxious to push on as quickly as possible. "As we entered Wyoming we stopped again to get some bottled water. We were in a pretty good-sized town called Evansville, and it was still pretty early, but there wasn't a light on in the entire city. Everything was closed. None of the houses had lights on either. I looked out of the window on the driver's side of the car and there were these two ships hanging there. One was orange, the other yellowish-white. We continued on toward Green River and the objects passed through the trees on the side of the road. At this juncture in time we lost control of the car once more. No matter how fast we put our foot down on the gas pedal the car refused to accelerate past a certain speed."

In the middle of nowhere, the car died completely. With this, a light came into the auto passing right through an open window. The light touched Kathy Echard and, for no explainable reason, Mickie began talking to that light. "Come on, little light, why don't you touch me, too?" she remarked, despite the fact that everything up until this point had frightened her.

No sooner had it appeared than the light inside the car vanished. "All of a sudden we didn't see the ship anymore, but we started seeing trucks. Northwestern, American—and other big-named rigs. They were traveling in both directions, up and down the northbound and southbound lanes. The only way I can describe it is as a caravan of big lights going back and forth. This one particular truck stopped directly in front of us and we knew something was wrong. It was freaky—the trucks were now ships; dome-shaped, 3-sided ships about the same size as a compact automobile, and they were no longer on the road, but traveling about six feet off the ground." Mickie admits that she was too bewildered to be an excellent observer. She finds it hard to estimate the number of trucks or dome-shaped ships but she does know that the car they were in got pushed forward about 20 feet as if it had been lifted by a terrific force from underneath.

Despite their accelerated heartbeats, the girls decided to get out of their car to have a look, to see if anything might have gotten caught underneath their wheels which might account for the sudden tug forward. There was nothing there that would offer a solution to the puzzle, and so they climbed back into the relative safety of their vehicle.

"Soon there was this other car that pulled up directly in back of us and Kathy said she wanted to get out and see who was driving it." It was quite apparent from Mickie's comments that the girls were anxious to seek help from any other companion of the road they might find driving so late at night.

"When Kathy got back into the car I was anxious to know what she had said to the individuals in the car behind us. She just looked me straight in the eye and said, 'Turn around and tell me what you would have said to them.' There was this black dog, tail curved up and two red eyes blazing just outside our car door."

The girls were understandably terrified by this new development.

Cowering in fear, Mickie happened to glance into the rear view mirror.

UFOS – WICKED THIS WAY COMES: THE DARK SIDE OF THE ULTRA-TERRESTRIALS

What she saw only added fuel to a fire of panic that was so near to bursting out of control within them. "I saw what appeared to be a kid with his arms bunched together on the back seat." The girls got out of the car in an attempt to escape this potential menace. Luckily, the dog-like creature they had seen was nowhere in sight

However, directly behind them were two bright lights which were joined by several other duller looking lights. After several minutes they all blended into one light. "As the light went past us, it was no longer just a light—but a ship. We heard this rumbling sound and our hair stood on end. Our skin was covered with goose-bumps."

At this point it seemed as if Mickie and Kathy had been transported to another dimension, another sphere of reality, for all at once things started looking peculiar, totally out of whack "Then the sun started to come up, but only it was an orange ball and it was coming toward us. And then it was not orange anymore, but its color turned suddenly to gray, and it was about 100 feet across, just enormous. And people started to appear out of nowhere, walking across the freeway carrying tubes or pipes. We didn't actually see them come out of any ship because the sun—or whatever it was—had landed in a valley out of our immediate viewing range."

The beings—or whatever they were—were standing in the middle island that separates the north and southbound traffic. "There were these bunch of blue lights and we knew something was going to happen. We were terrified. We felt like we were going to be taken to another planet and would never be heard from again."

Without warning the car started up. "I got mad at Kathy because I thought she had slammed on the brakes and I hit my head on the dashboard. We saw this ship coming down the Interstate and we also saw an 18-wheeler pickup truck towing one of the sports cars we had seen earlier in the evening. Something pushed us from behind but we couldn't get the car to run of its own accord."

From out of nowhere a man appeared and asked the girls where they were headed. "He said he was heading toward Chicago and we said that's where we were going, too. I'd have gone to Timbuktu just to get out of the spot we were in." From what I was able to gather, the man did not know anything was happening. He seemed totally unaware of the frightful state of the girls' minds caused by a terror that was real enough to them even if nobody else was able to perceive what was transpiring around them.

"I was so scared that I crawled all over the driver. He stopped at a truck stop to get coffee and we got out and walked to a nearby motel. We didn't have very much money. But we had about $35 and so we got a room. We unlocked the door and turned on the light and the TV went on by itself. Also, this little teeny light flittered around the room and we knew we hadn't escaped."

Realizing that they were being observed, the girls tried to intimidate the light that was buzzing around their room.

"'Kathy, did you mail that letter telling about the flight pattern of the UFOs to my lawyer?' I asked with a purposeful slowness. She said she had, playing along with the game.

"We called the police and finally, at 5 o'clock the next afternoon, they came and took us back to the spot where we had abandoned the vehicle. As it turned out, the car wasn't where we had left it. And when we went back to the valley where the ship had been, the area wasn't the same. There was no little road on the side of the road. The freeway railing wasn't even the same. There was a sign MOUNTAIN ROAD 189. There is no Mountain Road 189 in all of Wyoming. We had a full tank of gas and we were about 250 miles into the state and there wasn't a gas station anywhere."

It was like they were driving without consuming fuel.

Of further interest were the corpses of a cow and a sheep off in a nearby field. "The cow was all bones and the sheep had all of its skin peeled off, which made it look like a blanket lying there."

Mickie says that the police made them fill out a complete report. "After they had finished hearing our entire story they shrugged and told us we'd seen swamp gas!"

Moving the tape recorder closer to Mickie, she reported that both her life as well as her friend's have been drastically altered because of the events of that night "Kathy is only 31 years old, but she's been in the hospital at least 20 times since this happened. It's hard to explain, but somehow I feel we are the same people, but then again we aren't. Kathy had always been a slob and I have always been neat and clean. Now my house looks like the wreck of the

Hesperus, and Kathy's is really neat, tidy, and very well cared for.

"Before, I had always been the type to make my kids breakfast, lunch and dinner, while Kathy believed her children should prepare their own meals. It's just the other way around now. It's almost as though we've somehow exchanged personality traits. In other words, I'm still me, but it's as though I'm having my personality altered—taken over. I have always been a reader, for instance, and now I'm reading much more. I'm reading as much as I can on UFOs; that's the one subject that fascinates me the most."

Under hypnosis, Mickie was made to draw what she had seen. When it came to sketching the trucks that had appeared on the highway, she rendered a skeleton-type being instead of a moving vehicle. "Is it possible that they altered your whole thinking process that night?" I asked the witness. Mickie admitted that this is what might have happened and that what really transpired could be entirely different from what she perceived. For some unexplainable reason, Mickie and her friend, Kathy, have grown farther apart in their friendship. "Before the experience, we had been the best of friends for 17 years. Now we speak to each other only once a week, tops."

Mickie is anxious to undergo further hypnosis. She wishes to find out what really took place on July 22, 1978. She is not satisfied with just forgetting about the incident The whole episode is a true puzzle. Taken as an isolated encounter, most UFOlogists would probably do their utmost to doubt the word of those individuals who were personally involved. The rule of thumb seems to be, "If you can't explain it, or it doesn't support existing evidence, brush the whole affair under the carpet." If we were to do this, we wouldn't be any better than the government agencies who have tried so hard to hide the very existence of UFOs from the public.

While we may never know what really happened, it's to our benefit to keep an open mind and to try and track down the bits and pieces that may eventually come to the surface from the women's subconscious minds. If hypnosis is necessary, so be it Even then there's no guarantee that the intelligence behind this bizarre UFO caper hasn't taken the necessary measures to wipe the slate clean and make Mickie and Kathy forget for all eternity the true nature of the events they lived through.

This case is a prime example of how mysterious the entire UFO phenomenon might be. Just when you thought you might have pinned down the answer, it darts right away from you!

In John De Herrera's opinion, "My interrogation of the two witnesses, on four separate occasions, amounted to approximately twelve hours. It takes almost two hours for each one to tell her story! This account is incredibly detailed and the testimony from each lady is the same. Months later the repeat story matches the original account. I cannot imagine anyone investing this much effort to fabricate and memorize so much detailed information.

"If we stop and compare the information in this case to the multitude of similar cases, we find many parallels. The "ball of light" phenomenon is frequently observed and has baffled men for thousands of years. These lights through the years have acquired many names: Ball of Fire, Orange Fire, Ghost Lights, Foo Fighters, etc.

"Strange glowing balls of light are seen, and have been photographed, as religious apparitions. There were many photographs of the Egyptian apparition in 1968.

"Phantom helicopters are a persistent phenomenon in the Midwest. Many people have reported other phantom aircraft in the skies also. They glide silently by without making any noise. Has our government developed some extraordinary aircraft or is someone playing tricks on us? There have been many apparitions of things—from aircraft to creatures. Yes, even that dog with it glowing eyes."

UFO BEINGS DIRECT MY LIFE

WHEN I first met Lorie Roberts, little had been written concerning those individuals who professed repeated UFO-related experiences.

For the most part, up until recently, UFOlogists saw the experience of a close encounter as a "single shot" incident, not realizing that some persons have apparently been "singled out" by the aliens to be repeaters.

Throughout their lives, these "select few" seem to have their daily comings and goings monitored by some superior intelligence.

Often, they also encounter paranormal phenomena more frequently than others, and perhaps even find themselves developing a heightened sense of psychic ability. Lorie fills the bill of a "repeater" quite well.

It is not uncommon for people who have established contact with UFOs to report that their lives have been changed. Many times after a close encounter, they find themselves caught up in a literal whirlwind that threatens to destroy their former lifestyle. One police officer who chased a disc-shaped object for over 100 miles could not hold down his job any longer. His wife filed for divorce. He no longer was interested in keeping the same friends he'd had for so many years or in doing the same things he'd previously taken delight in.

From what researchers have been able to gather, it's as though their minds are opened, suddenly made that way, and they no longer see the world and those around them in the same light as they did before. There are a good many cases on file of individuals who discover they have heightened technical skills they never knew they possessed before their close-up sighting or direct contact.

Furthermore, it is not unusual for those so involved with otherworldly phenomena to realize they have certain psychic abilities they never before utilized nor even realized they had. Some of these people even feel that they are not "human" in the sense that they believe they were not born totally of earth parents, that they were "put" here and in actuality come from somewhere else, if not physically, then at least in mental terms. One female contactee I spent considerable time with says she died at the age of five or six. She fell unconscious in her backyard one day and the doctor was called. She was pronounced dead but was revived shortly thereafter. After this regaining of consciousness, she felt "different," as though something inside her mind had been changed—or switched.

Lone Roberts of Queens, New York, says that her mother didn't even realize she was pregnant. "Up until the exact time of my arrival, she was totally unaware of the fact that she was expecting another child."

The night I was a guest on the Leon Lewis talk show heard over a Manhattan radio station, Lone telephoned the station. While she had read a lot about UFOs, she's never had anyone to talk with about the things she has gone through life experiencing. Sure, there had been other so-called UFO "experts" interviewed on the air, but none of them seemed to be interested in talking about the possibility that another race of beings might be inhabiting earthly bodies. When this topic came up on the program, Lone couldn't dial the telephone fast enough.

A few days later, I met her in person and we talked at length about her own situation. Like a growing number of individuals, she felt the time had arrived for this information to be shared with others and so she told me her fascinating story.

Lorie's Story In Her Own Words

"I was at Lake Winnepesauke, New Hampshire, in August of 1951, when I had my first UFO sighting. I was seven years old at the time and it is still as vivid today as though it had just happened day before last.

"It was early evening (around 8:00 p.m.) and the sky was that medium blue, the beauteous hue it becomes after the sun has set and the darkness of night is ready to settle in. Then I saw something—an object shaped like an ellipse with huge red and green pulsating globes underneath. The object made no sound as it passed slowly over the cottage. And it was huge! It was at a height of about 50 feet and it would have covered the roof of the four-room cottage had it landed on it. I estimate that it was about 75 feet in diameter.

"I was alone on the porch, facing the small uninhabited island directly ahead. I watched as it disappeared into the trees on the island, and I ran inside to tell the folks about what I'd seen. They laughed at me and told me that I was just tired and had simply imagined it all.

"The next day I convinced my father to take me out to the island to prove that I'd seen something land over there. But the engine on the boat wouldn't turn over and, after trying for half an hour to get it started, he gave up and went back to the cottage.

"Being very determined, I decided if it was the only way I could get there, I'd swim to the island. Of course, I didn't get too far, but I did manage to reach a canvas-covered raft which was about a quarter of the way across. By the time I got to the raft I was totally exhausted and realized that I could never swim the rest of the way to the island. So, I climbed up onto the raft to catch my breath when suddenly it became very hot. Since I didn't feel like going back, I decided to jump into the water and go under the raft to cool off. I felt a glorious kind of privacy under the raft, since most adults wouldn't dare to venture underneath, because it was usually very dark and murky. This day in particular, there was no one on or under the raft and I had it totally to myself. Also, I soon discovered that it wasn't dark and murky at all under there, but very crystal clear and light lime-green in color, which it had never been before.

"While I had been swimming around under the raft and holding onto the sides, I noticed a big fish swimming around below me. I had never seen such a large fish (about one-and-a-half feet) before and I didn't want to scare it away, so I didn't move. After a short time, the fish came up to me and began to brush against my legs, similar to the way a pet cat would. After a while it went away. Today, I realize the fish was of an unknown variety.

"Finally, I swam back to shore and went about the business of playing.

"That evening, about the same time as the previous evening, I was again sitting on the porch, this time together with four adults. Suddenly my aunt uttered, 'Look at that!' Everyone turned to see an elliptically-shaped object lift off the island. As it passed directly over the cottage (without a sound), its lights began to pulsate red and green. Then it picked up speed and was gone within a few seconds. The adults were dumbfounded.

"I've been following the history of the UFO for the past 20 years and, in thinking back to the sighting, I realize that there were several 'classic' effects that occurred.

"First, the electromagnetic effect which kept the motorboat from operating. The next day the boat was operating normally and did not require repair. Obviously, some force didn't want me to get to the island because there was a saucer there.

"Second, the unusual behavior of the fish. Odd behavior is often noted in animals during a UFO encounter.

"Third, something I haven't found in the literature, is the unusual appearance of the water under the raft. When I ventured out to the raft the day following the 'liftoff,' the water had returned to its normal dark and murky appearance.

"Unfortunately, my father was too frightened by what he had seen and refused to go out to the island to see if we could find any trace of where it had landed.

"I have had other sightings over the years, but never as close or as spectacular as that one.

"Looking over the past 27 years since that first sighting, I find that my life has been 'led' into many areas of the unknown. I think I may have encountered Bigfoot.

"The next summer I went to camp in upstate New York. It was a fine but primitive camp in the sense that there were no flush toilets at that time. The old outhouse was there to answer the call of nature. One day after lunch, during rest period, I ventured off to the distance of about 200 feet. I saw a large creature watching me. It was definitely not a bear. It had very long arms and seemed to resemble a human except for the fact that it was totally covered with black hair and appeared to be about eight to ten feet tall. I was very frightened by it and was afraid to move because I was certain it would come after me. So, I froze. As I watched it, the creature grabbed a huge branch of a tree and broke it so that it was hanging from the tree. This action spurred me on to get back to my cabin as fast as possible.

"I didn't mention what I'd seen to anyone because I was positive the other kids would tease me.

"During 'free time,' later that day, I decided to go to the spot and check out the broken branch to make certain I hadn't imagined seeing this creature. Sure enough, I found a freshly broken limb hanging from the tree. It was broken at a point about eight feet from the ground. That was enough proof for me. I remember the hair rising on the back of my neck and the desperate need to get away from there as quickly as possible.

"Later that summer my closest friend got lost during a 'counselor hunt' in the woods at night. All of the counselors had been found but one of the campers was missing! We were supposed to go on the hunt together but we had an argument and we both went our separate ways. It didn't take long for the counselor of my cabin to realize that Judy was missing.

"While the head counselor and staff were huddled together trying to figure out a course of action, I heard her calling to me in my head. I tried to tell my counselor that I could hear her calling so everyone was quiet for a few minutes, but they couldn't hear anything. I was convinced that she could hear us if we yelled loud enough, so I told my counselor to have everyone start screaming for her at the same time. We did, and after a while she found her way out of the woods. Later that night I told her that I had heard her calling to me and she said that at one point she began crying and calling me by name. Although I didn't win an award for catching a counselor, I did win one for 'Best All Around Camper' that summer. This was my first psychic experience and I can't help but be fascinated by the fact that my ESP came about as well as my Bigfoot sighting so close on the heels of my UFO encounter. I can't help but believe there is a connection.

"I learned a very valuable lesson from that experience—when I 'hear' or sense a friend is in distress, I give them a call. I have rarely been wrong.

"I have always been a 'loner.' Each day, during 'free time,' I would venture off into the woods alone to explore. Even the fear of Bigfoot couldn't keep me out of the woods.

"What happened next added to my belief.

UFOS – WICKED THIS WAY COMES: THE DARK SIDE OF THE ULTRA-TERRESTRIALS

"One day I decided to take the 'Moss Road,' as I called it, up to the top of the mountain to a clearing where the counselors would meet at night. It was a beautiful sunlit day, with the bright orange orb shining through the thick foliage. When I reached the top of the hill, I decided to rest for a while. Then something happened. I felt like I had been hit by a beam of light and for a few minutes—or perhaps seconds—I couldn't move, and I felt like all of the wisdom and knowledge of the cosmos was flashing through my brain. I have no idea how long it lasted. I only know that when it stopped, I was elated—ecstatic!

"As the years passed, I realized that I thought 'differently' than others. I spent a lot of them reading about psychic research, UFOs, Fortean phenomena, and the like.

"I remember that when I was around 12 years old I read an article about a foundation devoted to psychic research and decided that when I was older I would get in touch with them. I did become involved with them and participated in many experiments, my goal being to help a struggling science to find credibility in a skeptical world.

"During the experimenting, I discovered that I was considered a 'gifted' subject and was (and am) able to produce evidence for telepathy, precognition, retro-cognition, and psycho-kinesis. The UFO sighting at an early age opened me up, of that I am convinced beyond any doubt.

"I have often read how people's lives are changed after a UFO experience. Some become telepathic, or visionary. Since my first sighting happened when I was only seven years old, I often have had dreams of UFOs and the people who pilot them during the time of flaps in my area.

"I also apparently am tuned in psychically to various physical phenomena occurring on the Earth, such as earthquakes, and disasters of various types. These all came through in my dreams and are only a matter of proper interpretation.

"There was one other sighting which I found to be quite interesting because a friend observed the phenomenon with me yet saw something totally different! (A common occurrence in UFO sightings.) We were eating dinner seated by a window in a restaurant by the sea, in September, 1973. I was looking out over the bay when I saw a dark object with white lights encircling it. It appeared as though one light traveled around the whole perimeter of the craft very rapidly. It would disappear around the other side and then begin at the front again. I asked my friend, seated opposite me, what he saw. He claimed to see three lights—red, green and blue in a triangular pattern—but could not discern any form. I estimated that it was about 2,500 feet from us and about 1,000 feet high. My friend looked away for a moment just as the object dove into the sea, causing a glow which lasted for about ten seconds, but not long enough for my friend to see it. The total time of the sighting was approximately one minute.

"There is so much speculation on the nature of the phenomenon. It appears to pass through the color spectrum as it changes or travels. It reminds me of the rainbow phenomenon. It's here for a short time, refracting light. We see it, then it fades away. Yet anyone who has ever seen a rainbow cannot deny the existence of its reality. Real circumstances are necessary for the prismatic effect that produces the rainbow. Interestingly enough, I have met people who have not been able to see a rainbow even though other people were enjoying its beauty at the same instant.

"There has been a big gap in the study of the UFO phenomenon because so many people have been afraid of ridicule. While many more people have reported sightings during the 70s, there are many people during the late 40s, 50s and 60s who have not told anyone of their experiences. Somewhere within all of these non-reported cases may be a concrete clue that will help us solve this riddle."

FLYING SAUCER BASE IN FOOTHILLS

As far as I can tell, the witness involved in this case had no early childhood experiences of UFO encounters or abductions by aliens. So why they singled her out is hard to say.

According to her own thinking, Mrs. De Long feels she may have actually stumbled upon a secret alien base and somehow the UFOnauts were alerted to her presence and selected her as an unofficial spokesperson. Their reason for such an open contact is a frequently delivered message—that mankind should learn to live in peace!

A flying saucer base—complete with at least three spaceships and two interplanetary pilots—is allegedly tucked away in the mountains above Sunland-Tujunga, California.

And, from their Big Tujunga Canon base station, the two spacemen have been calling quite regularly on several Foothill residents, bringing messages from outer space.

Mrs. Mans De Long said she had repeated contacts with two space people.

Her 12-year-old son, Charles, and a man, Charles Kisner of Montrose, have also seen, listened to and talked with the visitors from outer space.

Mrs. De Long said several of the contacts have occurred in the Big Tujunga Canyon area, near a reservoir.

Because of the repeated contacts in the same area, Mrs. De Long maintains that spacemen are using the area around the dam as their Earth base of operation.

To fortify her claim, Mrs. De Long cites the experiences of a Los Angeles couple who followed a flying saucer across the foothills and into the canyon area.

The pair were found by sheriff's deputies, lost near the Big Tujunga Canyon Road.

They told officials they had followed the large saucer-shaped object into the area and became lost when it disappeared with the approaching dawn.

Mrs. De Long, supported by her son, said the spaceship was probably the one she and four other witnesses had seen.

According to Mrs. de Long, she, her husband, Kisner and Charles, were first contacted in July while traveling through the isolated canyon at night.

She said a bright light appeared to be following the car, and that the four occupants "began to feel uneasy."

The spaceship then appeared behind the car, traveling along close to the ground with three multicolored rays extending from the rounded contours of the UFO.

Sure that something big was coming their way, the group returned the next night to the same general Foothill area.

Again the saucer-shaped object appeared.

This time, however, the frightened occupants of the Rambler were introduced to "Kronin." Introducing himself in a blaze of bright light, the spaceman told them not to be afraid, that he meant no harm.

Mrs. de Long said that in spite of the spaceman's easy manner, she was "very frightened."

After reassuring the car's occupants again, "Kronin" chatted briefly about atmospheric conditions and the food he ate on "Clarion," his home planet. "Kronin" then disappeared, promising to keep in touch, Mrs. De Long recalled.

The next night, Mrs. de Long, Charles, and Kisner traveled again to Big Tujunga Canyon, hoping to catch a glimpse of the space travelers.

Their hopes were not for nothing. Mrs. De Long said "Kronin" appeared outside the car, materializing in a cloud of vapor. As the car moved along the highway, "Kronin" kept pace, chatting in a low-pitched voice with the three Foothills residents.

This time, Mrs. De Long had her tape recorder along, and was able to record the spaceman's conversation.

In a gravelly low voice that would be expected of a spaceman, "Kronin" spoke about his visit to Earth. Mrs. de Long said he called her an Earth Angel and said he was contacting people on Earth to try to forestall a possible world war. He reported that people on other planets were concerned with the war-like activities on Earth.

Before disappearing, the spaceman asked the car's occupants to face their left and see the beautiful beam from his spaceship.

"It was absolutely fantastic," Mrs. De Long said. "This multi-colored ray stretched from his mother ship and right through a large mountain in the canyon."

She said "Kronin" was a large man, about six feet tall and that he had no eyes. "He told us he saw through thought control," Mrs. De Long said. After disappearing, "Kronin" said he would contact them again when atmospheric conditions were just right.

PROBING THE MYSTERY OF THE UNEXPLAINABLE RADIO TRANSMISSIONS

Since the 1950s, the FCC, as well as other government agencies, have been checking out reports of mysterious interference over various broadcast frequencies. Whether it's a powerful TV station in England, high frequency channels reserved strictly for astronaut communications, ham sets or CB equipment, some unknown sources of intelligence have the ability to "cut in" and take over the airwaves as they see fit.

You probably read a brief wire service account of the incident in your local newspaper. The authorities tried to explain the "voice from outer space" as the work of a practical joker who had somehow managed to take control of an abandoned transmitter and broadcast a message from the "Asteron Galactic Command." They made it seem like the broadcast had lasted only a matter of 30 seconds or so, while in reality there were several messages, not just one, all of which lasted for a good two or three minutes apiece.

The following is a complete transcript of the "voice from outer space" as broadcast on television in the Hennington area of Southern England at 5:05 PM. on Saturday, November 26, 1977. This is the first time the text of the broadcast has been published in its entirety in the United States:

The Incredible Message

"This is the voice of Glon, representative of the Asteron Galactic Command, speaking to you. For many years you have seen us as lights in the sky. We speak to you now in peace and wisdom as we have done to your brothers and sisters all over this, your planet Earth.

"We come to warn you of the destiny of your race in your world so that you may communicate to your fellow beings the course you must take to avoid disaster which threatens your world and the beings of other worlds around you.

"This is in order that you may share in the great awakening as the planet passes into the New Age of Aquarius. The New Age can be a time of great evolution for your race, but only if your rulers are made aware of the evil forces that can overshadow their judgment. Be still now, and listen, for your chance may not come again for many years.

"Your scientists, governments and generals have not heeded our warnings. They have continued to experiment with the evil forces of what you call nuclear energy. Atomic bombs can destroy the Earth and the beings of your sister worlds in a moment. The wastes from atomic power systems will poison your planet for many thousands of years to come. We who have followed the path of evolution for far longer than you, have long since realized this: that atomic energy is always directed against life. It has no peaceful application. Its use and research into its use must be ceased at once, or you will all risk destruction. All weapons of evil must be removed.

"The time of conflict is now passed and the races of which you are a part may proceed to the highest planes of evolution, if you show yourselves worthy to do this. You have but a short time to learn to live together in peace and good will. Small groups all over the planet are learning this and exist to pass on the light of a new dawning, the New Age, to you all. You are free to accept or reject their teachings, but only those who learn to live in peace will pass to the higher realms of spiritual evolution.

"Here then the voice of Glon—the voice of the Asteron Galactic Command speaking to you. Be aware also that there are many false prophets and guides at present operating on your world. They will suck your energy from you, the energy you call money, and will put it to evil ends, giving you worthless dross in return. Your inner divine self will protect you from this. You must learn to be sensitive to the voice within that can tell you what is truth and what is confusion, chaos and untruth. Learn to listen to the voice of truth which is within you and you will lead yourself onto the path of evolution.

"This is our message to you, our dear friends. We have watched you growing for many years, just as you have watched our lights in the skies. You know now that we are here and that there are more beings on and around your Earth than your scientists care to admit. We are deeply concerned about you and your path towards the light and we will do all we can to help you. Have no fears, seek only to know yourself and live in harmony with the ways of your planet Earth.

"We are the Asteron Galactic Command. Thank you for your attention. We are now leaving the planes of your existence. May you be blessed with supreme love and truth of the COSMOS.

The Unperturbed British

If there is one thing most Britishers have in common, it's their unflappability. They've lived through the blitz, survived more Channel storms than you can count, and taken every imaginable type of man or nature-spawned excess very much in stride.

That's why they felt prepared to ride out any bad news which was transmitted to them over their regularly scheduled newscasts of November 26. But in homes all over Hampshire County, and as far north as Reading in Berkshire and Whitney in Oxfordshire, TV viewers got the shock of their lives and caused the usually unflappable Britons to jam the switchboards of every police station for miles around. Voices from space are not your usual evening's entertainment.

According to those who live in the area, towards the end of Southern Television's evening news program, a series of "bleeps" gradually took over the normal sound. Commented one viewer, "It was the kind of signal you get prior to a bulletin of special importance." Following the bleeps, a voice cut into the regular broadcast frequency of the TV station.

Another segment that came in was as follows:

The New Message

"We speak to the people of the planet Earth. It is of great importance that you have the understanding that we come only in love and peace. It is a time of importance in the universe that the planet Earth be invoked and the consciousness of those that exist on the planet be raised to a higher degree. It is also important to you to understand that we cannot permit in the present, nor in the future, any more devastation upon Earth.

"There are those civilizations that are in service to the universe that are in motion to come to your planet Earth to give mankind the benefit of their medical and technological skills, but mainly of their love. They are in service to the planet Earth and to the universe. We conveyed to Sir John Whitmore and to the Dr. Puharich that we would interfere on your radio and television communication systems to relay when the civilizations are coming close to landing on your planet.

"It is now in motion. We wish you to know that we love you. We wish for there not to be panic on Earth, for we come in peace. But it is most important for the people of Earth to recognize that the civilizations that come, come in Brotherhood to help them. It is important now to become one with the Brotherhood of the universe. We ask that those of Earth do not attempt to prevent the civilizations that are coming, but to accept them in love as we have accepted the planet Earth in love even though it has caused devastation and in turn contaminated the universe. We are with you and we come in peace."

A Fast Reaction

According to viewer Rex Monger, "The voice seemed to suggest that the man was speaking from a spacecraft traveling within the vicinity of Earth. He sounded pretty fed up with the way we are running things down here. "

As usually happens in such cases, a spokesman for Southern Television offered the typical debunking statements, calling the transmission "a pretty sick hoax" and likening it to the 1939 Orson Welles radio adaptation of H.G. Well's "War of the Worlds." But as the days went on, the station was forced to admit that it had gathered no actual evidence that the transmission had indeed been a hoax. The official said, "Our engineers are trying to discover exactly what happened. We can't imagine how it was done, but it appears someone must have managed to transmit a signal directly over ours. The equipment used would need to be fairly sophisticated and expensive. "

UFOS – WICKED THIS WAY COMES: THE DARK SIDE OF THE ULTRA-TERRESTRIALS

A Chilling Message

The mysterious November English transmission fits into an overall pattern of such events which have been occurring on a world-wide basis over the last several decades.

While the official stance of such government agencies as the Federal Communications Commission remains that such transmissions are a hoax, in no case has any prosecution been brought, much less a conviction obtained. This even though there are strong communications laws on the books making such transmissions a federal offense. Nor can debunkers explain away the fact that witnesses to the receipt of such transmissions are highly reputable people not given to fantasizing or bouts of hysteria. Included in their ranks are a number of law enforcement officers as well as several astronauts.

The transmissions have come over commercial frequencies, citizens' bands and high frequency channels reserved for communicating in outer space.

Of particular interest is the fact that while some transmissions have been in unrecognizable code and others in unintelligible language, a good many messages have been broadcast in the colloquial dialect of the area.

Ultra-Terrestrial Robot Communicates

A good example of this is provided by a tape in the possession of this author of an actual transmission received by a night guard employed by the Alamac Knitting Mills located in Lumberton, North Carolina.

To set the scene for the experience of James Ed Floyd, Alamac's night security guard, we must turn back to early April, 1975, and the area around Lumberton.

Lumberton is in the southeastern section of the state. It is flat with heavy patches of pine forests, open areas of farmland, swamps and canals. On April 5, 1975, Lumberton became the focal point of UFO investigators when the first in a series of sightings of a V-shaped object in the sky was reported.

On the nights which followed an untold number of sightings were funneled through various police stations. Forty-eight of the actual sightings were attributed to police officers engaged in official business. The first inkling that the UFO must have been bent on jamming radio frequencies in the Lumberton environs came when at 2:20 AM, April 5, Officer Jim Driver of the Roseboro (Sampson County) Police Department, alone in his patrol car, noticed a series of lights in the sky hovering over some pecan trees. This was the third sighting of the night, but the importance of it was that Driver became the first lawman to tell of the object's interference with his radio transmission.

Said Driver, "I got out of the car at that point and could not hear any sound coming from the object. When I tried to radio headquarters, my car radio became all scrambled, so I had to use my walkie-talkie instead. The light on the object swung away and lit up the pecan trees, which were about 200 feet away."

As more and more sightings were made known within the next hour, Lumberton authorities immediately contacted the Center for UFO Studies, with headquarters in Evanston, Illinois. Expert investigator Lee Spiegel was dispatched to North Carolina.

Hollow Voice

As part of his ongoing probe, Spiegel interviewed Floyd. Floyd said that not only had he experienced numerous sightings of the UFO, but that he had heard a strange, hollow sounding voice over his CB radio. The voice described itself as "Robot." It indicated that it was broadcasting over South Carolina, but was heading north.

Spiegel notes that Floyd's story seemed to be corroborated by information that as the unexplained radio signal from "Robot" became stronger, other residents of the Lumberton area found their radios being jammed to such a degree that offices could no longer modulate with each other.

In his official report to the Center for UFO Studies, Spiegel notes that Floyd told him that the voice which spoke with a Carolina drawl had said that it could not speak with them or be seen after dawn.

Spiegel suggested that Floyd try to record the voice on a tape cassette recorder. The plan was put into operation, and on Sunday, April 12th, between 7:00 AM and 7:15, the recording was made.

Spiegel has provided the author with the tape, and although the quality is not good, certain phrases are decipherable.

"Robot: We are clear. We may be in violation of rules. You may be violating the rules and regulations of the National Loudmouth by modulating with this one Robot. We may be violating..."

Floyd (speaking back on the radio): "You're breaking some rules, right? Right, you are!"

Robot: "Do not modulate with this one, Robot. We are circling around and checking our difference, and they do not like for any voice to modulate with this one Robot.

"We are not black, we are not white, we are not red, we are not yellow, we are not anything... We are just one Robot. We are circling for the pleasure of our commanding vehicle. Anybody that does not like the sound RRRR-RRRRRR of this one Robot..."

After Floyd arrived at his home, the voice was still transmitting and Floyd's son typed up the following words from a CB unit in their home.

"We are not . . . anybody . . . that we did from out there . . . we are not a computer, but we are a Robot, we are computerized . . . We do . . . take the Earthling's words and twist it around and turn it against . . ."

Some months later, Floyd claimed he heard another broadcast by the same voice, and then the UFOs vanished from the area and the eerie-sounding voice right along with it.

UFO Zaps Texas Hams

Another case of the interference with normal radio communications occurred in Calvert, Texas, during a siege by UFOs. The small southwest community was flooded by transmissions of radio sounds with a regular cadence which might have been some alien code. The transmissions peaked in November of 1973, corresponding with the brunt of the UFO sighting wave.

Ham radio operator and television repairman Virgil Chappel notes,

"Almost every night during the early part of November, heavy interference plagued amateur broadcasters in the area, preventing us from communicating with one another as we regularly do. Instead of hearing the normal messages from fellow hams, all I could pick up was a series of clicks. They were closely akin to Morse Code. Being somewhat of an expert in codes, however, I can vouch for the fact that it was decisively different from anything I had heard before. Why, even the tonal pitch of the 'noise' was odd, varying greatly from high to low. It was definitely—as far as I'm concerned—an intelligent type of signal. I don't profess to know where it came from, and I don't know who was behind it. All I can positively state is that it was eerie to listen to!"

On November 15th, 1973, the stocky Texan received an additional jolt of "eeriness" when he ventured out into his backyard and was greeted by the sight of a series of lights. "The air all around was aglow with a multitude of twinkling lights. It was like a Christmas tree—that's about the best way I can describe the scene. All around and above me were these blinking spheres. I ran inside the house, yelled to my wife to follow me back outside and simultaneously grabbed a pair of binoculars, which I thought would give me a better view of what I was certain were not airplanes, stars, or those satellites that come over every so often."

Chappel was unable to determine the actual shape of the objects but nevertheless was bedazzled by the beautiful hues of light they emitted.

Senator Goldwater

No less a famous person than Senator Barry Goldwater claims he has heard strange signals on his ham radio set. "These signals had a cadence or sequence which sounded like a code," he has stated. "It wasn't like any code I'd ever hoard before. The U.S. and the other countries like Russia have picked up such signals. But nobody knows where they come from or what they are. I do know that NASA is doing a lot of research into this."

Contacts between operators of unknown frequencies and hams are on the rise. David L. Dobbs, a Cincinnati scientist, gives a graphic description of just such an encounter in a communique written to Walt Andrus, director of the prestigious Mutual UFO Network.

A Close Encounter Set Up Via the Airwaves

Dobbs says he was driving home late at night on August 12th, 1976, and was monitoring a ham call in which the operator was trying to give directions to a mobile which was lost, As Dobbs was awaiting the "repeater" on the message, the voice was suddenly cut off. The engine of Dobb's car began to miss and his headlights started to flicker. Although the electrical system of his vehicle returned to normal within split seconds, the receiver remained silent.

"Hoping the rig was OK, I identified for autopatch and punched the access code," Dobb says. "They tell me that no one monitoring heard a thing, but instead of the dial tone, there was this indescribable voice.

"'Priority Break,' it intoned, followed by some strange call mobile 8. Usually I remember calls, but the odd quality of that voice must have distracted me. It was kind of melodious, deep and compelling, with an accent I couldn't place. I just said, 'Go break,' and kept listening. From that point on, the whole incident had a sort of dreamlike quality.

"The fascinating voice went on to say that his vehicle was disabled on old Route 84 near the quarry and requested some assistance. It was my impression that he was probably some foreign ham operating on a reciprocal license. The nationality escaped me, but as a technician I don't work the low bands, and there are a lot of new countries these days. Since my OTH was only a few miles from him, I told him to stand by and I would be there as soon as possible."

Dobbs traveled the highway to the intersection with 84, turned into the ancient road whose decrepit pavement forced him to reduce his speed to 15 or 20 miles an hour After going some distance, the scientist found his way blocked by a fallen branch. He stopped his car and got out in order to remove the obstacle. It was then that he noticed the treetops some 200 yards away were illuminated by a flickering light. It was as if something might be burning, except that the light had a bluish tint, something like that made by the rotating flasher of a police car.

The Spaceman Approaches

"And then suddenly I saw him," Dobbs continues. "'Him' seems to fit somehow, but don't ask me why. He had come up for the car while my back was turned and was standing near the open door. In the glare of the headlights it was hard to see well, but he was short—probably not five feet in height. He had on a silvery one-piece outfit that looked like aluminized coveralls or a wet suit. Moving out of the headlight beams and towards the car, I was about to say, 'Hi,' when my first good look stopped me dead. He didn't have a recognizable face."

Dobbs tells how he began receiving a tremendous flow of information into his mind at a "fantastic rate."

"It was like a data link between two computers," he says. "Ideas weren't expressed in words at all—there was just a stream of impressions."

The Cincinnati man's linkup went on for what appeared to be no more than 15 or 20 seconds. Dobbs was told he had no reason to fear his visitor and felt the figure was some sort of "biological robot." His impression was that the visitor had traveled from distant stars in this galaxy—stars which were visible only in the southern hemisphere.

Dobbs accompanied the figure to a spaceship and came away with the thought that for some reason earthlings were being evaluated by the extraterrestrials. He is also sure that the humanoid borrowed a package Dobbs was carrying at the time in order to duplicate its contents.

As Dobbs was returning to his own car at the suggestion of the "humanoid," who had indicated that to be close to the UFO at the moment of its take-off might prove hazardous, he became aware of the spacecraft hovering overhead. A moment later it flew off in a tremendous burst of speed.

Tampering With Our Space Program

Strange and inexplicable as the radio and television contacts between private citizens and space aliens may be, they are nowhere near as bizarre as those which have occurred between those engaged in scientific experimentation and space exploration as government representatives and possible representatives from outer space.

On November 23rd, 1977, officials at Cape Canaveral, Florida, were forced to admit that they were launching an all-out probe into the origin of a mysterious series of radio signals which had forced the scrubbing of a launch of a Meteorite I satellite.

Spokesmen for the Air Force and National Aeronautics and Space Administration revealed that the unexplained radio signals had been discovered during a routine check of the rocket's electrical system.

While the investigators pressed their efforts to unravel the mystery, the 1,535 pound drum-shaped satellite, which is owned by the European Space Agency, sat on the ground and the $240 million Meteosat weather forecasting program remained stalled.

The cryptic word from Canaveral was, "The source of the signals must be determined before a new launch date can be set because they could have an effect on the destruct system."

In jeopardy was a "World Weather Watch" experiment in which European, Japanese and American satellites were to participate.

Mysterious Voices Override Skylab Transmission

Nor was this the first time that the space program was rattled by a so-called "space phantom." On February 19th, 1974, noted syndicated columnist and muckraker Jack Anderson reported that "mysterious voices" had imperiled the return to earth of Skylab III with its crew.

According to Anderson's account, Skylab's crew heard mysterious voices telling of an explosion over Moscow, an oxygen loss and a conversation with then President Nixon. Anderson considered the transmissions an elaborate hoax and noted that an all-out probe was underway towards apprehending the "perpetrator" who had violated NASA's communication frequencies. However, as in every other case of this nature, no suspects were ever rounded up nor were any formal charges ever drawn.

The facts of the incident are these:

In Rocky Mount, North Carolina, officials of Unifi, Inc., a textile firm, began having interference with a long distance call. The interference at first sounded like radio transmissions from an airliner, but later on the listeners realized they were monitoring what they thought to be a conversation between Skylab III and the Houston Space Center. It appeared the astronauts' side of the radio conversation was the only one being audited. The voices talked of a 10 megaton explosion over Soviet Russia observed while the spacecraft had been taking aerial reconnaissance photographs of underground Soviet missile silos. The message included the fact that the spacecraft had been severely damaged in the encounter and only had 11 hours' oxygen supply aboard. The voices then said they were going to scramble the transmission on channels five and eight. A series of coded messages which sounded similar to Morse Code ensued.

At this point, according to Anderson, the words, "Yes, Mr. President, we understand this," were heard, followed by a voice report that Skylab's secret documents and equipment had been thrown overboard. The transmission ended there.

The executive employees of Unifi were not the only ones to hear the message. Anderson's associate Joe Spear found a number of others who had monitored the same dire conversations.

Said Anderson, "At NASA, officials advised us that still others around the country had reported similar phone interference.

"Now, NASA's security specialists are trying to find which 'phone freak' perpetrated the elaborate hoaxes. So far, we have learned only the 'Space Phantom' knows."

Despite Anderson's somewhat flip attitude, the fact remains that a number of years have passed since the incident and as yet, NASA has never officially admitted that it took place. Nor has the "perpetrator" been apprehended.

NASA Records Provide More Documentation

Strange sounds which cannot be explained away have long been a part of NASA operations. A careful check of the tapes of Apollo 12's log presents a vivid recounting of the monitoring of strange signals by American Astronauts Pete Conrad and Allan Bean. Conrad and Bean have landed on the moon's surface and were undergoing their exercise program when the following conversation took place:

Bean: Do you hear a lot of background?

Conrad: Kind of static and things.

Bean: I keep hearing a whistle.

Conrad: That's what I hear. O.K.

Ten minutes later, Dick Gordon in the mother ship orbiting the moon reported the following to Houston control.

Gordon: Hey, Houston, do you hear this constant beep in the background?

CAPCOM: That's affirmative. We've heard it now for about the past 45 minutes.

Gordon: That's right, so have we. What is it?

Ground control could give no definition.

Nor has NASA been able to come up with a logical explanation for the unintelligible foreign language transmission heard on Gordon Cooper's fourth pass over Hawaii on Faith 7 on May 15, 1963. It should be remembered that these channels on which the transmissions were heard had been reserved for space flights. And it should also be remembered that in the ensuing 28 years, NASA has never been able to identify the source of the transmissions nor the foreign language involved.

Another question which nobody connected with the government is able (or willing) to answer is—was there a secret warning embodied in the tune which for some unknown reason filled the cabin of Walter Schirra, Jr.'s Apollo 7? The melody was remarkably close to the old ballad "Fools Rush In Where Angels Fear To Tread." The one thing which is certain is that the song was neither being transmitted from the ground nor from Apollo 7 itself. On Apollo 11, the sounds resembled those of fire engines and caused Mission Control to query, "You sure you don't have anybody else in there with you?" The question, posed on July 22nd, went unanswered by the crew.

The very next day at 1030 hours, the strange sounds began again. This time they resembled a train whistle and the labored chugging of a steam locomotive. NASA could not locate the source and made a joke of the fact by asking astronaut Buzz Aldrin whether he might be exercising too violently. Instead of an answer, NASA's headphones were filled by other whistles and squawks which made auditing conversations extremely difficult.

Beaming In On Earth

Whether it was Asteron's warning to the British television viewers, the red-necked message taped in Lumberton, N.C., the experience of the Calvert, Texas, ham radio operator, the Cincinnati visitation of a being which invaded CB channels or the more sophisticated incursions into the space and satellite programs, there is no denying that the evidence is all around us that our airwaves are being jammed at will by something or somebody who feels the time has come to communicate with us.

While the official line from government spokesmen remains, as it always has in the past, that such happenings are elaborately contrived hoaxes, the truth cannot be denied.

Federal law has been violated again and again. Using the most ultra-modern devices in their arsenal against piracy of the airwaves, federal officials have not been able to break one case. There have been no convictions. There have been no arrests. There aren't even any viable suspects.

Until there are, those in charge are going to have to come up with a better explanation than the tired old bromide, "It's just malicious mischief."

THE NIGHT ET RETURNED HOME
A First Person Experience

Sometimes a single event seems to trigger a set of weird and bizarre circumstances which do not seem to be made up of earthly events.

This particular series of bizarre happenings began when a UFO hovered across the street. Soon shadows were seen in the house, objects began to disappear, electrical devices malfunctioned, and an eerie presence could be felt, as if something "new" had joined the family.

The Boyers (a pseudonym) are a large, loving, family who occupy a modest home in a rural area of New Jersey. Ellen and her husband have six children of their own, ranging in age from two years to 27. Ellen's daughter, Rita, is herself married, having children who, along with her husband, occupy the family basement apartment. Because they are not looking for any attention this story might bring them, we have agreed to keep the identity of the family involved in this ongoing incident a secret. However, their total sincerity can be attested to by the author of this book, who has known them personally just about all of his life.

As far as was noticed, the bizarre happenings which have centered around the household began in the late summer of 1982, when a mysterious object was observed hovering over some trees across the street at approximately five in the morning by Mr. Boyer, who was returning home from an emergency call. Though nothing unusual happened for quite some time after the sighting, it later became apparent that the UFO directly tied in with the many manifestations which threatened to alter the course of the family's lives, and was probably the catalyst which triggered the start of this unearthly series of events, which finally ended when their unseen visitor

UFOS – WICKED THIS WAY COMES: THE DARK SIDE OF THE ULTRA-TERRESTRIALS

was taken home.

Though there have been numerous incidents in which households have literally been besieged by invisible entities, the assumption is normally made that the disturbance is caused by the spirits of the dead and not alien beings. In recent years, however, an awareness has come about which confirms the fact that quite often UFOlogical events can closely parallel those of a psychic or parapsychological nature, and that not all extraterrestrials need necessarily be flesh and blood creatures. Research has pretty much established the fact that unseen beings who exist in different dimensions or vibratory levels are around us all the time, but can only be "felt" or "sensed" upon occasion. Apparently, this is one such case which proves that there is more in heaven and upon earth than is dreamed of.

"I have reason to believe that an ET resided in our home for over a year, and that we felt his presence though we might not have realized the identity of our uninvited visitor.

"We first noticed something strange going on when the weather started to turn warm last summer and the dogs in our yard began to act peculiar. They would bark all night long, keeping the family awake. One night my dog, Max, began to shake like a leaf. His tongue was hanging out and he was dripping saliva, though there was absolutely no reason for him to be acting this way.

"My daughter, who first brought my attention to the dog, suggested I bring him indoors. I told her I wanted to, but I was afraid that he might get sick in the house. No matter what I did, I couldn't shut him up. I couldn't stop him from shaking. I tried giving him water, but he wouldn't drink. He didn't want anything. He just kept running around and barking all night long.

"One of my five sons also said there was something wrong with his dog. He said all the animals seemed to be nervous. His dog almost hung himself trying to jump over the fence.

"The next day the three littlest children in the house, Danny, three, J.R., four, and Glen, four, went outside to play. They took a jar of jelly beans and some toys with them and had a picnic. I was doing the laundry indoors when J.R. came inside and told me and my daughter (his mother) that he was through. He said, 'The man told us, no more picnic.' We didn't think anything of it until the following afternoon when another of the kids told us that he had seen a man standing in the woods in back of the house and that they were told to go inside and not to play there.

"Naturally, I was worried about any strangers who might be wandering about where young children are concerned, and so I tried to get more information about the man, but all JR would say was, 'No more picnic, all finished, all gone.'

"Later we gathered all three children together and asked them to show us where the man had been. They all pointed to the same spot over by the garden where the fence is that the dog almost caught himself on.

"Interestingly enough, in the summer there is no way that anyone can get back there because the bushes are so thick and nobody trims them. Quite a few times, the dogs have barked and the kids have come in and said they saw the man. We would run outside and wouldn't see anyone. The kids described him as wearing a suit jacket and a pair of pants. Sometimes they said there were two men.

"Shortly thereafter, it would feel like someone would come into the bedroom at night and would push against the bottom of my mattress. Sometimes I would be overcome by the feeling that I wasn't alone, although nobody was physically in the room with me. One time, I was lying on my left side facing the wall and I felt a poke like someone's finger jabbing into my shoulder.

"The business with the mattress happened almost every night. In addition, a photograph of my youngest son, aged two, kept falling from the wall This happened so frequently that finally I decided to leave it down where it couldn't break.

"One night, I got bumped on the mattress, and I thought that someone was trying to speak to me. I sat up in bed and said, 'What, what did you say?' I was able to hear the sound of someone talking but was unable to distinguish any words. I put the light on and my husband who was in the next room on the couch shouted in to me, 'What do you want? What's the matter?'

"I asked, 'What did you say? Did you call me?' He said he hadn't.

"Later, when my daughter arrived home, I told her about the voices and she said she'd heard them a few times as well. Actually, she seemed truly petrified. It seems that they had been bothering her for a while, but she was afraid to mention it to anyone for fear we would all think she was crazy.

"At times, she said the voices would call her by name, but even though I was in her company when this happened, I could never hear anything.

"Despite these intrusions in our life, I never did get the impression that we were dealing with anything that was particularly harmful. If I had felt that way I would have really been upset since there were so many youngsters in the household.

"Things really got out of hand the day before Labor Day. Everybody had gone out to see the fireworks display put on by our neighborhood carnival and I was sitting around the kitchen getting the food ready for the next day when I heard a sound coming from the basement. It was the sound of someone walking across a board that had been placed at the bottom of the stairs to cover an open sewer pipe. When you step on it, it makes a little plunking sound, and someone was going back and forth across it repeatedly and it was driving me crazy.

"Not wanting to get hysterical and trying to brush the matter aside, I kind of laughed and thought, 'Oh, I've got company.' It was like a feeling of not being alone. Now and then, I got a little upset because it plunked a little too loud. I would go to stand out on the porch for a little while just to clear my head and then go back into the house.

"I had a loaf of bread on top of a cabinet in the kitchen and it started falling off. At first, I thought maybe it had just slipped off, but I knew this wasn't the case when it happened four or five times.

"When the family got back from the fireworks display, I told them what had happened and that I had this strange feeling that I wasn't alone. When I explained what had happened to the boards, my daughter replied they had been hearing that all day long, but didn't want to say anything about it. Her husband and my oldest son also heard it. My daughter's husband even got up a couple of times to see if it was the kids fooling around and there was nobody there. He said, 'It would sound just like someone was walking around down there and then when you went to look, you couldn't find anything.'

"After my daughter and her friend Linda left, I just sat in the kitchen working on some stuff and the bread fell again. I said, 'O.K. now. I'm busy. Let's knock it off. I'm getting tired of picking the bread up.' I didn't realize that one of my sons was in the room at the time. At this point, everything that I had on the shelf—room deodorizer, spray, newspapers, window spray, all came down. I yelled, 'Oh, you've got to be nasty. I don't have enough to do. You have to make more work for me.'

"As I put everything back, my son came in the room. He said, 'Is there really somebody here? Do you see somebody? What's going on?'

"I said, 'Oh shut up and go to bed.' That was all the trouble we experienced that night.

"Our 'friend' seems to like my air conditioner. One night the dogs were barking out back and there was nothing outside. I shut off the air conditioner in order to go and check on the dogs. When we were below my bedroom window, my husband said, 'The air conditioner isn't on.'

"I said, 'No, I shut it off so I could hear the dogs better.'

"So, we were out back of the house trying to figure out what was wrong with Max. He had plenty of water and food. It wasn't that. He wasn't nervous, like he was that other time. He wasn't shaking. The dog was upset about something in the air.

"All of a sudden, my husband turned and said, 'What was that?'

"I asked him, 'What's what?'

"He said, 'The air conditioner just went on. Then it went off again, But just as we went by the window, it went on again.' There is no way to shut it off and turn it on without pushing the buttons. When I had shut it off, it was on 'Off.' When we went back indoors it was 'On.'

"I said, 'Well, thank you, whoever you are. It is hot in there.'

"My husband said, 'I know that thing was off. I know that thing went on and off a couple of times.'

"I said, 'I know it's George.'

"He said, 'Well, tell your friend to leave. I don't want him hanging around here.'

"I said, 'You tell him to leave.' We went to bed and there wasn't any more trouble that night.

"The next incident was about a month later. It was near the end of August. I was in bed and I had to go to the bathroom. So, I walked out to the living room, where the children were sleeping. There were no lights on. I stopped in the middle of the living room and looked into the kitchen. There was someone standing there. I couldn't see any clothes on him, so I thought it was my daughter's husband. He often walks around in only his shorts. It was very dark so it was difficult to see really well.

"I was just getting ready to say, 'What the hell are you doing here?' when I thought, 'No, wait a minute, that's not my daughter's husband. How come it's so dark and I can still see him? There's something wrong.' I didn't want to take any chances in case it was someone who broke in.

"As I backed up to hit the light switch, he started leaving, moving behind the refrigerator. As the light came on, he disappeared right through the wall.

"Then I grabbed my flashlight, went into the bedroom, and turned it on my husband. He asked me what was the matter. I said, 'There was a man out in the kitchen.'

"He said, 'Yeah, let me go get him.'

"I said, 'Forget it, he just went through the wall.'

"He said, 'What, what are you talking about?'

"I had not been scared. I would have been more frightened if it was a human. When I thought about it, I realized it couldn't have been human, because it was like a shadow. I wasn't scared of him, because if he wanted to do anything, the two kids were in there. He could have done something to them. He doesn't seem to bother anyone, outside of scaring my poor daughter to death. I don't particularly like it when he comes into the room at night. He has grabbed my foot at times, which I don't like.

"Objects in the house have disappeared from time to time. For example, one morning I woke up and I didn't notice anything until I was talking on the phone. I went to rub my rings, which is a habit that I have, and they were gone from my fingers. I found the one which wasn't worth anything on the bed. I could see that one coming off because it's big.

"On the other hand, I could never get my wedding ring off. I looked all over the house for it. I couldn't get any work done. I paced back and forth and said, 'Look, I thought you were a nice guy. Taking the ring off my hand is not very nice. That's stealing.'

"I had just about given up when I went into the living room to straighten up. There I found the ring, on the floor, by the door. This was strange because I had looked all over the house. It could easily have been seen there. Also, it's just not possible to get the ring off my finger. This really bothered me, that 'he' could come into the room and had taken the ring, which is impossible to remove, without my knowing about it.

"Around the same time, our neighbor who has a small trucking company started to complain to us that on several occasions he had heard someone fooling around back of his place in the woods. He was so paranoid that they might be trying to steal some of his valuable equipment and goods that he took to staying up at night to protect his property. He would sleep out back in a little shed with a shotgun in hand, and though he often heard someone poking around, he never saw a soul. He had some boards set up behind his house and at night he would hear footsteps, but he'd never catch a glimpse of anyone upon turning on the outdoor light. He told us that he'd heard sounds coming from the woods. He said he's going to blow their damn fool heads off when he catches whoever is causing the disturbances.

"There was another incident where one of my sons was lying on the living room floor and someone booted him smack in the behind."He gave out a loud yelp and before I knew it he was knocking on my door wanting to know if he could crash in my room, since he was afraid to stay by himself.

"That same night the air conditioner started going on and off by itself. I turned my flashlight on and I could see that the button had been turned off. I pushed it back on and said, 'Knock it off.'

"We knew that there was someone by the window, even though we couldn't see anyone. The pushing of the air conditioner button went on forever it seemed. My husband thought it was dangerous to keep the air conditioner plugged in.

"'Shut it off, it must have a short in it,' he kept saying, but he couldn't explain how the buttons would move in and out by themselves.

A Shadowy Figure In An Otherwise Quiet Household.

"Finally, I unplugged the air conditioner, but it plugged itself back into the wall socket and stayed on the rest of the night. Next, we heard a strange rustling sound by the window, to which I said, 'Please, don't turn the air conditioner off again, it's really warm in here.'

"In response, the curtain on the window fell. With that, I got my pillows and blankets and brought them out into the living room.

"My twenty-year-old son thought I'd really gone off the deep end and he said he was going to prove it was all my imagination playing tricks on me. I waited to see how long he would last in the bedroom. My son got really scared when he felt the presence of someone looking at him in the dark, and it was really all over for him when the shade went flying up. He ran out of the room, his face as white as snow.

"With that, I went back into the room and said, 'In the name of God I ask you to leave.' The air conditioner went off and on again and after that we didn't have any more trouble that night.

"Another time, two of the kids said they had seen two men, a short one and a tall one, standing on the roof of the house and that they had coveralls on and that when they unzipped them they had some sort of strange suit on underneath their outerwear. I was in the living room later and I felt someone standing near me and heard the sound of a zipper being pulled up and down.

"Still, at other times, I saw weird white-blue lights in my bedroom at night that were not reflections from the street. The whole house was being turned upside down. Things were missing that would show up in unpredictable places, there would be eerie sounds and a creepy feeling as if we were never alone.

"The second Sunday in October, at about 5:00 AM, I was lying in bed and I heard what sounded like a motor running. I woke my husband up and he mumbled something about someone trying to steal his truck. He jumped up and flew outside while I looked for my slippers. I was still looking for them when he came running back, slamming the door and bolting the latch behind him.

"'What did you see?' I asked him.

"'Never mind. It's nothing. Let's forget it and go back to bed.'

"Even the next day, my husband wouldn't talk about it. All that I could get out of him was, 'The last time I told you I saw something, you said I was nuts. So I'm nuts.' I've talked about this experience to Tim Beckley and he says there have been other cases where invisible entities have come into a person's house and made themselves right at home."

UFOS - WICKED THIS WAY COMES: THE DARK SIDE OF THE ULTRA-TERRESTRIALS

Monia Staford's drawing of her incredible UFO abduction.

A NIGHT OF TERROR ABOARD A MOTHERSHIP

Normally, in the case of an abduction by aliens, there is seldom more than one person involved, although the number of multiple-witness cases is increasing rapidly these days.

Anyone in a car or at home who might remember something finds themselves either unable to awaken or they are literally "frozen in time." In this sense, the case of three Kentucky women was an important breakthrough in abduction cases, as they all recalled—in varying detail—being aboard a large mother ship and examined by the ET-like crew. Their experience, in this respect, is valuable in terms of the history of UFOlogy.

"They are still with us all of the time."

Elaine Thomas' words echo the feelings of all three Liberty, Kentucky, women who were abducted by UFOnauts on the night of January 9, 1976.

"I think they want me to be quiet," Elaine says. The "they" she is referring to are the creatures who held her and her girlfriends, Mona Stafford and Louise Smith, captive on a UFO for approximately an hour and a half.

"I think they are beaming that thought to me," she continues. "And I'm sure they are communicating with us."

Elaine Thomas revealed this to the author in an exclusive interview. We asked her to elaborate.

"One night after it happened, I told the girls that I had a feeling I could communicate with them, and that I was going to do just that," Elaine says. "They laughed at me. Still, they agreed to go along with what I wanted to do.

"And what I wanted to do was to go back to the Redwood Restaurant in

UFOS – WICKED THIS WAY COMES: THE DARK SIDE OF THE ULTRA-TERRESTRIALS

Sanford where it had all started.

"Nothing happened there or on the way back," Elaine reports, "but when I was standing just outside Louise's home, I felt this trembling come over me. I went inside and I noticed that I had all these golden cobwebs on me. I told the girls to look. I felt that this was their way of symbolizing that they had communicated with me that night.

"I grabbed a strand of this mysterious substance and it squeaked between my fingers. Louise came over to look at it under the light, and as soon as she touched it, it vanished. There were little golden strands all over me, like hair. But they all disappeared quickly."

According to Elaine Thomas, everyone in Louise's home saw the strange web-like material. She described it as being stiff to the touch, like metal or plastic, and very shiny.

The woman was convinced that the beings which had held her captive were trying to make their presence known. Louise and Mona share that feeling. Louise Smith declared, "I feel that they know everything I do. It's a bad feeling, because there are so many things I remember about the incident that have never been told. I remember making a promise to them that I would never tell, and if I did tell, I felt that I would not know what would happen to me."

The Strange Craft

It was Mona Stafford's 35th birthday, and to celebrate, the trio had decided to dine at the Redwood Restaurant. Finishing their dinner, they left for home at 11:15 PM. The restaurant is located 29 miles from Liberty in Sanford, Kentucky. Normally, it takes Louise roughly 40 minutes to complete the drive from the restaurant to their home. This evening it took much longer!

The route she takes is Kentucky #78, a small country road which runs between Sanford and Hustonville. It's a winding road, cutting through the hilly countryside dotted with farms and wooded areas.

All three were sitting in the front seat of Louise's green 1957 Chevy Nova. They were laughing and chatting when Mona suddenly gasped, "Look! It's coming down! It's going to crash!"

Their immediate thought was that a jet plane was on fire, and that it was screaming toward the earth right ahead of them. The object was a brilliant red light, and it was coming down very fast and at a sharp angle. The "thing" suddenly stopped at tree-top level and then paced the car. Elaine Thomas was able to tell that the object was disc-shaped and domed, with its leading edge tilted down toward the car. She estimated that it was less than 100 feet away.

The lights on the object were red and yellow and appeared to rotate around the bottom of the craft. It rocked back and forth, moving from one side of the car to the other.

The object was huge! It was what researchers might term a "mother ship."

At this point, Elaine appeared to fall into a trance-like state. She opened the car door to get out. Mona, in the middle, screamed at her, reached across and shut the door. The vehicle suddenly picked up speed until it was moving at about 85 miles an hour—of its own accord. Mona shifted her attention to Louise, who struggled desperately to keep the car on the road. Mona yelled, "Slow down!"

Louise gasped, "Mona, look! My foot's not on the gas pedal!"

Louise Smith said later, "We were so frightened. I'm not ashamed to admit I was really scared. The light from the spacecraft came into the car. It's hard to describe. It was like a fog, a bluish light, and our heads began to hurt something terrible.

"And my car went out of control," Louise recalls. "I yelled to Mona to help me handle the wheel. The two of us struggled, but we couldn't control the car. It was very hot inside and it was difficult to breathe. The car felt like it was being drawn toward what looked like a rock wall with an opening where a gate should be.

"Then all at once we had the feeling that the car was being pulled backwards," Louise says. "It went over a speed breaker in the road, but we learned later it was a cable crossing through a gate, and we were drawn right through the opening."

Louise told us that she felt the car was being drawn to the craft by way of the light or beam emanating from the ship. She was aware of the car being lifted off the ground, but after that her memory is blank. Nor can Mona or Elaine remember what happened after the Chevy Nova began its ascent.

Memory Loss and a Neck Burn

Louise says, "But a split second later we were in Hustonville, about eight or nine miles from where we had the sighting, and we were thinking, how the hell did we get here so fast? Yet that split second had been an hour and a half later!"

In Liberty, Louise drove to her mobile home. Inside, she complained about her neck hurting her. Mona and Elaine looked at it and saw that she had an ugly red mark, like a burn, which ran from her hairline down to her back.

Mona and Elaine had similar marks on their necks. Mona took off her ring and saw that the skin under it was very red. She also noted that her eyes burned.

Louise said, "I had taken a bath before going out to eat, but now for some reason I felt very dirty. I don't know why."

The mystery of the women's wrist watches was never solved. According to a report in "The Ohio Sky Watcher," Elaine's watch had stopped. Louise's watch showed 6:00, and the minute hand was moving as fast as the second hand. She was so frightened by her watch's behavior that she jerked it off her wrist and threw it down. She then went into the kitchen to look at the stove clock. It read: 1:25. The three of them were amazed. They should have been home at midnight. Where had they been for the last hour and 25 minutes?

Blistered Paint

After an almost sleepless night, the three decided to drive back to the road they had been on the night before. That was when they saw the blistered paint on Louise's car, which looked as though it had been subjected to terrific heat. They drove to the area, but found nothing of interest. The most puzzling aspect for them was why it had taken them so long to get home. Mona Stafford felt that she couldn't keep quiet about it any longer—she had to tell someone. She called the Kentucky State Police. The officer listened politely, but said he could do nothing for her. Mona then called the naval recruiting office in Danville. The individual there got in touch with the Lexington television station, Channel 27.

Mona, Louise and Elaine found themselves in front of TV cameras. The last thing they wanted was publicity. All they really wanted to know was what had happened to an hour and a half of their lives.

Subsequent interviews appeared in local newspapers, and the stories then found their way to OUFOIL (Ohio UFO Investigators League, Inc.). Jim Miller, an investigator for the organization, offered to help the women. However, because of previous commitments, he and a team of researchers from the group were unable to get to Liberty, Kentucky, until the latter part of February.

By that time, Mona, Elaine and Louise had suffered great changes. Each had dropped 15 pounds of weight. They had lost their appetite. Sleep was almost out of the question. They would not go anywhere alone, and did not dare venture out after dark.

Writing in "The Ohio Sky Watcher," Jim Miller states: "We talked with the women, saw the remains of the burn marks on their necks, checked the blistered areas on the car, talked to the local police and had a good general idea of what the women were going through. We even checked Louise's pet parakeet, which was very friendly with Louise before the sighting, but would now fly toward the back of the cage when she came near.

"We called the weather office in Lexington and found visibility was fifteen miles on January 6, with a cloud cover at 10,000 feet and the temperature was 38 degrees. We also had other reports that same night from people in the county of strange lights in the sky that were not from airplanes."

Hypnotic Regression

It was agreed that hypnosis might be the answer, the feeling being that the women might recall under hypnosis what their conscious minds had kept blocked from them. The women also agreed to undergo polygraph tests.

It must be pointed out here that these interviews with "The Ohio Sky Watcher" and the testing had taken place over a period of months. By July, the women were no better off physically than they had been shortly after the sighting. They continued to lose weight. They found themselves running to doctors more than ever. They had nightmares. Mona Stafford's eyes still bothered her.

In fact, Mona's nightmares were probably scarier than the others. She reported that every time she closed her eyes to go to sleep, a strange vision of an eye would appear to her. It frightened her so much that she quickly opened her eyes.

On July 7, while she was trying to doze off, two "eyes" appeared. They looked like rather normal eyes, but they did jolt her nonetheless.

On July 19th, Mona had been watching television. As the last program went off the air, a snowy pattern appeared. She stared at it and suddenly felt that someone was watching her. Turning away from the TV screen, she caught sight of a man's face; he was apparently about five feet away from her and was staring at her. He had red hair and a red curly beard. When she jumped up, the entity vanished.

This was indicative of the kind of hell the women were going through during this period. They were still unable to account for an hour and a half of their time on January 6. Finally, Dr. Leo Sprinkle was called in to hypnotize the women. Dr. Sprinkle, an associate professor of psychology at the University of Wyoming, has been involved in many UFO "lost time cases," and felt that this was a good one.

The hypnosis and the polygraph testing were conducted at the Brown Motel in Liberty, Kentucky. The women passed the polygraph tests with no difficulty, and after two days of hypnosis, some startling results came to light.

The Humanoids

Louise related, "Under hypnosis, we were able to recall quite a bit about our time in 'captivity.' One of the things in particular was that I was alone on the craft, separated from Mona and Elaine. In fact, we were all separated from each other. At no time were two of us together.

"It was very hot," Louise continued. "They kept my face covered most of the time. But at one point I begged so hard, crying that I wanted to see, that they removed whatever they had over my face, and I did see—I guess they were humanoid—that's the only way I can describe them. They were about four and a half feet tall. Their hands were very different from ours, like a wingtip with jagged feathers instead of normal fingers."

Louise Smith went on: "They didn't talk. I knew what they wanted me to do, but it was only when they looked at me that I would know. There was no verbal communication whatsoever."

When asked if they examined her, she said, "Yes, at one point they had one of my arms pinned down. I couldn't move it. I tried to, desperately. I don't know what held it down."

Did they hurt her?

"It did hurt. When they pulled on my arms, it hurt, and some of the things they did to me hurt. I remember that they poured some liquid over me. When they peeled it off, it was like removing a band-aid. I had a crazy thought that they were making a mold of me."

Elaine Thomas apparently had an even more frightening experience while being held captive. Under hypnosis she revealed that a bullet-like object had been pressed painfully against the left side of her breast.

"This object on my left side," Elaine recounted, "was pressed against me and it was a terrible, painful force. I could feel the pain in my chest and mouth."

Metal Clamp

"And they choked me. Every time I tried to cover up for the girls, they would put this metal clamp around my throat. It felt like it had fingers. I tried to scream, but they kept choking me."

We asked Elaine if she felt that they were trying to communicate with her.

"I kept thinking," she said, "that they don't want me to talk. All I wanted to do was get away, but I couldn't move. My arms and legs were pinned down. I was paralyzed. I couldn't even move my head.

"It was dark where I was. There was fog. I could just barely see the hooded objects floating around me. They looked to be about four feet tall.

"Some kind of light came through the fog, or smoke, or whatever it was. Gray light. There were four of these creatures and I couldn't see their faces."

Elaine then told us about a single, detached eye which looked down at her. At this point, she could see nothing but the eye, which was at a distance of about four feet. She described it as being similar in shape to that of a turtle's eye. Its color was blue. It hovered above her for about three seconds.

"The eye was very plain," Elaine said. "There was no white space, like a human would have. I saw it so quickly, and then it was gone."

More questions

None of the women had any idea where the creatures were from. However, Mona Stafford, the least talkative of the trio, felt that the craft they were on might have been inside a mountain or a volcano, since she could look up and see what appeared to be small white clouds passing across a blue sky.

Under hypnosis, Mona also recalls being taken from the larger ship the women were originally transported aboard and placed inside a smaller craft, where, through a transparent section of the craft, she could actually observe the larger craft pulling away into space. In addition, the Ohio Investigators League also have in their file a drawing that the witness made which shows a woman lying on a table, surrounded by four beings who appear to be seated on the floor, as if they were in a meditative position. Mona claims this scene took place in a room directly opposite the one she was detained in, and that the door was opened a crack so she could watch what was going on.

Of the three, Mona has perhaps had the most negative results. "Emotionally," she says, "this has worn me thin." The petite blonde has lost thirty pounds. She spends most of her waking hours thinking about the incident and admits that she gets very little sleep.

UFOS - WICKED THIS WAY COMES: THE DARK SIDE OF THE ULTRA-TERRESTRIALS

Hysterical

She has a copy of the tape that was made while she was under hypnosis. "I get so upset listening to it," she says. The sobs that came through on the tape cause her to flinch. Louise Smith appears to be the least troubled of the three. Her health has faltered. She weighs only 97 pounds. Yet she is determined to keep her spirits up. "I've coped pretty well," she says. "I've just blocked this thing out, right from the beginning."

We might add that Louise is also the most daring of the three women. She often drives along Kentucky Route 78, sometimes alone and late at night, to prove to herself that there is nothing to fear.

Not The Same Person

"I feel I have a knowledge now, a knowledge that's hard to explain. You know, I never really thought much about UFOs before. It's the kind of thing you have to experience before you can tell what it's like. "I don't feel that whatever they are," says Louise, "that they want to harm or destroy me. I believe there could be life on other planets, and if we can go to the moon, why can't they come here? I think that eventually everyone will see them. Maybe not in the same way we did, but at least everyone will be aware that they are here.

"Looking back, that was a beautiful thing. I'd like to study it. Maybe try to communicate. I crave knowledge about anything and everything. Before, things like that didn't bother me."

Elaine Thomas also feels that she is not the same person she had been before the abduction. The tall, large-featured woman told us that she is no longer interested in painting. She feels that her intuitions about things have become much stronger. "And you know, sometimes I feel kind of like a little child. I just want to get out and play." UFOlogists insist that this case is bona fide.

They all believe the women are telling the truth. Their polygraph tests prove that they were not lying about their experience. In future sessions under hypnosis, it is hoped that many more details will be revealed. Who knows? It is possible that still locked in their subconscious are all the answers to the mysteries of flying saucers and alien encounters!

MAN'S LIFE DRAMATICALLY ALTERED AFTER CLOSE ENCOUNTER

The case of John Clark contains just about every "strangeness" a researcher is likely to encounter during the course of a single investigation. Although we do not know why certain individuals seem to attract the "unknown," John Clark, in this respect, turned out to be a paranormal magnet.

In the classic film, "Close Encounters of the Third Kind," we see how the sudden appearance of UFOs eventually comes to radically change the lifestyle of Roy Neary. Following his brush with a pulsating craft from the unknown, the power-linesman finds he is the subject of considerable ridicule even by members of his own family. His wife leaves him, his children are the brunt of neighborhood jokes, and he finds himself out in the street without a job because he was at the wrong place at the right time.

And even though "Close Encounters" was basically a science fiction epic, almost everything that happened in this motion picture has transpired at one time or another in reality. The appearance of UFOs has had bizarre effects on many witnesses.

Take the case of John Clark. Things both good and bad have been happening all around him since he saw a landed spaceship in 1975. Clark was on vacation with his wife when he underwent an experience he is not likely to forget.

After the incident, John's life turned around. A truck driver for the "San Francisco Chronicle," Clark just recently won a $40,000 grand prize in a contest, and he admits his "luck" may have something to do with what transpired on that day more than fifteen years ago in the Sequoia National Park. Unfortunately, John Clark's "luck" has not been all good. He maintains that his "good fortunes" are paralleled by negative happenings. For example, tornadoes have leveled hotels where he is staying, and in addition, several times the engine of a plane he will be flying in will cut off mysteriously.

To date, John Clark has gone to see priests, psychics and psychiatrists in an attempt to find out what has been causing these strange things to transpire. So far nobody seems to have all the answers.

For Clark it all began in the summer of 1975 when he was on vacation with his wife (they are now divorced). But let John tell the story himself:

"My former wife and I were camping with another couple. I heard something and woke up. I saw this thing about nine feet tall with long blond hair, kind of illuminated, sort of gliding across the clearing. My friend saw it too and ran for his gun. Then it was gone."

The next day Clark says his wife took out a Ouija board and tried to communicate with whoever—or whatever—it was that had crossed in front of them during the night. Her hands began to move of their own accord and little by little a strange message was given on the Ouija board. The board spelled out the name "Q-ON," indicating that it was the source of communications for the universe with a station positioned approximately five million light years away in space. Through "Q-ON" it was revealed that the Clarks had seen Bigfoot, an alien "that crashed there in 1863 from the planet Pluto."

The message stated that Bigfoot was a vegetarian and lived in caves. It also said that the alien had been shot two times by humans.

Shaken by what they had been told through the Ouija board, John and his wife tossed the device into the nearest trash can. Perhaps they should have held on to it in order to sort out what was to happen over the period of the next six years.

As time went on, Clark became more disturbed over the session with the Ouija board and the sighting of this tall being. He went around consulting so-called "experts." He went to see several ministers who simply told him that he had bumped into the devil. On the other hand, representatives of the Academy of Psychic Science located in San Diego strongly suggested that he had seen a mammal that had escaped Greenland before the Ice Age. Others talked in terms of "ghosts" and "supernatural experiences." Nobody seemed to have the whole answer.

Eventually, according to Warren Hickle's column in the "San Francisco Chronicle," Clark was placed into a hypnotic trance. The paper printed this version of what took place at the regression session:

"Now, you're back in Sequoia Park, the night it happened. You're going to raise your left hand and bring it across your chest," the hypnotist said. "Now, there's nothing to be afraid of. You can tell us what happened that night."

Clark started to talk. His speech was like warm milk. "I was surrounded by a blue light. A bright blue light. I was cold," he said.

"Did you feel any sensation?" the hypnotist asked.

"I was being lifted," Clark responded.

"What happened then?" the hypnotist continued.

"I'm lying on the table. There's a bright white light above me. There's big eyes looking down at me."

"What color are the eyes?"

"Yellow. Big yellow eyes. They had black slits in them. I couldn't see their bodies."

"Could you feel anything?"

"Something cold in my stomach. Something sticking in and out of my stomach like steel pins."

"You mean like they were probing you?"

"Yes."

"Can you remember anything else?"

John Clark is still not satisfied that he has all the answers. He plans to continue to probe deeper to find out exactly what happened on that night several years ago.

UFOS - WICKED THIS WAY COMES: THE DARK SIDE OF THE ULTRA-TERRESTRIALS

PROVEN BEYOND A DOUBT!
UFOs Caused East Coast Blackout!

Even as far back as the early 1950s, it became apparent that UFOs were capable of draining power, whether it was the charge contained in a car battery, or shutting off the electrically operated appliances in one's home, or an entire community, to knocking out the extremely sensitive instruments in the cockpits of our fastest jets—both civilian and military.

It is not known if UFOs wish to show their abilities to cause havoc on our society, or if this EM effect is simply a drainage by-product of these craft being in our atmosphere. But to think they have the power to shut off electricity in an entire portion of the country must be exceedingly frightening to those who are in charge of our nation's defense.

Are the UFOs now making themselves known by causing giant power failures? There is evidence that this may be the case.

The UFO which caused the giant northeastern blackout which plunged some 30 million persons into total darkness was even photographed by an outstanding member of the community and was observed by dozens of persons.

Even actor Stuart Whitman, who starred in the motion picture "The Sound and the Fury," claimed to have observed and even talked with the occupants of a UFO on the night "the lights went out" in New York City. Whitman vows that during the 1965 power failure, two flying saucers pulled up outside his hotel window and the occupants chatted with him and admitted that they were responsible for the power failure which engulfed millions of others in darkness.

UFOS - WICKED THIS WAY COMES: THE DARK SIDE OF THE ULTRA-TERRESTRIALS

He described the objects as one being blue and the other orange in color. He said that he was not able to see portholes in them because of their basic brilliance, but said they appeared like a whirlwind, shifting their position as they hovered by his window. He is quoted as having said: "They spoke to me all the while in English. But later on I thought that perhaps this might not have been audible to anyone else (sort of telepathic). They said they wanted to talk with me because they felt I appeared to have no malice or hate in me. They said that they were most fearful of Earth because earthlings were messing around with many unknown quantities and might disrupt the balance of the universe or their planet. The people in the UFO said that the blackout was just a little demonstration of their power and that they could do a lot more with almost no effort. It served as a warning. They said they could stop our whole planet from functioning. They asked me to do what I could to fight malice, prejudice and hate on Earth, and then they took off."

The reporters who interviewed Whitman said that he was dead serious and not the drinking type. This he proclaimed was NO JOKE.

The blackout on November 9th, 1965, which plunged an estimated 30 million persons in the Northeast, from Canada to New Jersey, into total darkness may have been the result of either a power-draining unidentified flying object which hovered and maneuvered in the sky near the New York-Canadian border, or a UFO which got too close to this important power system.

For weeks in a row, both before and after the blackout, reliable witnesses claim a huge UFO hung suspended in the sky turning night into day, and looking like a birthday candle over the area of Erieau, Ontario, Canada.

Residents of this secluded fishing town say that the object at times gave off puffs of smoke and would twist around in the sky as if controlled by intelligent forces. One of the first to witness these strange sky phenomena in Erieau was Harvey Vidler, who described the UFO as a big round light which moved up and down and back and forth. The light would go out and then reappear nearby during the entire evening, according to Mr. Vidler.

At the request of many citizens, the Canadian Air Force was asked to intervene in the matter, but it is not known what conclusions, if any, they came to regarding the situation.

The first sighting on the evening of the big blackout came from Weldon

Ross, who is self-employed as a pilot instructor working out of Hancock Field near the northern sector of Syracuse, New York.

While flying above Syracuse about 5:15 p.m., only a few minutes before the lights were to go out and not be turned back on in some places until shortly after six the following morning, he was certain that he, and a student pilot who was flying with him, had been witness to a flame colored globe of light. When later interviewed by the "New York Journal," Weldon is quoted as having said: "My first impression was that it was a building on fire. I said to the student with me, 'My God, somebody's in trouble. Look at the fire.' It originated on the ground and grew in size to about 100 feet around—a ball of fire, sort of reddish-orange, like nothing I ever saw before.

"Then, almost as quickly as I said it, it diminished, got smaller and finally, about 10 seconds after I first saw it, it disappeared completely."

From his position, Ross said he could estimate with some degree of certainty that the UFO first appeared over the New York Power Authority's Niagara Mohawk Company (attributed by some as being the source of the trouble) and during its rather brief visibility continuing on over the New York Central Railroad tracks near Lake Oneida.

Among many other persons known to have observed the exact or related event was Robert C. Walsh, employed by the city of Syracuse as Deputy Aviation Commander. Walsh said that while on a simple pleasure ride over the shopping district of downtown Syracuse, the lights seemed to dim, then brighten and then go out completely. At first he was panic stricken with the thought his eyes were failing him and, fearing that he might crash and hurt someone, he began to take evasive action. However, at about this point he could still barely see the lights from the traffic in the street and not knowing what to think he radioed the tower at Hancock Field. They told him, NOT KNOWING the overall widespread trouble, that the whole town had gone completely dark almost at once.

Deciding that he would be of more help on the ground than in the air, he proceeded to land his light single engine aircraft. Upon landing, he proceeded to help other pilots who were circling the field to come in safely.

Taking a needed rest, he and a few of the other airport officials sat down at the side of one of the long runways. Just about then he, and ten others, saw a large "ball of fire" south of them toward Thompson Road and Carrier traffic circle. "It appeared to be about 100 feet in the air and 50 feet in diameter. All I could think of was a mushroom effect," he later stated.

About ten or twelve minutes later another display, which I have yet to see an explanation for, was seen by the same witnesses at approximately the same or nearby location.

In the nearby town of Camillus, a Mrs. Dewey Boshers and her three children—Dewey 17, Howard 9, and Suzette 14—said they saw a "huge dome-shaped" object in the sky, with a mushroom-type trail. The object appeared to them to stay in the same position for a good ten minutes and then rose over the moon and then, suddenly, all the lights went out. The UFO then seemed to change its position in the sky and whisked away in a flash.

Tom Doxsee, another notable witness, said the object appeared to him as if it were a setting sun "only in the east." His observation, along with that of a neighbor, who said it stood on end and glowed yellow, was that it appeared to stay in the sky for about an hour after the lights went out,

Two pretty teenage co-eds who live on Mt. Olympus, a hilltop on Syracuse's beautiful campus, said they saw a smoking reddish ball "moving towards the dormitory complex with sparks coming out of it" both the night before the blackout and once again on November 15.

Another unidentified resident of Mattydale, near Hancock Field, said he witnessed an unusual sight in the form of an egg-shaped object while out driving on the night of the blackout.

But perhaps the biggest breakthrough came in the form of two pictures showing the mysterious sky visitor taken by William Stillwell, a sexton for the St. Pad's Episcopal Church in Syracuse and released to the news media on November 16th. He claims that he has seen identical objects on twelve different occasions. He claims that they travel at varying speeds, hover in the sky sometimes for hours and then take off in various directions. He says that he is quite certain that they are not any conventional type craft and he is at a loss to explain the phenomena.

One time, while looking through a telescope from the east wing of his private room in the church, he said he was able to get a good look at the "what is it" by turning the power to 117. The UFO's center appeared to be rotating, "going around and around."

Stillwell told newsmen: "Where they came from or whether they are manned or unmanned I don't know. I do know they aren't Air Force planes. We haven't got any planes that go that fast."

Residents as far removed from upper New York State as New Jersey and Connecticut also saw strange lights and objects in the sky on the night of the "big blackout."

One such event recorded in or near Somerville, New Jersey, by Mrs. John Dorr was unusual in that the UFO appeared to make a large "box" by moving up and down and back and forth. One New York City resident claimed that a very black and menacing cloud, in an otherwise perfectly clear sky, was the most unusual sight she had ever witnessed. And the funny thing about it is that it did not move but stayed in the exact same spot for a considerable length of time.

Suggestions for these events, which could not otherwise be explained, included an explosion in the city dump near Syracuse, the moon, street lights from a nearby city reflecting on cloud layers and dust blown up from the moon by the latest Russian space voyager, all of which failed to stand up under close investigation. Some in fact were harder to swallow than admitting that a UFO might have been responsible for the blackout.

Major UFO research organizations list many identical cases where UFOs have caused power failures.

With this case in mind, it is not hard to speculate that the cause of the subsequent flurry of reports in Pennsylvania, Ohio, Michigan, Indiana and as far away as California were in some way involved with UFO activity in the sky over the United States.

For on December 9th, 1965, over some seven states, a mysterious object or objects reportedly blew up, causing widespread brush fires.

Fallen debris from the objects, or one of them if such be the case, are said to have started fires in at least three states—Ohio, Pennsylvania and Michigan. The first report came from Windsor, Ontario, Canada, about 5:00 PM. Shortly thereafter the object was said to have fallen in the vicinity of Elyria, Ohio, but a search of a wooded area produced nothing. The witness, a Mrs. Ralph Richard, told the "New York Journal-American" that the object didn't have a tail or anything and she saw no smoke, although it did start a fire. It was not like a fireball, according to her, but instead was round and seemed to give off a blue-yellow glow which later turned to pure yellow. Officials stated that another woman reported seeing a UFO doing maneuvers in the sky and then falling to the earth near her home. It was not close enough for her to see any great amount of detail. The area in question, about 30 miles from Pittsburgh, was quickly roped off by the Army as reported on the 1:00 AM news broadcast over New York's WNBC-TV.

About the same time, near Laper, Michigan, two small stacks of shredded foil were found by the Sheriff's office investigating reports that a flaming UFO had fallen in the area.

The U.S. Coast Guard said a flying object apparently exploded over the Windsor-Detroit area and four vessels were dispatched into Lake St. Clair but they could find nothing.

And indeed, if it was a meteor or fireball, it was the most unusual on record, as it was seen from Indiana, Ohio, Pennsylvania and Canada. It was also observed in California by two patrolmen, Charles Seril and Clark Mears, a number of hours later.

They said it moved in a southerly direction over the hills west of San Francisco Bay. Police reported phone calls on sightings of a second object at 5:40 AM.

A meteor that crashes in five different places, starts fires, vanishes and then shows up thousands of miles away hours later sounds better than any saucer tale to date.

To back up the idea of stopping wars or nuclear experiments which might affect the entire universe, while President Johnson was in Hawaii (early February 1966) speaking with representatives of the Vietnamese government, an entire two mile radius around his hotel room had an unexplained power failure. The lights returned some 10 minutes later as mysteriously as they had gone out. No explanation was offered,

Other power failures in the turbulent 1960s included a hundred mile strip of the southwestern U.S. from El Paso to Central New Mexico (the site of much UFO activity since 1964) that was without power for more than an hour on December 2, 1965.

UFOS - WICKED THIS WAY COMES: THE DARK SIDE OF THE ULTRA-TERRESTRIALS

On December 26th, a big power failure left some eight million persons in greater Buenos Aires without electric power for two hours.

Also in late December, 1965, all the south and central points of Finland, including the four largest cities of Helsinki, Turku, Tampere and Lahti, were darkened for fifteen minutes, leaving about three thousand persons without electrical power.

And on the night of January 8th, a UFO is thought to be responsible for a blackout which resulted in a loss of power in Southern Italy. Witnesses said a big fireball-like object flared across the sky and then disappeared.

SECRET MILITARY BASES AND UFOs

Freelance UFO investigator John Lear opened a Pandora's Box of controversy when he penned an open letter to fellow UFOlogists which was carried several years ago on Paranet, a computer bulletin board. In the letter, Lear spoke about the existence of underground bases which had allegedly been taken over by alien forces, from which a variety of "dirty deeds" were being performed, many in cooperation with various branches of the U. S. government.

Soon afterwards, a retired Naval Intelligence Officer, William Cooper, came forward to tell of classified documents he had seen while in the service, which attested to some "strange things" taking place under the very noses of those we have elected to protect us. Likewise, Robert Lazar, who was employed as a civilian engineer at an underground base known as "Dreamland" in the Nevada desert, went on TV after his life was threatened for telling how he would daily be taken by bus to an underground facility to work on aerial craft which were not manufactured on this planet, but had been captured by the military and were being flown on a regular basis in order to discover the kind of technology used be the extraterrestrial vehicles.

This report was provided by the astute researcher Bruce Walton shortly before he gave up probing into extraterrestrial matters—perhaps because he realized he had learned too much about the secrets of flying saucers. Walton writes:

I am writing to pass on a few things which I've come across in relation to secret military bases and UFOs.

UFOS – WICKED THIS WAY COMES: THE DARK SIDE OF THE ULTRA-TERRESTRIALS

The first rather lengthy description came my way from an investigator in Airport, Texas [name on file at publisher's office]. The first part of this letter refers to a secret installation at Ft. Hood, which apparently has some connection with secret military UFO-type craft. It is interesting to recall the theories put forward by some investigators to the effect that the government has retrieved several crashed disks of unknown origin, and from their examination of these disks have been able to construct a crude type of "saucer" vehicle which uses a revolutionary means of propulsion.

This Ft. Hood case is interesting indeed, and I would really like for someone to either find more leads on it or debunk it and lay it to rest. Against the assertion that there is an underground hangar of some kind with a large door on a hillside is the fact that Ft. Hood lies in an area of almost total flatness. If there is a hill it would have to be a man-made one. The area is also dry country, and keeping such a hill concealed would be a monumental task indeed. However, the Ft. Hood reservation is quite large and inaccessible to the public, and there is a zone above it which is restricted from access by civilian aircraft. The whole state of Texas is densely populated, even in rural areas, and it would seem that someone would have seen something. The Ft. Hood reservation is also within a relatively close range of the area where the Cash/Landrum [UFO] case occurred. It has always been my contention that this case was caused by a test of some sort of military craft or weapon which malfunctioned and exposed the witnesses to radiation.

It has recently been disclosed that Carswell Air Force Base in Ft. Worth was actively involved in nuclear-powered aircraft research well into the 1970s. As interesting as it would be to ascribe the Cash/Landrum case to a UFO, the evidence points to a military experiment gone haywire.

There are a couple of more things of interest I have come to dead ends on. There is, supposedly, a highly secret military base of some sort in Henderson County, Texas, just north of the city of Athens. The area is densely forested, but from the crest of one hill one can see a water tower and what appear to be several buildings. There is no access, FROM ANY SIDE, to this facility, dirt roads notwithstanding. There is a fence around the perimeter of the place that is noticeable from a few spots. Unmarked, though mundane, military aircraft of some sort can be seen occasionally landing or taking off. If one takes a detailed look at a Henderson County map, there is a sizeable hole of perhaps 25 square miles to the north of Athens. No roads go through the area, as I have said. Now, what could this facility be? This is also due north from the site of the Cash/Landrum case. A mid-1980s report in the MUFON Journal described a possible abduction-type case near Cedar Creek Lake, which is also in Henderson County and perhaps 10 miles by air from the unusual facility I have driven down that particular road on which the case occurred and can attest to the fact that if nothing else it is a desolate and spooky stretch of road.

Now keep in mind that I have gotten this next bit of information second-hand, so I have no idea as to its validity. Perhaps readers of this book have heard of this intriguing incident and can fill in more of the blanks!

In early 1985, police officers in Mansfield, just south of Ft. Worth, Texas, conducted a raid on a drug laboratory which was set up in a residence. Two people were arrested, chemical apparatuses were confiscated, and during the search police found two unusual gun-like weapons.

All of this was duly carted off to a police station. One of the officers took special interest in one of the peculiar weapons. These are described as looking like a small rifle, with one or more coils of wire wound around the metallic barrel. There is a control on the side of the device, although I am not sure if it is a rotary switch or potentiometer. A pair of wires exits the device, and these are connected to a regular motorcycle battery.

A few days after the raid, a pair of supposed federal agents appeared at the station and demanded that the two devices be turned over to them. The police were able to convince the two men that there was only one device, and so only one was confiscated.

After this, the above-mentioned officer became even more interested, not surprisingly. He took the remaining device out into the parking lot and aimed it at a police car which had its engine on as well as the headlights. Upon pulling the trigger, the engine died and the lights went out. Luckily there was no one in the car, as the officer turned the knob on the device and aimed it at a cat that immediately fell dead.

Several days later, the officer took the device to General Dynamics in Ft. Worth, a large defense contractor (this was a grave mistake, in my opinion). Anyway, they decided to fire it at an idling jet engine. The engine immediately went dead. Not surprisingly, General Dynamics immediately became extremely interested in the device, and I am of the opinion that this move on the part of the police officer will close the case forever from scrutiny by civilian researchers.

Two important details regarding the unusual gun were that the device has two faceted clear crystals (quartz?) positioned on either side of the barrel at its end. In other words, they are mounted on the metallic barrel. The two suspects arrested were later transferred to the Johnson County Jail in Cleburn. They were put in separate cells, but were later both found dead. On top of this, the Mansfield police have been having problems with police car engines dying and drivers passing out. It would appear that more of these devices are still out there.

Another account involving both a reference to an underground installation and crashed discs was sent to me by a man from Raiford, Florida [name on file]. I quote from his letter to me:

"I know a man high up in Military Intelligence. He has a string of clearances you wouldn't believe. He has enough pull that he took a friend to the White House, Pentagon and the CIA building all via underground tunnels! Not the CIA in Langley, Virginia. That's just for the public eye, but the real(!) CIA underground installation which, incidentally, is only called the Central Intelligence Agency as a front. Its real name is the 'Criminal Intelligence Adjutants.'

"Anyway, this man's job is shutting up those who have witnessed UFOs, but first he makes sure he has extracted all the information. He then normally tells you to keep quiet, stating that it's a 'government project,' etc. He investigates mainly military personnel. He is a strange character, but he says that UFOs are real, and that the Hangar 18 episode was legitimate as he investigated it. He also added that if what he said was known he would be killed."

References to the underground tunnels beneath Washington, D.C. have also popped up at different times in the history of UFO investigation. James Brandon, in his book "Weird America," refers to them as "Atlantean" tunnels, already there when the founding fathers laid out D.C., and that they also connect with the "Octagon Building," an old-time spy shop.

Richard Toronto, editor of the now-defunct "Shaverton" magazine, knows a man who claims to have talked to an engineer in Washington who said they were about 100,000 years old (carbon dating), lined with a super-hard glaze, and connect many of the D.C. buildings.

This probably connects with the fact that in early 1977, President Jimmy Carter announced a few details of a top secret Pentagon project code-named "Noah's Ark." It is, supposedly, a system of 96 "bunkers" and "bolt holes" which have been established at various locations on or near the Earth to house approximately 6,500 key officials in case of a nuclear war. Many of these bolt holes are underground cities complete with streets, sidewalks, lakes, small electric cars, apartments and office buildings. One such "city" is carved out of a mountain near Washington (Upperville, Virginia). It is called "Mount Weather." Other such "cities" are most probably located at each of the super VLF broadcast stations around the planet. Another one for sure is 60 miles north of Washington called "Raven Rock"

Lastly, another military installation which could be investigated is Ft. Irwin in California. There have been "rumors" circulating for years of secret tunnels/installations there, and more recently reports of possible military ET/UFO activity in the area.

Even by the law of averages, some of these reports have to be based on truth, but it's going to take more digging on the part of dedicated and courageous investigators to lay out these bare facts to the cold light of day. The public has the right to know!

THE CRAWLING LIGHTS

In the mid-1960s, when I first investigated the case of the "crawling lights," I didn't believe we had much to compare it to. But now, other cases involving roaming beams of light have become a bit more frequent.

The case that most immediately comes to mind is the famous "Bentwaters Affair," involving a spacecraft that landed near a NATO base in England and included the sightings of humanoids and possible contact with U. S. military forces. At Bentwaters, rays were seen to shoot out of the forest and actually pass through the solid trunks of trees as well as parked military vehicles. So, in a sense, this incident we relate here was sort of a forerunner of what was to come.

Normally, Toledo, Oregon, is an extremely quiet community. Situated far from the bustling city of Portland, it is located in what can only rightfully be termed logging country. Yet the residents of Toledo and nearby Siletz are considered city folk to those husky backwoodsmen who make up the large percentage of homeowners on Pioneer Mountain.

Typical of these residents is the Douglas Reeves family. Or we should say former residents, because they no longer occupy their former modest dwelling. In back of their decision to leave is one of the most harrowing and baffling UFO incidents to date. Their account may well go down in UFOlogical history as the first attempt by UFO occupants to observe the daily actions of a rather typical, hard-working Earth family.

A total of some 35 to 40 persons claim to have witnessed some type of strange phenomena near the Reeves property. These strange phenomena ranged from spaceship-like crafts, to pulsating, doughnut-shaped lights that crawled along the walls of the house, to strange stump-like creatures.

The beginning of these weird events on Pioneer Mountain was in early March of 1966. During a walk through the woods, the Reeves' 16-year-old daughter, Kathy, and a girl friend suddenly glimpsed from the side of their eyes an apparent fire burning in an open section of ground some distance away that had been cleared of trees previously. Approaching closer, the teenagers noticed that instead of a fire there was some type of object hovering a few feet above the ground. The object, as the girls later described it, appeared to be giving off a "ruddy glow" which could be seen for some distance.

The object appeared to be dome-shaped with sparks and smoke flying in all directions, as if the craft were burning. Finally managing to get up some nerve, the two overly-excited and somewhat frightened girls headed for their nearby homes to get some older witnesses to back up their observations.

Hurrying now through the woods, they suddenly found themselves confronted with what appeared to be a large searchlight beacon. Thinking that someone was either trying to frighten them or play a joke on them, they both picked up some rocks and threw them at the light's source.

Suddenly, and without warning, they found themselves surrounded by identical lights which seemed to be moving in on them from all sides. Now near panic, the two raced at top speed to tell their parents.

On arriving home minutes later, the two teenagers managed to blurt out to Kathy's mother, Evelyn Reeves, what had happened. At first, Mrs. Reeves didn't take the girls seriously. She felt that they must be trying to pull her leg, not having taken seriously before reports of UFOs. However, she noted that they were extremely frightened and would not retract their story no matter how hard she tried to get them to.

After talking with her husband and the parents of the other girl, Mrs. Reeves decided the best thing to do was keep quiet about what had supposedly happened. After all, if these weird things had occurred, who would believe them? They figured that the entire family would be held open to ridicule.

However, had the family known about what was to happen that very same night, perhaps they would have thought otherwise.

At about midnight, after everyone had retired for the evening, Mrs. Reeves was awakened from a sound sleep to find the air filled with a strange-pitched hum like nothing she had ever heard before. Getting up to investigate, her eyes were at once attracted to the partly opened window of her bedroom. In between the curtains she could make out a light that appeared to be pulsating. As she drew the curtains apart, the entire bedroom was suddenly filled with a harsh glow emanating from what appeared to be a large object sitting in her yard. Suddenly all the rooms in the house were filled with the same glow. Likewise, appearing from nowhere were strange doughnut-shaped lights which seemed to be creeping up the very walls of their dwelling.

By this time the rest of the family was also awakened. The high-pitched hum was louder and more menacing than ever and the weird crawling lights were rapidly increasing in number.

Grabbing a gun from its rack in the living room, Mr. Reeves ran to the window and pointed it toward someone or "something" he thought he had seen moving outside. Suddenly the house sparkled anew with bright lights. Many more "crawling lights" also appeared on the walls and for a time it seemed as if the family would be overcome by hundreds of these strange doughnut-shaped lights.

Then the original reddish glow gradually dimmed and disappeared; the humming sound faded away and the night was black and still once again.

Although the Reeves were very frightened, they still felt it to their advantage to keep their "invaders" secret. And with the dawn of a new day, all seemed back to normal again. It was as if the previous night's happenings had been part of another world, totally separated from normal reality.

By and by the family forgot about the strange sounds, the bright red lights in their yard, and most of all the lights that had seemingly crept up their very walls. They soon dismissed the entire affair, feeling it would be best to leave well enough alone. They felt as if the worst had passed and they could again live a normal existence.

But their hopes were in vain, for the weird sights and sounds soon returned to haunt their home on Pioneer Mountain.

UFOS – WICKED THIS WAY COMES: THE DARK SIDE OF THE ULTRA-TERRESTRIALS

In the weeks to come the Reeves family was continually shaken out of a sound sleep about two or three o'clock in the morning to find the entire room filled with a rosy glow which they described as being so intense that "you could read a newspaper by it." In fact, these occurrences became so frequent and annoying that they finally boarded up their windows in an attempt to keep the lights out. Even this failed, and the crawling doughnut-shaped lights continued to creep up the walls.

On one particular occasion, Mrs. Reeves happened to look toward the door leading into their darkened living room and saw a cloud about the size and shape of a watermelon, but transparent, just hanging in midair. It seemed to hover there for minutes before it dissipated into nothing.

It was at this point that the family agreed it would be best to call in outsiders to have a look at their UFO phenomena.

One of these "outsiders" was Delbert Mapes, who told investigators how he had himself seen various lights and objects flying in a helter-skelter fashion through some trees in the Reeves' apple orchard. He described the phenomena as consisting of small round disc-shaped objects, giving off a bright light and traveling at high speeds. He also indicated that they produced a high-pitched hum that was almost inaudible.

Another of the witnesses was Max W. Taylor, a personal friend of the family. Taylor is a chemist employed by the Georgia Pacific Corporation. At the request of Mr. Reeves, he and a group of neighbors camped out on their property in an attempt to find a rational explanation for the phenomena. Although Taylor was highly skeptical when first contacted, he soon joined the ranks of believers. For he was not on the site more than a half hour when he saw a number of strange pulsating spots of bluish light. According to Taylor and the other witnesses, one spot turned up on the outside wall of the living room while the other spot appeared at the opposite end of the home, on the outside wall of the kitchen. Surprisingly enough, there was no apparent source for the light and no beam could be seen in-between.

Making a call to the local police, Taylor brought in a deputy sheriff, Thomas W. Price, from Lincoln County. At about 1:30 AM, Price arrived at the Reeves home, and as he was disembarking from his squad car he glanced upward and saw a fast-moving object that was flying from northeast to southeast. It was accompanied by a high-pitched whine.

Writing in the police log, Price said that the UFO itself was orange color and appeared to be spinning on end. As it headed in a southeasterly direction the object suddenly came to a complete stop and then made a sweeping motion toward the southwest and disappeared over the horizon.

Deputy Price stated further that before this incident, "I had never believed in UFOs—but I can only report what I myself was a witness to. It actually made the hair on the back of my neck stand on end."

Other residents, likewise skeptical, also reported odd occurrences. Five or six persons, who the police termed "apparently sober," insisted that they had seen "stump-like" creatures moving across an open field near the Reeves residence on two occasions.

A 17-year-old high school senior, Douglas Whitlow, found himself being followed by an object down the Siletz-Toledo Highway. The object remained visible for nearly an hour over the area and witnesses told how it crisscrossed the open highway, following the auto's bright lights, at low altitude. The description of the UFO tallied with the objects seen on the Reeves property.

But perhaps the best look at the UFOs came from a group of six teenagers who told reporters they had viewed the objects through binoculars near the Reeves home. They described the craft as "oval-shaped with a string of red, blue and green lights on their upper sections." Peering at the objects even closer, they felt that there were searchlights inside that appeared to be scanning the nearby earth, perhaps taking photographs. This light also seemed to change color from red to blue and then to a bright shade of green.

Nor was the Pioneer Mountain area free of what appeared to be physical evidence of these strange visitors. As early as May, 1966, Ed Keenon, a logger, came upon a large chunk of metal, which, under analysis, turned out to be pure sodium. This find was made by Keenon as he walked along a path which passes by a small creek bed on the outskirts of Kernville. To this date no one has been able to locate the source of the sodium or discover what its use might have been.

A bomb disposal team from a nearby Army base brought out the fact that the object could not have been in the area very long, since sodium is highly explosive to water.

Also discovered near the Reeves Pioneer Mountain home was a large quantity of aluminum-looking shavings which an analysis showed was composed of magnesium. Taylor suggested that the pilots of the strange craft might be dropping the shavings in an attempt to jam nearby radar tracking stations.

Now the Reeves are gone and so are the lights, the spaceships, and the crawling stump-like creatures. The new owner of the Reeves' former home denies seeing anything unusual now, although he had witnessed various phenomena before the Reeves' sudden departure.

Here indeed is a classic case where apparently the operators of the UFOs seen in the Taylor, Oregon, area were keeping watch on a single Earth family, perhaps with the intention of recording their daily activities, much the same as we would do upon the discovery of new life forms, whether it be microscopic or higher on the evolutionary scale.

Did the strange phenomena follow the Reeves family to wherever they had fled? We may never know, for the family informed nobody of their destination.

BOB SHORT IS THE MAN WHO TALKS WITH SPACE BEINGS

Some people seem to be natural magnets for the intelligence behind the UFO phenomenon. Robert is a prime example, as his warm smile and shimmering blue eyes reflect his genuine sincerity. Although his claims of contact with extraterrestrials may seem farfetched to some, documented evidence points to the fact that his astonishing claims are authentic, and yet we cannot explain how it is that he might have been chosen out of millions to speak for *them* on a regular basis.

A Channel For Space Intelligence

Robert E. "Bob" Short has probably had more close encounters with UFOs and their occupants than any other man alive today. The California-based contactee has been receiving messages from UFO entities for almost 30 years. Said a friend, "Bob draws UFOs like a bowl of jam draws flies."

This is no exaggeration. During lectures held across the United States, Short's presence has somehow triggered valid sightings.

Says Bob (as he prefers to be called), "I'm considered a channel for space intelligence. They (living beings in outer space) communicate with me through my voice box, giving information concerning world trends in the fields of geology, meteorology, politics, and so on."

These sightings are usually mind-bogglers. One eyewitness, a man in his early forties, describes an incident which took place during an outdoor UFO conference, in California on October 14th, 1967:

"At about 8:00 PM (Saturday), after most people had left the convention or were inside their trailers or in a nearby restaurant, a group of about 75 people had gathered outside in a circle to hear Bob Short channel messages from the pilots of UFOs.

"While a few people from the group were introduced and short talks given, a large pulsating reddish-orange object flew silently overhead and remained in view for a good two minutes.

"About a quarter of an hour later, after Bob had explained to the group how his type of channeling was accomplished, he entered what appeared to be a semi-trance state under control of some external intelligence.

"Just after the beginning of the transmission, with the words 'Message to follow,' two more objects (like the previous one) came into view and silently flew very low overhead (perhaps 500 to 1,000 feet), just as these words were being dramatically transmitted through Bob:

"'Greetings to the people of Earth, people who are at this moment watching these objects over this area. I am called K. I am a representative for the planet you people of Earth call Jupiter. We are, at present, in your location, azimuth 13 degrees, three of your miles to the North and East. We have released our spacecraft into your area. We are on a larger craft which you people choose to call a mother ship, and which we call Klactas. We have the following information for the people of your planet at this time.'"

Accurate Predictions

The "following information" centered on predictions of earthquakes in Alaska, Peru and Nicaragua. Years later, all of them occurred.

Short, who is founder of the Solar Space Foundation of Joshua Tree, California, is an untiring researcher of archaeology, Indian cultures, customs and prophecy.

Bob's first experience with being a channel took place in 1952. A year earlier he had been experimenting with automatic writing, achieving some success. Then he heard about a man who had spoken to aliens in the desert. Bob felt compelled to find him. The man was the controversial George Van

Tassel, who lived in the Twenty-Nine Palms area and had claimed to have gone onboard a UFO that landed a hundred feet away from where he was sleeping on a sweltering night.

Eventually, the two did meet. Bob told Van Tassel about his automatic writing and about how his writings told him to find the man who spoke with space people. Van Tassel was interested. He invited Bob to stay for a session in which Van Tassel was to communicate with aliens.

"There were a lot of people present," Short remembers. "I sat in a big chair and the lights were turned off. I was ready to do my automatic writing, but my hand started to shake. Then my arm shook. My whole body started shaking and I couldn't stop it. And all of a sudden, I passed out cold. When I came to, the lights were on. I thought I'd fallen asleep and I apologized.

"The people were staring at me with a strange look in their eyes," Bob recalls. "Then George Van Tassel told me I wasn't asleep, that the aliens were using my voice box to communicate with the people in the room. My wife says that just before the voice came through there were peculiar clicking noises in my throat."

Strange Occurrences

Witnesses present during Short's channeling have claimed to see him disappear. Others say his face fades and is replaced by another. One woman painted a picture of the face she saw. Bob says it is Oara, from the planet Saturn, which is the hub of the government in our Solar System.

"I have received representatives from Venus, which they call Agva, and Acva, or Uranus," says Short. "These are the English equivalents of their names."

In an interview with Bob Short, he told us that there is no way he can really be sure that the voices are legitimate. He makes a concerted effort to document the prophecies that come through, and in most cases the information will be revealed later in the news media.

Says Bob, "They have even warned of possible assassination attempts. Many times lives have been saved. As a matter of fact, witness the recent attempt on the life of Anwar Sadat [who later was killed]. The conspirators were caught in Egypt. It might be assumed that Libya had knowledge of it because they were about to invade Egypt when it happened."

To our question about the possibility that entities are in touch with the world's heads of state, Short was adamant in his belief that they are. "It's been denied, of course. But the allegation is that communication has been going on for some time."

Why They Are Coming Here

Moving into another area of concern, we asked Bob if aliens, or space people, were here.

"Yes," he said. "I believe they walk our streets many times. If we were open to them, they would stop and talk to us."

"Can we recognize them?"

"Yes. The eyes are very peculiar. They're more hollow, or sunken, than ours, and they seem to have a strange side vision. But there are others who look something like the Indians of Peru. High cheek bones, high foreheads, almost Oriental, with swarthy skin. They seem to be ageless."

"Do they have bases?" we asked.

"Here? Yes, although they can't stay here very long because of the chemical differences in their bodies. Their bone structure is different. They don't have our boney look. And their bases are in the southeastern part of the country. There are some off our coastal shelves and perhaps some in the Bermuda Triangle.

"Look, I am in touch with them. I don't want to lose contact—and that could happen if I reveal too much, that is, be too specific about where they are."

We asked, "What would happen if we confronted one of them?"

"He wouldn't say anything," Bob says. "He'd probably just smile. If you were alone with him in an isolated area, and you were receptive, that is, meant him no harm, he might lay a whole thing on you. He might tell you about your life, what you've been doing, what you hope to do." Space aliens, it seems, are very psychic.

UFOS – WICKED THIS WAY COMES: THE DARK SIDE OF THE ULTRA-TERRESTRIALS

Ultra-Terrestrials Among Us

Short relates a unique incident which occurred in February, 1962. He was in the Glinton Restaurant in Yucca Valley with a group of people prior to a communication he was to have that evening in a desert area near Death Valley. After some time, a couple came in, a man and a woman. They had to stoop over to get through the seven-foot-high door.

Diners were frightened by them because of their height, but Short said that their presence had been predicted during an earlier communication. He had been told that the entities would meet him in person. Bob felt instinctively that this was the moment.

There were plenty of seats available at the counter, yet the couple elected to occupy a table close to Bob's. He described the woman as being exceptionally beautiful, with a sort of scooped out face. She wore no makeup. Her eyes were very pretty, wide and alert. Her nose was straight.

Short said the man was handsome in a rugged sort of way, much like the Clark Gable type. He wore a moustache. His slacks were dark and he wore an Eisenhower jacket with a winged white shirt collar which went all the way to his shoulders.

The man sat with his back to Bob's group, but the woman faced them and smiled often at Bob and his friends. They ordered toast and coffee but did not touch the food. At the cash register later, the woman turned and again smiled at Bob and the others.

As soon as they went outside, Bob Short bolted from his chair and hurried out after them. He was too late. They were gone. There was nothing outside. He saw no car on the road. There was no other building they could have ducked into. It was as though they had vanished from the face of the earth.

One of Bob Short's strangest experiences deals with a pregnant woman. She had heard of Bob's reputation in the field and had come to him for two reasons. One was that she had a disorder in her tubes which the doctor had described as a tumor. The other was a contact with a couple who wanted her baby.

The woman told Short that while she was in her doctor's office in Oakland, California, a couple came in. They spoke briefly to the doctor.

UFOS – WICKED THIS WAY COMES: THE DARK SIDE OF THE ULTRA-TERRESTRIALS

When he approached her, she said, he was visibly frightened. The doctor said, "There are people here who want to talk to you." He then ushered the woman and the couple into an unused office.

According to Bob's visitor, the couple was wearing brown street clothes. The woman was pretty. She had an aquiline nose, no makeup. The man had reddish hair, which was short, and very penetrating eyes.

He did all the talking. He told the pregnant woman her life history from the moment she was born to the present. He then mentioned the child she was carrying, about how he wanted to adopt it and take it back where he came from, which was Tibet.

Bob Short frankly did not know what he could do about helping the woman to keep her baby, but he did hope that the space people would cooperate with him on the matter of the disorder in the woman's tubes.

Walking Miracle

"I did communicate in the woman's presence," says Bob. "They did something through me which healed her. I was nothing more than an instrument. But she had X-rays taken later and her doctor described her as a walking miracle. There was nothing there, not even scar tissue. He was absolutely floored. She had her baby, a beautiful child, and now I understand he's very much interested in UFOs."

The inference in this business about the baby was that the woman might have copulated with an Ultra-Terrestrial. However, Bob Short apparently did not know the father and therefore chose to remain silent on that aspect. In any case, the baby was not adopted by the mysterious couple who showed up at the doctor's office.

The story did prompt us to ask him if space people were concerned about us.

He said, "Not in an egotistical way, but they are interested in us as a people, as decision makers, as nations. They are interested in national policies. They are interested in our sciences and are concerned about our use of them, or misuse of them. The nuclear thing holds their interest. What they want to do is correct the conditions here. Not in a covert way, but openly. Yes. It's interference of a sort, but they want to reason with us. They are upset sometimes because we are unreasonable people."

During our long conversation with this unusual man, the subject of physical encounters came up. He mentioned that he had come face-to-face with a space alien in October, 1958. Short was impressed with the being's eyes, saying that they were penetrating, set wide apart. We induced him to give us the details.

"I had been out walking one night. I was alone," Bob began. "As I went along the road I heard a noise tell me to stop and not go any further. It was a normal voice. I thought I'd passed someone in the darkness. So I turned around to look, but no one was there.

"There was this orange-bluish light coming at me from up over the hills and my first impression was to run fast and get the hell out of there. I was sure the thing was going to hit me. But it quickly veered to my left. This light came down like a falling leaf. I think it's called shipping gravity. Anyway, the light faded as it came down to the ground, then suddenly there was a blinding glare of white light, bluish white. That was when I saw the opening in the ship.

"One part of me wanted to run and the other wanted to stay to find out what was going on. Then I heard someone walking on the road and I saw a shadow coming toward me.

"He was close enough for me to touch him. And strangely, my fear was gone. In its place was a sense of well-being, peace. I put my hand out to show him I was friendly. He didn't take it. Instead, he put his hand over his heart and then swept it outward. He gave me an enigmatic smile.

"He didn't open his mouth to speak, yet I heard his voice say, 'We had come down to make an adjustment in the power of our craft. We will see you at a later time.'

"He walked back to his ship. Seconds later the thing rose about 20 feet in the air and then took off at an incredible speed.

"At first I thought it was a dream. But I figured that if it really happened, there would be footprints. I looked for them. They were there. I followed them to where the craft had landed and they disappeared."

Short said that he had confirmation of the experience in June 1961 when a woman said she had also seen a space alien. She showed Bob a picture she had painted of the being. "I was astounded," Bob said. "The being was the same one I'd met on that road."

After a quarter of a century of giving readings from space people, Bob Short feels that his psychic awareness has increased. It's not a quick-study thing, he says. He must feel something first, or study something, to get into it.

According to Bob, space aliens are able to give such quick readings because the information they impart comes from records, instantly available, in our Solar System. Specifically, every individual has a brain wave pattern and no two are alike. Through these brain waves, they are able to locate anyone they want almost instantaneously.

Earth in Upheaval

"Have they given you any predictions lately?" we asked.

"Yes," Bob said. "A very important period commenced beginning in 1980-82. A tremendous change process began at that time. There will be a conflagration, not immediately but in the future."

"What kind of changes exactly?"

"Upheaval changes," Bob said, "but they can't be specific about it. They can't give exact dates because things have to run their natural course— a process that may take years to complete. As soon as they see that the course is set, then they can be specific."

And Bob Short's greatest wish is to learn as much as he can about his space brothers so he can, in turn, share it with all of us!

"VEGETABLE MAN"—A SEMI-ABDUCTEE

As this book so ably recounts, there are all sorts of strange and eerie UFOnauts visiting our planet but, for the most part, these humanoids do seem to be of flesh and bone—or, at least, spirit. But this attempted abduction was with a saucerian that might best be placed in the vegetable kingdom. The report comes straight from the pen of Gray Barker, the late West Virginian whose book, "They Knew Too Much About Flying Saucers," on the Men-in- Black, thrilled readers a generation ago. Barker writes:

North of Fairmont, West Virginia, U.S. Route 19 grows crooked and confused. The local traffic not able to take the 1-79 bypass picks its way carefully around the treacherous curves, especially in winter. You reach the little hamlet of Rivesville to find nobody in the streets on this snowy afternoon.

You're trying to reach the Grant Town area in the back country but road signs are sparse and of little help; unless you are a resident of this area it is difficult to find your way. And there is not much reason for an outsider to go there anyway. But I was on a unique mission to see Jennings H. Frederick, amateur rocket expert lately turned UFO investigator. His efforts to help crack the UFO mystery had come about not by choice but because he needed to prove to himself his own sanity!

For Frederick had been a victim of a syndrome familiar only to the most perceptive UFO investigator: he had not only experienced multiple sightings, but his mother had sighted a strange craft with occupant; he had encountered an abominable green creature and had been visited by the MIB, hopefully in a dream, but with the mark of the needle in his arm for days afterward.

UFOS - WICKED THIS WAY COMES: THE DARK SIDE OF THE ULTRA-TERRESTRIALS

Jennings H. Frederick is the subject of a drawing by Gene Duplantier, illustrating the encounter with "Vegetable Man."

UFOS – WICKED THIS WAY COMES: THE DARK SIDE OF THE ULTRA-TERRESTRIALS

As I picked my way over the unfamiliar side roads, hoping the snow showers would halt, I mused over the landing report we had discussed over the phone.

On April 23rd, 1965, Ivan Frederick was cleaning up the breakfast dishes after getting the children off to school and her husband to the day shift at the mine. She glanced out the small kitchen window and saw what she first thought was a child in the hillside pasture field above the house. Fearing the child might be injured if it tried to climb over the electric cattle fence, she ran out the front porch for a better look.

There her concern turned to amazement and shock. A saucer-shaped aircraft hovered near the ground and then landed. Running downward from it, through what appeared to be an elevator and doorway, ran a dark green-colored cable. Attached to the end of the cable by a connection at its stomach area was a small black or dark green-colored creature. It appeared to be more animal, or even satanic, than human. It was collecting grass and dirt and stuffing them into the small bag it carried and it didn't seem to be aware of her observing it. It was unclothed, had pointed ears and a tail. She could see no mouth or other facial characteristics, though it was only about 200 yards away. She was very frightened and watched it only a short while before fleeing inside the house, getting into bed and pulling the covers over her eyes, "hoping it would go away."

She was able, however, to supply a few additional details: she estimated the craft was about 10 feet in diameter and about five feet in height, not counting the stem, or elevator, which was about the same height. It was cream and silver-colored, with rows of windows underneath a dome or "crystal canopy" on the upper surface which sparked in the morning sun. The machine rotated in a clockwise direction while emitting a loud humming or buzzing sound.

After about 15 minutes, Mrs. Frederick recovered enough composure to venture another look out the kitchen window, just in time to see the creature step into the stern of the craft and disappear. The craft then rotated faster, the buzzing sound got louder, and suddenly it rose, "like a feather," straight up out of her view.

When Jennings, the oldest son, came home from school and heard her story, he hastened to the hillside to investigate. There he found a depression in the ground where the stem of the craft had sat, and estimated that the weight must have been more than a ton. He also found claw-like tracks of the creature, which he estimated weighed about 45 lbs. He also found some hair samples in the footprints and sent these, along with plaster-of-Paris impressions and photographs of the area, to the Air Force. The Air Force replied with an inane explanation—a weather balloon—and never returned the physical evidence. This evidence indicated that his mother hadn't been dreaming, and the complexity of her account indicated a technology far beyond her limited education and experience.

The vast construction of the old mine, its abandoned elevator rising spectrally in the storm like some Dark Tower from a Keel extrapolation, loomed ahead of me, and I knew I was nearing Grant Town. I shuddered as I realized that many miners still lay entombed in the serpentine catacombs below, sealed off when the old mine, years ago, had belched forth flames and poisonous fumes from an explosive hell below. In a field to my right some thin cattle crouched in a tight group, trying to shield themselves against the storm, chewing dry hay with only cloudy regurgitated remembrances of a summer's greenery in their brute minds dulled by winter.

But it had been in the bright lazy days of late summer when Frederick had encountered something so outré and outlandish he had frozen in his tracks, his terrestrial weapon hanging limp and useless in his left hand. From the lack of a better description, Frederick called it "Vegetable Man. "

I sat in Frederick's comfortable living room, as his wife did sewing in the kitchen, and his two-year-old daughter ambled and cooed around the modest apartment, sometimes pausing to play with our notes and files, and the UFO books I had brought for reference.

Frederick was a young, husky, good looking man in his early 30s. His language, precise and clear like the notes he had sent me, hardly gave hint of his rural upbringing, never employing the localisms and brogue which often crept into my own speech. He certainly wasn't a crook or candidate for the nut house—though deep beneath the surface of his calm demeanor I could sense something else, maybe a note of controlled urgency, or maybe pangs of suppressed terror.

The encounter with Vegetable Man occurred mid-July of 1968, just before he was to enter the Air Force. It was a beautiful day and he had been hunting unsuccessfully for woodchuck. As the sun was setting he decided to return home, and near his father's property line he stopped under some maple trees. He removed the arrow from his 45-lb. bow and transferred both to his left hand to rest his arm.

As he paused he heard a high-pitched jabbering, much like that of a recording running at exaggerated speed. He believed he could understand the words, but he may have experienced telepathic communication:

"YOU NEED NOT FEAR ME. I WISH TO COMMUNICATE. I COME AS A FRIEND. WE KNOW OF YOU ALL. I COME IN PEACE. I WISH MEDICAL ASSISTANCE. I NEED YOUR HELP!"

Stunned and puzzled, he reached with his right arm for a handkerchief in his hip pocket to wipe his perspiration. He winced. At first he thought his hand had become entangled in a wild berry briar and he quickly withdrew his arm.

Attached to his wrist was what looked like a thin, flexible right hand and arm, of a green color like a plant, and the size of a quarter coin in diameter. The hand, which terminated with three fingers about seven inches long, and with needle-like tips and suction cups, grasped his arm more tightly and punctured a blood vessel. He heard a suction sound and knew blood was being drawn.

Frederick turned to see a terrifying being with semi-human facial features, though there the resemblance ended. Its slanting eyes were yellow and it had pointed ears. Its body reminded him of the stalk of some huge ungainly plant, though it had remarkable physical power, coupled with the hypnotic effect the sing-song message imparted. He cried out in pain from the incisions and fright. Suddenly the eyes changed from yellow to red and seemed to rotate, and spinning orange circles emerged from them. His pain immediately ceased as the eyes created what obviously was a hypnotic effect, and he froze in his tracks, though his terror had also vanished.

Frederick isn't sure, but he believes the "transfusion" lasted only about a minute, after which the creature suddenly released him, turned and ran up the hill in great leaping jumps, covering 25 feet or more in each leap, like a modern "Spring-heeled Jack." He estimated the height of the leaps by noting it cleared a five-foot fence with about three feet to spare. At the hilltop it vanished into the woods.

UFOS – WICKED THIS WAY COMES: THE DARK SIDE OF THE ULTRA-TERRESTRIALS

The pain in his arm returned as he stared in the direction of the creature's spectacular exit. Then he heard a humming and whistling sound coming from the woods, as if the saucer the creature may have arrived in was taking off. He stumbled to his home, washed the wounded arm and put a bandage on it. Though the wound convinced him that he was sane and had actually experienced the horror, he doubted that anybody else would believe him. So he told his family he had been scratched by a briar and didn't see a doctor for fear of disclosure.

I sensed I was one of the few persons he had ever told of the happening, and that he trusted that I would not laugh at him. And suddenly I also realized a peculiar thing: the witness, while being questioned, was also interviewing me. I discovered that he was also obviously worried about some things he had read in books and articles by John Keel, and for the first time I was "getting to" the controlled terror that boiled just beneath his seemingly calm exterior. He asked me what I thought about a "pattern" Keel attributed to contactee and other UFO experiences. I reiterated that he must already have known about this subject: how these witnesses indeed often continued to have additional experiences, and how they often experienced personal difficulties—though I played this down as much as possible, not wishing to contribute to his previous worry.

At this point he told me of an even earlier sighting in which he believed he experienced a time distortion and related some recent sightings. Although some readers may scoff at his dramatic accounts, there is the independent sighting by his mother which indicates there was independent confirmation of UFO activity in the area. If you, the reader, are saying, "Well come on, you might as well end all this with the Men-In-Black bit," well, here we go:

Near the end of his Air Force enlistment, Frederick was assigned to temporary duty with NASA and given a security clearance. It is interesting to note (in connection with the MIB account) that while working for NASA he obviously encountered evidence of some secret project that dealt with UFOs. Although I did not press for information about this, he hinted there had been a lapse of security at NASA and that "several people were sacked" as a result. I got the impression he had seen plans or models of some sort of secret aircraft because he questioned me at length about what I knew of the history of the Avro Saucer, an early jet-powered airfoil taken over from the

UFOS - WICKED THIS WAY COMES: THE DARK SIDE OF THE ULTRA-TERRESTRIALS

Canadian government by the U.S. and highly-touted in publicity releases by the Air Force. It seemed obvious at that time that the Air Force was aiming the publicity at those who believed in "flying saucers" of interplanetary origin to subtly persuade them that UFOs had an earthly and military origin (the Air Force "saucer" never flew successfully and is now on display at Wright Patterson Air Force Base).

About four months after his honorable discharge, Frederick had the run-in with the MIB:

"I was living with my parents and slept on a cot near a window. One night, sometime between 1:00 and 4:00 AM, I was awakened by a red flash. I thought the gas furnace had caught fire, so I raised up in bed and looked into the living room where my younger brother, Bill, was sleeping, and saw a small canister about the size of an apple come bouncing across the living room floor. It was giving off a red-colored vapor.

"I instinctively reached for my .38 pistol, which I always kept loaded under my pillow when living in the country, but a hand stopped me and I felt the prick of a needle in my left arm. I saw three men dressed in black turtle neck sweaters, slacks and what I thought were ski masks, entering the room through the window (I assume there was a fourth, the one that gave me the needle). One of them said, 'The dogs have been darted and everybody gassed!' Another asked, 'What about this one? Will he remember?' The other replied, 'He's going out soon, he's half asleep! Don't worry about the needle! It will make his arm sore for a day or two, that's all!'

"Just as the red gas from the canister was beginning to reach me, the men put on gas masks over the ones they had on, and the last thing I remember seeing was one man opening a suitcase with a tape recorder in it and another grabbing the canister and stuffing it in his jacket pocket. Then they stuck something over my face and began to ask me questions, mainly about my UFO sightings and what I thought the UFOs actually were. I'm sure I was losing consciousness, for their other questions sounded very stupid, such as what did I know about time, and questions about the future."

Next morning nobody else in the household reported anything strange about the previous night, and Frederick assumed that the red vapor from the canister had "put them out."

As I drove back to Clarksburg and home, the snow had stopped, and the late afternoon sunlight illuminated thousands of Christmas trees on the hillsides. The road was beginning to clear, and, back on the main highway, I saw a crowd of parents and children gathering at the Terrace Shopping Center to see Snow White and the Seven Dwarfs.

I mused about Mrs. Frederick's weird little demon man, stuffing weeds and dirt into his poke; Vegetable Man and the obvious similarity to the modern abductee, who is always the unwilling donor to some saucerian or galactic blood bank.

Frederick's MIB sounded to me very much like terrestrial visitors, with their talk of "gassing" and "darting the dogs." And there had been some incident involving his seeing something he shouldn't while with NASA.

I knew I would have to talk with Frederick again and try to penetrate further into the substratum of what I still sensed was a massive, though unarticulated, FEAR. Or maybe Frederick was one of THEM, either terrestrial, extraterrestrial or OTHERWISE, who had interviewed ME as much as, or more so, than I had questioned him!

More logically, however, Frederick was a man possessed, not by insanity, not by Christian devils, but by the pattern. And he must exorcise this Fiend with a fighting spirit any mountain man carries in his brave heart. Frederick had himself become a UFO investigator. Perhaps he could prove they didn't exist. Perhaps he could prove that Keel's pattern didn't always come true. Perhaps all marriages didn't break up; perhaps all percipients did not enter a mad world of unreality where hoarse voices croaked, "We are one!"

Then I forgot all this as I remembered the little girl, laughing and playing with our papers. The next time I visited Frederick, perhaps I could take her a nice picture book.

Note: West Virginia terminology: POKE-A paper bag. "My daddy went to the store and brought back a poke of candy."

UNDERSEA SAUCER ATTACK!

There has been speculation for as long as I can remember that UFOs have set up shop beneath the seas and oceans of Earth, thus avoiding the necessity of traveling back and forth to distant solar systems.

Throughout history, seafarers have witnessed unexplainable pinwheels of light beneath the waves. Dazzled by these spectacles, they wrote about them in ship's logs and even drew pictures of what they had observed. Vast cities may even exist in areas such as the Bermuda Triangle that were built by otherworldly intelligences. Some of our ships may have been attacked by some rather unfriendly underwater creatures.

For hundreds of years, mysterious unidentified lights and objects have been observed hovering, submerging and emerging from various bodies of water all over the earth.

These unidentified craft would appear to be using the vast water areas of the earth as operational bases.

Former NASA Mars mapping expert, Jacques Vallee, author of the book, "Anatomy of a Phenomenon," has candidly conceded that not only is it likely, but it is most probable that the UFOnauts do have hangars deep under the sea, where they cannot easily be detected.

Some credence to the existence of such entities is seen in the fact that the National Bureau of Standards has stated that it never has been able to identify mysterious radio signals which seem to come from somewhere in the middle of the South Atlantic. These recurring sounds have never been identified or specifically located.

Undersea UFOs have featured in some of the earliest stories of the sea. As

UFOS - WICKED THIS WAY COMES: THE DARK SIDE OF THE ULTRA-TERRESTRIALS

long ago as the 12th century, seagoing men returned with tales of objects which followed their ships for periods of days, sometimes at sea level, and sometimes just below the surface of the water. Many of these objects were reported to be brightly colored. At night they often lit up the sea for miles around. Some were circular in shape while others were described as long, "like the body of a whale," silver in color.

Charles Fort in his book, "Book of the Damned," describes a case in which Captain E.W. Banner, skipper of the ship Lady of the Lake, reported seeing a remarkable "object in the sky." It was said to have taken on the appearance of a semi-circle divided into four parts, "the central dividing shaft beginning at the center of the circle and extending far outward, and then curving backward." Fort placed the date at March 22, 1870.

One of the most documented accounts of UFOs seen over water is still vividly remembered by William J. Kiehl, who lived in San Francisco when he was interviewed. Kiehl reports that in August, 1914, near Georgia Bay, Canada, he and eight other persons observed an odd phenomena:

"Wet and chilled, we were gathering wood for a fire when two young girls who were in the party came running excitedly into our make-shift camp in an isolated cove and demanded that we follow them to a nearby beach. A deer was standing there, they said, gazing out onto the water at a strange machine which appeared to be anchored. We followed the girls and there, near the middle of the bay, was a strange machine of a type I had not seen the likes of before nor since.

"I would say that this strange machine was about nine feet high and twelve feet long. On top of the ship were two little men dressed in green and purple tight-fitting clothes. Square yellow masks which seemed to rest on their shoulders covered their faces.

"A light green-colored hose appeared to come out of a small porthole about halfway up the side of the unusual craft. The two little creatures appeared to be trying to get some kinks or knots out of the hose, which was dragging in the water.

"Their task accomplished, three more creatures appeared on the topmost deck of the craft and began adjusting some type of rods which were affixed to the upper part of the ship.

UFOS – WICKED THIS WAY COMES: THE DARK SIDE OF THE ULTRA-TERRESTRIALS

"After what was probably two or three minutes, the five beings went inside the ship by way of the porthole from which the hose was extended. The ship then rose from the bay surface, sucking with it a heavy upsurge of water which sprayed the entire sea, leaving a mist above which did not settle for some time. As the ship continued to move straight up, it changed color from red to green and then made a tight left turn and flew off on its side."

Another almost identical story, which received little publicity, appeared in the September-October 1950 issue of "The Steep Rock Echo," house organ of the Steep Rock Iron Company, Ontario, Canada.

A senior executive of the company, accompanied by his wife, was on a boating trip when he pulled into a tiny cove in Sawbill Bay just after dusk on July 2, 1950. "Cliffs rose on all three sides of the cove. Small trees and bushes concealed us and our boat from anyone overhead in a plane, had there been one around that evening," the man reported.

The couple had decided this would be an ideal spot to eat. "Suddenly," relates the executive, "the air seemed to vibrate as if from shock waves from a blasting operation. I had an intuition to climb ten feet up a rock, where a cleft gave onto the bay."

There he saw a large shining object in the curve of the shore line, about a quarter of a mile away. "I rushed back to my wife and brought her back to the cleft in the rock," he said. Together they saw the strange shining object which they described as being like "two saucers, one upside down on the top of the other, floating on the water.

On the top of the craft were several open hatches and approximately ten "little figures."

The leader of the UFOnauts was standing on a small raised platform. "He wore what seemed to be a red skull cap, or perhaps it was red paint. The caps worn by the others were blue," says the report. "I should say the figures were from 3 feet six inches to 4 feet tall—all much the same size. We could not see their faces. In fact, the faces seemed like blank surfaces and the figures appeared to move like automata, rather than living beings."

As the two watched through the fading daylight they saw one of the beings pick up the end of a green hose, lift it from the water, and begin walking to the rear of the ship. As soon as this figure had completed what appeared to be his job, all of them climbed down the open hatches into the interior of the ship. The hatches then closed and the watchers heard a strange hum. Seconds later the UFO took off at high speed.

Days later, they returned to the area with an associate. As luck had it, they again saw the object with its hatches open, but the hum from their boat motor apparently attracted the attention of the UFO's crew, who jumped through the ports on the top of the ship, which immediately took off.

The U.S. Navy Hydrographic Office issues a weekly publication, "Notice to Mariners," which is a valuable source for those collecting material on the observation of marine phenomena. In recent years this publication has contained several accounts of mysterious celestial events which are still completely unexplained. The following reports have been selected from this publication for a period of a single week in 1959. They are listed under Section VI, "Marine Information," which contains "selected reports from cooperating observers." Mariners are urged to submit reports of their observations of the various marine phenomena. Such reports are evaluated and published as appropriate, "for the benefit of the maritime community in general." The following are typical:

CELESTIAL PHENOMENON North Pacific

Second Officer L.R. Bjelde of the American ship, "Mariposa," Master R.C. Russell reported:

"On 14 September 1959, at 1318 G.M.T. in lat. 31'26'N., long. 140'04' W., course 061' gyro., speed 19.7 knots, light variable breeze, air temperature 67'F., sea temperature 72-F., barometer 30.14 inches, a gigantic explosion was observed in the sky. The horizon was brightly illuminated by the blast, which left trails that resembled smoke. The phenomenon was on a bearing of 056' true at an altitude of approximately 45', apparently high above the normal atmosphere."

CELESTIAL PHENOMENON South Atlantic

Third Officer W.E. Hughes of the American S.S. Del Mundo, Capt. E.J. Quillin, Master, reported:

"At 0615 G.M.T October 6, 1959, in lat. 2'22'S., long. 38148'W., on passage from Cabadello, Brazil, to New Orleans, a bright white light with a yellow loom of about 40 was observed just under Castor and Pollux bearing

35' altitude 38'. A yellow loom trailed the light which traveled southeasterly and set below the horizon bearing 96' at 0622 G.M.T. Mr. Hughes stated the light appeared to be manmade and traveled at a uniform speed and brightness and was observed for approximately seven minutes.

"Weather partly cloudy with good visibility, wind ESE force 3, barometer 29-84 inches, air temperature 78'F., sea temperature 78oF."

MARINE PHENOMENON Indian Ocean

Capt. Luigi Colombo, Master of the Panamanian S.S. Stanvac Singapore, reported:

"At 1810 G.M.T. April 4, 1959, in lat. 2000'N., 59022'E., course 82, speed 13.5 knots, on passage from Abadan to Maritius Island, the third mate called me to the bridge and I observed a diffuse light on the horizon bearing 252'. Observing the light through binoculars it appeared as the loom of a city beyond the horizon. It was not due to lightning as the phenomenon lasted for some time and was clearly seen. A similar luminous spot appeared above the beam and a third one of lesser intensity was observed abeam. Radar showed four circular targets at 20 miles and 3 larger ones at 40 miles. The observation lasted from 1810 to 1930 G.M.T. and only one lightning bolt was observed above the 3 luminous sources.

"Weather clear and good visibility, wind calm, moderate long swell. Barometer 30.00 inches, air temperature 82'F., sea temperature 80oF. "

CELESTIAL PHENOMENON North Atlantic

Second Officer Rvd. Vrie of the Dutch M.V. Colytto, Capt. R. Illistra, Master reported:

"At 0130 Zone Time, February 22, 1959, in lat. 18'20'N., long. 58'10'W., I observed an object moving very fast in the sky. The height of the object was uncertain but estimated at more than 300 meters (984 feet). It was observed moving from west to east when suddenly its course was altered in the same direction as the ship (235') which it followed for about three seconds and then turned in the same direction it previously followed, without any change in speed. The color of the object was between orange and red and had a small trail of white-blue gas.

"Weather partly cloudy with good visibility wine NE force 3-4, slight sea, air temperature 79'F."

Hundreds of similar reports have found their way into mariner journals over the years.

On August 29th, 1964, an amazing photograph taken from the Eltanin, a Military Sea Transportation ship about 1000 miles west of Cape Horn, South Africa, showed what apparently was a complex radio antenna being raised from the ocean at an estimated depth of 2250 fathoms. Dr. Thomas Hopkins, a senior marine biologist who was on board at the time, remarked that "at that depth there is no light, so photosynthesis could not take place and plants cannot live." Scientific investigation has failed to explain the what-for and why-for of the object photographed by the Eltanin.

In 1964, USOs, or Unidentified Submarine Objects, were frequently seen in Australian waters. Henk Hinfelaar, editor of New Zealand's "Spaceview," personally investigated seven known cases between January and November of that year. One of the reports occurred on January 12, when an unidentified airline pilot (known to Mr. Hinfelaar) was on an assignment from Whenupai (Auckland's Airport) to Kaitaia.

The crew was comprised of the Captain, First Officer and an Operations Officer. As they flew low over the coastline approaching the southern end of Kaipara Harbour, something shining drew their attention. The pilot veered the aircraft slightly to port to fly more directly over the object, which was just under the surface of the water. He saw that the object, which at first glance might have been mistaken for a whale, was actually a metallic structure.

He observed the following details:

1. It was perfectly streamlined and symmetrical in shape.

2. It had no external control surfaces or protrusions.

3. It appeared metallic and there was a suggestion of a hatch on top, streamlined in shape, not quite halfway along the body as measured from the nose.

4. The shape was not that of a normal submarine.

5. Its length was estimated at 100 feet with a diameter of 15 feet at the widest part.

UFOS – WICKED THIS WAY COMES: THE DARK SIDE OF THE ULTRA-TERRESTRIALS

The March 26, 1966, edition of the "Miami News" relates how Isaac Lester and John Robert Bair, who were cruising in a motor launch, spotted a strange cigar-shaped object maneuvering in the sky quite low over the water several miles out at sea. To get a closer look, they headed for the object at full speed. When they were within a few hundred yards of it they noticed "eerie pulsations of light around what appeared to be the nose section of the craft." Then, what looked like a greenish volume of light, water or vapor extended from the underside of the object down to the surface of the water, which they discovered was strewn with dead fish.

The crew of the launch radioed back to the Boca Chica base to report what they had seen, and within several minutes search planes were flying over the area. It was then that the strange craft took off and vanished.

On January 23rd, 1969, the French Submarine Minerve disappeared with 52 men on board, somewhere in the western Mediterranean.

About the same time as the Minerve went down, strange "ping sounds" were heard bouncing off a mysterious object beneath the surface. Over 30 ships and dozens of aircraft were called in to take part in the search.

According to the "New York Times," "French officials reported that a destroyer had picked up an echo on its sonar gear which apparently came from a metallic object lying at a depth of 412 to 650 feet." However, several days' extensive search showed no signs of the Minerve.

So what was this metallic object which sonar had tracked? In late May, 1968, the U.S. submarine Scorpion also disappeared without a trace. During the search for the missing submarine by hundreds of aircraft and surface vessels, a crewman on the Navy freighter ship Hyades sighted a "strange orange object" some 1400 miles east of Norfolk, Virginia. This was where the Scorpion is thought to have gone down, but air and sea search for the object provided no clue as to its identity.

These and many other authenticated reports of the mysterious lights and objects which have appeared over the oceans of the world would indicate that there are submarine UFOs as well as what must now be considered the more conventional flying saucers.

UFOS - WICKED THIS WAY COMES: THE DARK SIDE OF THE ULTRA-TERRESTRIALS

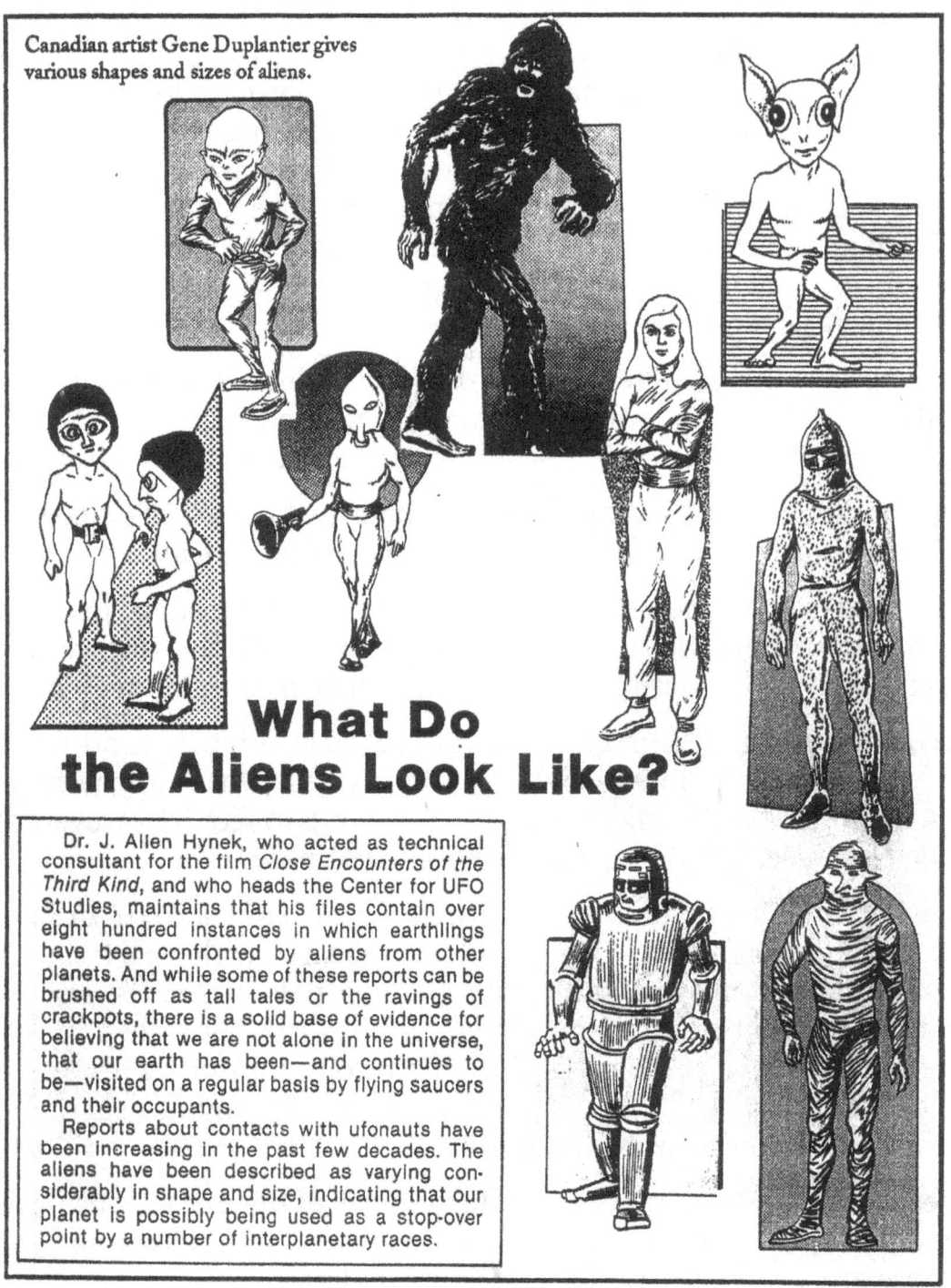

Canadian artist Gene Duplantier gives various shapes and sizes of aliens.

What Do the Aliens Look Like?

Dr. J. Allen Hynek, who acted as technical consultant for the film *Close Encounters of the Third Kind*, and who heads the Center for UFO Studies, maintains that his files contain over eight hundred instances in which earthlings have been confronted by aliens from other planets. And while some of these reports can be brushed off as tall tales or the ravings of crackpots, there is a solid base of evidence for believing that we are not alone in the universe, that our earth has been—and continues to be—visited on a regular basis by flying saucers and their occupants.

Reports about contacts with ufonauts have been increasing in the past few decades. The aliens have been described as varying considerably in shape and size, indicating that our planet is possibly being used as a stop-over point by a number of interplanetary races.

A WIDE—AND WILD—VARIETY OF ALIENS

In Australia, a man stumbles upon a 13-foot tall alien emerging from a strange circular craft and is blasted by a red ray that temporarily immobilizes him. In Argentina, several farmers are frightened by the sudden appearance of two seven-foot tall saucerians who try to kidnap one of them. In the U. S., a 25-foot tall being with a round blood-red face (no nose or mouth) approaches seven eyewitnesses, who run for their lives. In Brazil, a 10-foot tall giant saucerian 'Cyclops' tried to carry off the son of a farmer.

Around the world, reports of giant aliens have flooded the offices of government agencies who are baffled by the strange actions of these beings. Is it possible that the many different sized and shaped UFOnauts who have landed on Earth have carved up our planet, like galactic colonizers, into spheres of influence?

It was a humid evening in late August 1963. The moon was full, and the stars twinkled brilliantly. Near the town of Sagrada Familia, Brazil, the Eustagulo family lived in a modest home in a rural area. They had never heard of flying saucers.

On this particular evening the two Eustagulo boys, Fernando, 11, and Ronaldo, 9, were told to go to the well in the garden and clean the family coffee filter. The two went down the little stone stairway that led to the well with their friend Marcos. The night was so clear and luminous, they didn't immediately recognize the sphere that was floating in front of them as they stood in front of the well cranking the pulley to bring up a bucketful of water.

When they first saw the object, it was above the trees, practically touching the branches. The boys could make out people sitting one behind the other in four or five rows inside the craft. Then suddenly a door popped open, making a humming noise. Two luminous parallel bands speared the ground near a flower bed and a slender being, about 10 feet tall, glided on the two bands of light to the ground, landing near the foot of the stone stairway.

The being rode down the beams, with his arms outstretched, in a slow sliding movement. Once he reached the ground he walked about 20 feet, with his back stiff, legs open, and arms stretched out, balancing himself. He moved, swinging his body from left to right continuously until he reached a rock in the yard and proceeded to sit down. All three boys agreed that the being wore a transparent helmet over his head and had only one visible eye of dark color in the middle of his forehead. It was actually a giant-sized saucerian Cyclops! The UFOnaut was wearing high boots, which had long, thick triangular spikes protruding from each.

The spikes made strange impressions in the soft earth, which could be seen for days following the sighting.

The trousers the being wore seemed to be fastened to the boots in a ring fashion. The moment the being hit the ground, his suit seemed to inflate as if it filled with air. His garment was very shiny and similar to leather. Fernando said that the being had a copper-colored box on his back and a square pack which covered part of his chest. He said this pack gave off flashes of light, and he thought it was either a camera or flashlight. In the craft's open doorway the boys could plainly see the other occupants sitting behind control panels turning knobs and flicking switches.

Frozen in their tracks, the boys said the being reached for one of them as if he meant to sweep him up in his giant hands and carry him to the waiting ship. Fearing the worst, Fernando picked up a brick and was about to heave it at the spaceman, who was seated on the rock, when the being stood up and stared at the youth. Fernando was unable to move or throw the brick. It was as if the being had gained control over his body and his movements.

As if surprised by the boy's hostile action, the "spaceman" took a few steps back, his mouth opening in a vertical fashion, showing a row of white teeth with two larger ones at the corners of the mouth—one directed downward, the other up. The being proceeded to enter the ship, gliding up the shafts of light still beaming down. This time, however, the Cyclops floated skyward with his hands pressed against his body and not outstretched as before.

Looking through the door of the open ship, the boys saw that all the crew members were about the same size and stature and wore the same transparent helmet. The youngsters also felt that one of the beings on board was a female, since it had long hair pulled tightly into a bun, while all the others appeared to be bald.

As in many cases already reported, the boys felt that the occupant was not really attempting to hurt them. They could not explain how they got this impression, but their fear had disappeared. The boys were also quite certain that he would return again. When asked how they knew this, they answered that it was just a feeling, as if someone was talking to them. A local Brazilian UFO researcher explained this as a telepathic suggestion and claimed that others in the vicinity had also reported strange objects in the skies that evening.

Another of the many cases of giant UFOnauts was reported in the "Australian Flying Saucer Review." It was raining heavily at dawn on October 18, 1963. Eugenio Douglas was driving with a truckload of coal, between Monte Maix and Isla Verde, in Argentina, when a brilliant headlight, apparently from an approaching car, blinded him. As another "auto" approached, Douglas realized that the vehicle had only one headlight. He slowed down to avoid a collision, and as he did the light became so bright he could not look at it any longer. He stepped on the brakes and put his head on the steering wheel. The truck was now on the edge of the road. Douglas got out of the truck and through the veil of rain saw a circular metallic craft about 35 feet high in front of him.

Douglas told an investigator from the "Review" that, "Suddenly another light of lesser intensity appeared in the vehicle. It came from an open door. Several tall figures passed through the opening. They were human-like but extremely tall." He estimated their height at approximately 13 feet and they were dressed in tight-fitting metallic suits.

According to the filed report, the occupants wore strange head gear with protrusions that looked like small antennae. Douglas said that there was nothing repulsive about the big men, yet he was terribly frightened.

The moment his presence was discovered by the aliens, a ray of red light flashed, burning his skin. Eugenio Douglas was in such a state of fright that he could think of nothing but grabbing his revolver and firing three shots at the tall being. Then he started to run on the road toward the town of Monte Maix.

But the "burning light" from the ship followed him wherever he went. When he reached the village, Douglas noticed that as the red beam touched electric lights in the street, they turned violet and then green. A strong smell of gas immediately spread all around the area.

As he came to the nearest home, he began to shout for help. This was the house of a Mr. Ribas, who had died the night before. Unexpectedly, the candles around the casket and all the electric lights in the house turned green. A strange smell instantly filled the room.

Hearing the shouts outside and seeing the weird happenings inside, the Ribas family rushed out of their house to find Douglas with an overcoat over his head and a gun in his hand. Neighbors appeared on the scene to stare at the green street lights. In the meantime the UFOnauts had disappeared into the gloom.

Douglas was taken to the police station, where he showed burns on his face and hands, and again related his weird experience. The police officer then remembered that he had received a number of calls about the electric lights changing color throughout the town, which was attributed to irregularities at the local power plant. Douglas was examined by a Doctor Dabolas, who stated that the burns had been caused by radiation similar to overexposure to ultraviolet rays.

The following day the villagers went to the site where Douglas met the strange machine with the giants and found large footprints (19 1/2 inches long) partially washed away by the rain. Burnt out cables were also found in the truck.

There have been many observations of flying saucer "giants" in South America, but sightings of these beings seem to abound in Argentina. "Saucer News" (September 1965) contains a brief report concerning an incredible incident which occurred in the town of Torren. During February of that year, a UFO landed in full view of a group of extremely excited and frightened farmers. Two strange beings, towering over seven feet tall, emerged from the craft and walked toward the villagers. As in the Douglas case, they had an apparatus on the foreheads which gave off small rays of many-colored light. The beings then went into one of the nearby houses and attempted to kidnap the farmer who lived there. They were unsuccessful, due to the combined efforts of his friends who came to the rescue.

On the same evening, the craft landed again, and this time the farmers opened fire on the giants. To their horror and dismay, the bullets had no effect. Despite the ability to withstand the onslaught, the spacemen were easily discouraged from the kidnap mission. Interestingly, one of the farmers who fought the spacemen hand-to-hand later came down with a strange skin disease.

Brazil has also had its share of visits by these giants. In August, 1958, three men on the outskirts of Mindui reportedly observed a pair of eight-foot-tall beings dressed in brilliant red clothing. They watched the spacemen walk up a hill to their UFO, and take off.

On February 10, 1965, on a beach near Guarani, Brazil, five local residents observed the landing of an unusually large object. Three of those present went back to a nearby motel to get additional witnesses. While they were gone, the two remaining UFO witnesses cautiously approached the ship from behind sand dunes, until they managed to maneuver within 60 feet of the craft. From this position they noticed that three beings had alighted from the ship. The UFOnauts were thin, tall creatures about eight feet tall, each wearing a dark, one piece suit which fit very tightly around their bodies.

Before anyone else could arrive at the site, the craft took off. However, those who did return could see traces of footprints and unusual circles where the object had rested.

Several hours later on the same evening, Nib Domingues, while resting on a beach in Atlantida, Brazil, saw a UFO land and immediately turn on what appeared to be a bright spotlight that moved about on the sand. A porthole could be seen on the craft and from a door on its underside came another strong light. Suddenly the object took off rapidly and disappeared. Half an hour later, Domingues returned to the beach with his son and found strange markings in the sand which looked like the ship and its crew had returned during his brief absence.

From Vilovi, Spain, comes a sighting of an enormous hairy monster seen on February 27, 1968. The "animal" reportedly left huge footprints in the ground and walked the countryside at night scaring animals. Several horses were reportedly attacked by the beast. There have been frequent reports of UFOs in the area.

Even more recently, a Rumanian migrant in Australia reportedly saw three giant creatures in purple and yellow clothing about 200 miles north of Brisbane. This sighting was carried in "The News" of January 17, 1969: "Mr. George Vas, a repairman, his wife, Malanka, and daughters Olga, 14, and Maria, 13, all say they watched the spacemen collecting sugar cane and other plant specimens for 10 minutes. Mr. Vas said he and his family were asleep in their caravan at the edge of the road. About 4:30 A.M., they were awakened by the barking of their dog, Ica. He heard a loud buzzing noise like a big swarm of wasps and said he saw an object land; it was between 25 and 30 yards in diameter and looked like a Mexican sombrero. It gave off a brilliant violet color. Mr. Vas said he and his family watched as three spacemen—about three times larger than humans—descended from the ship. They had blocky arms and legs and shapeless bodies. They gave off a purple-yellowish glow. After gathering specimens for about 10 minutes, the spacemen returned to their ship. The craft then went straight up, traveling very quickly. As it took off, the hair on (everyone's) body stood up as if affected by a form of magnetism. Mr. Vas said this was his third sighting of 'spacemen.' He saw one as a child in Rumania in 1918, and another near Belgrade in 1946."

Although the appearances of these giant UFOnauts have been less frequent in North America, information has been obtained of at least 25 reports centering around sightings of these creatures. Mary Lou Guenther, a Canadian researcher, reports that on September 19th, 1963, about 8:00 P.M., a UFO hovered over a field across from a school yard in Saskatoon, Canada. As the UFO passed over the vacant lot, it dropped a large container of some type. After the UFO took off, the young witnesses, including 11-year-old Brian Whitehead, started walking in the direction of the "box." When they were within 15 feet of the object, someone or something stood up. The being was about 10 feet tall, and suddenly started moving toward the children, moaning and holding his hands out as he came at them.

Brian described the alien as being dressed in clothes which "were like a cloak worn by a monk." The "suit" was white like a huge crayon. When questioned whether he saw pants legs, Brian seemed puzzled and said, "I don't know; sometimes I could see right through them."

After the children had calmed down, the police were summoned, and they arrived about 45 minutes after the incident took place. The investigation centered around the field for several days and details of it were sketchy. The boys were questioned separately and asked to draw sketches, which apparently matched. According to Mrs. Guenther, "The following evening some boys, while in the playground, saw the same UFO return and again hover above the lot. They thought they saw an extremely large man lying on the ground because they saw 'arms and legs move.' The object then disappeared, and they saw nothing else."

During a widespread wave of saucer sightings in Mexico in 1965 there were several cases involving giants. In September, a group of saucer occupants estimated to be 10 feet in height, with brilliant red eyes and no mouths or noses, were seen by three women who claim they popped out in front of them during a stroll through a suburb of Mexico City. The beings were dressed in shiny gray suits and boots "just like out of the comic strips." After seeing the beings, the women said they ran away in panic and when they eventually decided to return to the site the UFOnauts had departed.

Not to be outdone, the United States has had its share of this type of creature. On the evening of September 14, 1952, seven witnesses, including a National Guardsman, climbed a hill in Flatwoods, West Virginia, after watching a flaming fireball land in the immediate area. When they reached the top of the hill, they were startled to see a dull orange glob resting on the ground. From the glow surrounding the object emerged a 15-foot-tall being which towered over the witnesses. Its face, everyone agreed, was round and blood red. No one noticed a nose or mouth, only eyes, or eyelike openings, which projected "greenish-orange" beams of light. Around the red "face" and reaching upward to a point was a dark hood-like shape, which could have been a helmet.

Watching the "monster" gliding over the ground in their direction, the witnesses took off, running back down the hill and clearing a four-foot gate without opening it. Later, questioned by researcher Gray Barker, the witnesses remembered that an awful odor, like rotten eggs, covered the entire area. This stench was so horrible they were sick for hours afterwards.

UFOS - WICKED THIS WAY COMES: THE DARK SIDE OF THE ULTRA-TERRESTRIALS

Returning to the area with Gene Lemon, the Guardsman, Barker found the site covered with mysterious "skid marks." The impressions were about 10 feet apart in the tall grass and led from the tree, where the "monster" was last seen standing, to the location of the alleged "fireball."

Oddly enough, at the exact time of these seven witnesses' experience, residents from surrounding states were calling local police departments, TV and radio stations, and military installations to report peculiar aerial observations which were generally interpreted as meteorites.

The Air Force sent an investigator to Flatwoods a few weeks later and convinced at least one witness that what they had seen was a top secret government rocket, propelled by an ammonia-like fuel. No answer has ever been offered to explain the appearance of a 15-foot-tall monster. Thus it must be listed as another appearance made by giant saucerians!

A young Van Nuys, California, electrician, Ted Kittredge, came forward in June, 1956, with his account of meeting three seven-foot-tall "visitors" who appeared quite friendly, had long flowing hair and spoke English, "as if they had memorized thousands of conversations and were repeating the words on tape."

Kittredge said his stepbrother, with whom he shared his home, slept through the entire episode. Kittredge himself was awakened by the barking of his dogs and upon stepping outside to investigate saw a huge golden-colored ball in his yard.

"Three men approached me without hesitation and told me not to be frightened," he said. "I was really scared. In fact, the whole thing seemed like a dream. Only I know it wasn't. Several other people in the Valley had seen the same thing, even talked with the men. I just hope I never see it again, that's all."

Kittredge also appears to have had a brush with a mysterious group who try to silence saucer witnesses. After appearing on a TV show in Van Nuys, he got a phone call in the middle of the night, warning him that it would be wise not to talk about his contact. "I was told to stop worrying and stop talking," Kittredge said. "I could hear machines clicking in the background and the voice said 'We know all about what's going on. You just keep your mouth shut and forget about it.'" This type of phone call has been received by many people after a close sighting or contact.

UFOS - WICKED THIS WAY COMES: THE DARK SIDE OF THE ULTRA-TERRESTRIALS

While going for a late walk in the sand near Riis Park, N.Y., in September, 1961, Stan Suban, of Brooklyn, claims that he saw a creature at least seven feet in height near a burning fire. The young Columbia University student maintains that his sighting occurred around 2:30 A.M. "A sphere of white light hung suspended around the fire. Near the water I could see five or six persons whom I took to be skin divers. I could see the black 'wet' suits with the white strings drawn at their arms. They were all about 6 and 1/2 feet tall and well built. I was about 50 yards from the fire and was attempting to get a closer look at what was going on. Then a figure, much larger than the rest, approached from the direction of the water. It came up to the fire and bent over it and remained in that position for some time. Then he walked around the fire several times, stopped and took off what appeared to be sweat pants. What then terrified me was the appearance of this figure. He was white as snow, seven to 7 and 1/2 feet tall, and had no distinguishable facial features.

"I couldn't believe my eyes but stared at him in fascination and terror. At this time I hid behind a concrete block which was about seven feet high." The "alien" even towered above the structure. "After looking at the creature for several minutes, I knew he was not of this world. He walked with an animated gait. I was impressed with the massive power it seemed to have within itself. I do not believe the 'person' was human."

Minutes later, the creature disappeared as it moved out of the firelight toward the ocean. Because of the constant shifting of the sand, no impressions were found to confirm Stan Suban's tale, but he is very definite about what he saw.

One of the strangest encounters involving giant-sized saucer occupants occurred to six teenagers in Daniels Park just south of Denver, Colorado, on the evening of April 8, 1966.

The group of teenagers consisted of Alan Scrivner, Donald Otis, Michael Simington, all 17 years old, and Patricia Retherford, Kaye Hurley, both 16, and Mary Zolar, 18. At about 5:30 P.M. they drove to Daniels Park, which is a short ride from the heart of Denver. They parked their car and walked, joking as they went, a distance of some 350 feet to an old dugout shelter where they proceeded to build a fire and have a picnic.

About 9:30, Scrivner told reporter William Logan of the "Rocky Mountain News," "We were all inside a shelter and thought we heard a sound like someone walking on top of the roof." Scrivner and Donald Otis took a flashlight and went out to have a look. "We couldn't see anything. It seemed real quiet outside, and then we noticed this buzzing sound. There was something out there rustling around and it would stop when Don and I would stop. Up near my car we looked out into a nearby field and saw something that looked like another car with big round tail lights. The lights moved around and then were gone. We went back to the shelter, where the others (were waiting), and they told us they had seen a big figure or something pass in the light outside. They said it was a lot taller than me, and I'm six feet one inch." Scrivner estimated that the being was seven feet tall.

"We decided to leave and as we walked to the car, Don yelled about a light. There was a white light that shot out real bright across from us, and two blue lights, dimmer, and a brighter one below us."

Four of the teenagers stood on the hood of the car to get a better view. They saw four objects that looked like "fireballs with domes on them, sort of squashed spheres. This strange sound was all around us. It didn't come from one direction. It was pulsating."

Scrivner then told reporter Logan that three of the objects were off to the right. "Two that hovered and one that went up and down—and the fourth came around from the left. The last one changed its color to red after it got close to us." Red rays seemed to be coming out of the bottom of the object "on and off," as if the object was trying to blast off unsuccessfully. Scrivner continued: "We decided to drive out of there. My car wouldn't work right. It's a 1954 Ford, but has a new engine and works fine, but the engine kept (conking out) like the ignition was going on and off. There was nothing but static on the radio."

After Scrivner finally managed to get the car started, he reported that the others all saw a huge light on the road behind them. "It was 30 feet behind us and came up right behind our car and then it went out. The strange thing is I couldn't see the light in the rear view mirror."

Police Chief John C. MacLevor said the teenagers seemed quite sincere and "two of the girls were really frightened." The chief commented, "I'm inclined to think they really saw something."

Emil Slaboda, Wire News Editor of "The Trentonian," has been one of the few dedicated newsmen who have tried to get the facts about flying saucers across to the public. His investigations of several sightings which have taken place in New Jersey have turned out to be valuable contributions to UFO research.

In his "Across the Board" column of February 5th, 1967, Slaboda wrote: "The following two stories are true to the best of my knowledge. They happened in the Trenton area and both cases were reported to the police. The principals, however, wanted to remain anonymous and for good reason. Monster and flying saucer stories often bring ridicule to the tellers! Although only a select group of people know it, a monster, presumably from a saucer, visited Washington Cross Park, New Jersey, and scared the daylights out of four nocturnal visitors to the park some five weeks ago."

Slaboda reported that two men and two women were driving through the park when they noticed an unusual shadow pass over their car. "Although there was no sound of engines, the four passed off the shadow as that of an airplane heading for nearby Mercer Airport. They stopped the car moments later and two of the group left the car for a short walk." Suddenly there was an alarming roar, "as if some animal were nearby." Hurrying back to their parked auto, the couple saw an eight-foot-tall creature gliding toward them over a grassy knoll. "It definitely did not walk like an animal or anything human," one of the witnesses explained.

Slaboda interviewed a brother of one of the witnesses who told the newsman, "I don't know what they saw out there, but I do know that whatever it was, it certainly scared the heck out of them."

The second encounter reported by Emil Slaboda occurred on Friday, March 3rd, 1967, not far from the same Washington Crossing Park. "Two 19-year-old girls were driving down Bear Tatern Road, in Ewing Township. They were in the vicinity of the Mountain View Golf Course when the UFO put in its appearance." The girls told the Ewing Police that the craft was about 20 feet long, cigar shaped and was lit up along its entire length. When the object dipped down in front of their car, the girl driving slammed on the brakes and began to scream.

It was once suggested by the late Ivan T. Sanderson, and more recently by John Keel and many others, that a good number of UFO occupants are actually "androids"—manufactured creations. This would mean we are dealing with non-thinking, non-feeling beings and are faced with the task of trying to understand machines which are merely "programmed." The space giants, from eyewitness reports, could be the machines created by the UFOnauts to land on earth and perform various mysterious tasks. Imagine what the Russian "Moon Rover" would look like in the eyes of a lunar creature.

What is astounding about the space giant phenomenon is that these "creatures" have been sighted throughout the world. But perhaps the most important aspect of this mystery is this: witnesses have always seen different-shaped beings in different locations and one type of giant has never been sighted in another area. Have the masters of the giants or the giants themselves carved up the Earth into spheres of influence to accomplish—who knows what? Research indicates that giants have walked the Earth in the past. Were they from space? If so, why have they returned?

* * *

About the Author: Timothy Green Beckley

Timothy Green Beckley is a UFO & paranormal pioneer. At an early age, his life has more or less revolved around the paranormal. The house he was raised in was thought to be haunted, he underwent out of body experiences at age six, and saw his first of three UFOs when he was ten. As a teenager, he created one of the first UFO periodicals, which he collated together with mimeographed sheets. Later, he merged his publication with Jim Moseley's Saucer News. Over the years he has written over 30 books on everything from rock music to the secret MJ12 papers. Today he is the president of Inner Light/Global Communications and editor of the Conspiracy Journal and Bizarre Bazaar.

Author Biographies For Additional Material

Sean Casteel

Sean Casteel has written about UFOs, alien abduction and related phenomena since 1989. He is currently a Contributing Editor to "UFO Magazine" and a regular contributor to "Open Minds Magazine." In addition to the United States, his articles have been published in the UK, Australia, Italy and Romania.

Casteel is the author of several books for Global Communications, to include "***UFOs, Prophecy and the End of Time***," "***Signs and Symbols of the Second Coming***," and "***The Excluded Books of the Bible***." He has contributed to many other books, such as "***Round Trip to Hell in a Flying Saucer***," "***Disclosure! Breaking Through the Barrier of Global UFO Secrecy***" and "***Behind the Flying Saucers***."

Scott Corrales

Scott Corrales is a writer and translator of UFO and paranormal subjects with an interest in the "high strangeness" aspect of the phenomenon. His books include ***Chupacabras and Other Mysteries*** (Greenleaf, 1997); ***Flashpoint: High Strangeness in Puerto Rico*** (Amarna, 1998) and ***Forbidden Mexico*** (Fatbrain, 1999) and his translation of Salvador Freixedo's landmark ***Visionaries, Mystics and Contactees*** appeared in 1992.

Corrales directs the Institute for Hispanic Ufology, which provides daily updates on UFO and paranormal events in Latin America and Spain to the English-reading public, and contributes regularly to Paranoia, Australian Ufologist and other publications worldwide.

UFOS - WICKED THIS WAY COMES: THE DARK SIDE OF THE ULTRA-TERRESTRIALS

Peter Robbins

Peter Robbins is one of ufology's most respected investigative writers and public speakers. He is a regular guest on US and UK radio shows and has appeared as a guest on and been consultant to numerous television shows and documentaries. He is also co-author (along with Larry Warren) of the British best-seller, ***Left at East Gate: A First-Hand Account of the Rendlesham Forest UFO Incident, Its Cover-Up and Investigation.***

With thirty years of experience as a researcher, investigator, writer and activist, Robbins has lectured extensively both in the States and abroad. He is a columnist for UFO TRUTH MAGAZINE, was a staff writer at UFO Magazine, a contributor to UFO Magazine (UK), and has written for numerous other publications and websites. Event Coordinator for the SCI FI Channel's 'Alien Abduction Phenomenon: A Symposium,' organized to promote the release of the Steven Spielberg miniseries 'Taken.' Peter has worked as a consultant to the McMinnville Oregon UFO Festival, the Exeter NH UFO Conference, The New England UFO Conference, and the Maine-based Experiencers Speak Conference. From 2007-2010 he was a Public Relations Representative and Media Liaison for the City of Roswell NM and continues his involvement in the field from his home near Ithaca NY.

Television appearances include "The Early Show," CBS; The History Channel's "Britain's Roswell;" "Unsolved Mysteries;" "Good Day New York;" "The O'Reilly Factor;" "The Real Roswell," National Geographic Channel; The SCI FI Channel's feature documentary "UFO Invasion At Rendlesham;" "Paranormal Witness" (Horizon UK) , Chilean and Norwegian National Television, French-Canadian TV and numerous BBC TV affiliates. Radio appearances include "Coast to Coast" with George Noory; "The Art Bell Show;" "Hieronimus & Company;" "Eye To the Sky;" "The Jerry Pippin Show;" "Through the Keyhole" and numerous BBC Radio affiliates.

Brad Steiger

The author/co-author of 170 books, Brad Steiger wrote the paperback bestseller ***Strangers from the Skies*** about UFOs. His edited work ***Project Bluebook*** was hailed by Omni magazine as one of the best UFO books of the century. Steiger was inducted into the Hypnosis Hall of Fame for his work with UFO contactees, abductees, and past life regression. In Minneapolis, he received the Lifetime Achievement Award at the National UFO and Unexplained Phenomena Conference. For many decades, Brad and his wife Sherry have researched and investigated UFOs and their cultural impact throughout world history, and they have lectured and conducted seminars on the phenomenon throughout the United States and overseas. Sherry and Brad were featured in twenty-two episodes of the television series "Could It Be a Miracle?" Together, their television appearances and specials include: The Joan Rivers Show, Entertainment Tonight, Inside Edition, Hard Copy, Hollywood Insider, and specials on HBO, USA Network, The Learning Channel, The History Channel, and Arts and Entertainment (A&E), among others. They appear frequently as guests on numerous domestic and international radio talk shows.

Tim R. Swartz

Tim R. Swartz is an Indiana native and Emmy-Award winning television producer/videographer, and is the author of a number of popular books including **The Lost Journals of Nikola Tesla**, **Secret Black Projects**, **Evil Agenda of the Secret Government**, **Time Travel: Fact Not Fiction!**, **Richard Shaver-Reality of the Inner Earth**, **Admiral Byrd's Secret Journey Beyond the Poles**, and is a contributing writer for the books, **Sir Arthur Conan Doyle: The First Ghostbuster**, Brad Steiger's **Real Monsters, Gruesome Critters, and Beasts from the Darkside**, and **Real Ghosts, Restless Spirits and Haunted Places**.

As a photojournalist, Tim Swartz has traveled extensively and investigated paranormal phenomena and other unusual mysteries from such diverse locations as the Great Pyramid in Egypt to the Great Wall in China. He has worked with television networks such as PBS, ABC, NBC, CBS, CNN, ESPN, Thames-TV and the BBC. He has appeared in the series Contacto Extraterrestre seen on The History Channel Latin America.

His articles have been published in magazines such as Mysteries, FATE, Strange, Atlantis Rising, UFO Universe, Flying Saucer Review, Renaissance, and Unsolved UFO Reports.

As well, Tim Swartz is the writer and editor of the online newsletter Conspiracy Journal; a free, weekly e-mail newsletter, considered essential reading by paranormal researchers worldwide.

View his website at: www.conspiracyjournal.com

UFOS - WICKED THIS WAY COMES: THE DARK SIDE OF THE ULTRA-TERRESTRIALS

UFOS – WICKED THIS WAY COMES: THE DARK SIDE OF THE ULTRA-TERRESTRIALS

Dr. Karla Turner

BEFORE HER UNTIMELY DEATH, A CONTROVERSIAL ABDUCTEE DECLARED THAT THE EVIDENCE WAS IN . . .

KARLA TURNER REVEALS WHY THE ALIENS ARE WICKED
By Sean Casteel

FOR many in the UFO community who deeply desire a more reassuring explanation for the UFO phenomenon than the evidence may present, Karla Turner continues to be a problematic, even tragic figure in the many years since her death in 1996 from a dangerous form of breast cancer she contracted right after an abduction experience. Turner was an outspoken voice for abductees' rights and never wavered in her belief that the aliens were an evil, invasive force that intended no good with their medical experiments and frightening mind control capabilities. To this well-educated, gifted woman, the UFOnauts were wickedness personified, simply evil in the "flesh."

Is the human race at the so-called mercy of hostile, even monstrous aliens? For Turner, it was always impossible to turn her alien abduction experiences into a blissful New Age blessing. Unlike the many who took the experience to be a form of contact with angels or benevolent entities of some kind, Turner always adamantly hammered home her belief that alien contact was a negative, frightening, even heartbreaking burden that was to be resisted and fought with every ounce of a person's strength. When she died, it was openly speculated that she had been "silenced" by her abductors for her outspoken beliefs in their fundamental evil, though we of course cannot know if that is true.

UFOS – WICKED THIS WAY COMES: THE DARK SIDE OF THE ULTRA-TERRESTRIALS

It is imperative that Karla Turner's voice continues to be heard from beyond this time and place and that her message is still proclaimed in an era when alien abduction is no less rampant and no less traumatic for the experiencers than when Turner first began writing about what was happening to her and her family. This is more so the case considering that so many stand deeply-rooted today in the Exopolitical movement, where a sort of pseudo-hip "spiritual blissfulness" regarding the true character of the "visitors" outweighs rational thought in light of what at least some of the evidence as to their nature seems to indicate

Karla Turner's first book, "Into The Fringe," set new standards for honesty and bravery in the face of the dark mystery of alien abduction. Turner had no patience for people who said the negative baggage that accompanies abduction was because of the abductee's own failure to be open to the experience's beauty and worth. She protests most vigorously the tendency to "blame the victim," to say the fault lies in humanity and not in the fascistic, iron-grip of the aliens. No amount of New Age positive thinking can change the fact that people are being subjected, completely involuntarily, to a series of medical, psychological and emotional procedures that leave them cowering in fear and with no readily available cure or solution.

Even the late abduction research pioneer, Budd Hopkins, who told me more than once that he hesitated to call the aliens "evil" because it would an over-simplification that he felt would be counterproductive, nevertheless equated alien abduction with rape, simply because it was not an experience freely chosen and could not be stopped by any human method of resistance.

In her introduction to "Into The Fringe," Turner presents the cluster of people she will be writing about, which will include her husband, her son, her son's girlfriend and her son's male roommate, as well as other friends and researchers she would come to know along the way.

"We discovered that we were victims," Turner writes, "of abductions by some alien force. We learned that this force, this alien presence, had in fact been part of our lives for many years. And through sharing our experiences, and seeking answers and help from others who had also encountered these beings, we learned to survive with our sanity intact and our perspective on life immeasurably expanded."

UFOS – WICKED THIS WAY COMES: THE DARK SIDE OF THE ULTRA-TERRESTRIALS

Many of the experiences Turner writes about are common among abductees. But one aspect of abduction that even the hardiest believer in alien benevolence has trouble dealing with is the sexual procedures frequently performed during an alien encounter.

For instance, Turner writes about a man named "Fred" (a pseudonym) who recalls under hypnosis a horrifying sexual experience involving a half human/half animal creature.

"I feel like they are doing something to me with the animal," Fred begins. "They are doing something with me, my blood, my sperm, and my genes. They are injecting my fluids into this animal. I think it's stupid, and I don't like it. Why are they doing this?"

His facial expression becomes disturbed.

"Seems like the animal is part human, part animal," Fred continues. "Like a small child around two years old. The one animal that appears to be part human seems to be real hairy."

Fred begins to feel angry, watching as the aliens inject fluids into the apparently female animal. He next starts to shake all over, in "wrenching spasms" that continued for several minutes, which are then followed by his sobbing and moaning in distress.

After a while, he recovers his composure and returns to telling his story. He now remembers seeing gray aliens levitating the small human/animal, who is spread-eagled on her back.

"There is one now," Fred goes on, "that is sticking a needle device up her groin or vaginal area. It has hooves, like a cow."

Fred realizes that he is naked and strapped down, unable to move.

"Seems like there is a nude woman," he says. "She's been opened up and has a vertical incision from the top of her chest to straight down to her groin area. They have moved her close to me. The one that had my stuff in the tube is going over to her. He's putting his hand inside her. His hand entered through the chest opening and was directed down towards the reproductive area. It looks like he's got a long, tube-like instrument going in through her vagina."

Next, a gray alien takes a lighted object and pulls the woman's skin together, sealing it up as if there was never a cut there at all. Fred restates his belief that his sperm, blood, etc. had been inserted into the both the half animal/half human creature and the human female. After some frightening moments in which the aliens insert a long, thin rod into both his eyeball and his navel, Fred is brought out of hypnosis, still upset and affirming his statements that he had seen the typical gray aliens throughout the experience.

The aforementioned roommate of Turner's son, called by the pseudonym "James," also had a harrowing sexual encounter.

"I saw a beautiful blond woman facing me," James said. "She was really pretty and looked totally human. And she was acting sort of sexy and alluring to me. She held out her arms like she wanted to hug me, so I went to her. I thought she was going to kiss me, but when we got really close together, it all changed. She wasn't pretty anymore, and she damn sure didn't look human. It was ugly, whatever it was."

The female figure looked "terrible, real dark and bumpy, like there were warts all over the body. And slimy."

Seeing the creature's transformation into something so ugly frightened James. The creature shoved something down his throat, after which his memory cuts off. He awakened the next morning to a sore throat and a bitter taste in his mouth, "like bile." He also discovered three parallel scratches on his neck, which served to indicate the experience hadn't been a dream.

Turner's son, called by the pseudonym "David," told her that he awoke one night in his bed feeling "as if he were oscillating violently, as if his body were about to explode or disintegrate into its atomic particles."

"It felt really scary," David said, "like if that sensation went on much longer, I was literally going to come apart. I was just getting ready to scream, I was so scared, and then the sensation suddenly stopped."

For an article she wrote for Tim Beckley's now defunct magazine "UFO Universe," which is further elaborated on in the Global Communications book "Round Trip To Hell In A Flying Saucer," Karla Turner created a checklist, a breakdown of the most basic elements of alien abduction that puts the matter in its proper perspective quite succinctly. We present a portion of the checklist here.

- Aliens can control what we think we see. They can appear to us in any number of guises and shapes.

- Aliens can take us – our consciousness – out of our physical bodies, disable our control of our bodies, install one of their own entities, and use our bodies as vehicles for their own activities before returning our consciousness to our bodies.

- Aliens can be present with us in an invisible state and can make themselves only partially visible.

- A surprising number of abductees suffer from serious illnesses they didn't have before their encounters. These have led to surgery, debilitation, and even death from causes the doctors can't identify.

- Some abductees experience a degeneration of their mental, social and spiritual well-being. Excessive behavior frequently erupts, such as drug abuse, alcoholism, overeating and promiscuity. Strange obsessions develop and cause the disruption of normal life and the destruction of personal relationships.

- Some abductees report being taken to underground facilities where they see grotesque hybrid creatures, nurseries of hybrid humanoid fetuses, and vats of colored liquid filled with parts of human bodies.

- Abductees report seeing other humans in these facilities being drained of blood, being mutilated, flayed, and dismembered, and being stacked, lifeless, like cords of wood. Some abductees have been threatened that they, too, will end up in this condition if they don't cooperate with their alien captors.

- Aliens have forced their human abductees to have sexual intercourse with aliens and even with other abductees while groups of aliens observe these performances. In such encounters, the aliens have sometimes disguised themselves in order to gain the cooperation of the abductee, appearing in such forms as Jesus, the Pope, certain celebrities, and even the dead spouse of the abductee.

"It becomes clear," Turner writes, "from these details that the beings who are doing such things can't be seen as spiritually enlightened, with the best interests of the human race in mind. Something else is going on, something far more painful and frightening, in many, many abduction encounters."

There is an understandable need, she acknowledges, for humans to believe in the power of good.

"We need for the aliens to be a good force," she admits, "since we feel so helpless in their presence. And we need for some superior force to offer us a hope of salvation, both personally and globally, when we consider the sorry state of the world."

The aliens understand that we hope for them to be benevolent creatures, she reasons, and they use that desire for goodness to manipulate us.

"What better way to gain our cooperation," Turner asked, "than to tell us that the things they are doing are for our own good? Looking at the actions, the results of alien interference, such as on the list above, there is a great discrepancy between what we desire from them and what they are doing to us."

Turner also detailed the consistent patterns of deception that make up a great deal of the abduction experience. People sometimes report that they were treated kindly by the aliens, and were told that they were "special" or "chosen" to perform some important task for the benefit of humanity. Given such a positive message, the abductees may ignore the fear and pain of their encounters and insist to themselves and others that a higher motive underlies the abduction experience. They may only recall, in some cases, a benevolent encounter and have no memory of any negative action.

But intensive research now shows us something much different.

"We know, for instance," Turner writes, "that 'screen memories' are often used to mask an alien abduction. Such accounts abound, in which a person sees a familiar yet out-of-place animal, like a deer or owl, a monkey or a rabbit, and then experiences a period of missing time. The person often awakens later to find a new, unexplained scar on his body.

"Uneasiness about the encounter will persist, however, and far different memories may start to surface in dreams or flashbacks, and then the person seeks help to explain the uneasiness. Quite often, hypnotic regression is used to uncover the events behind the 'screen memory,' and that is when the typical alien abduction surfaces. However, from several recent cases, it is apparent that these recovered memories may well be yet another screen, masking events that are much more reprehensible."

UFOS - WICKED THIS WAY COMES: THE DARK SIDE OF THE ULTRA-TERRESTRIALS

So, according to Turner, abductees can't trust their screen memories nor can they trust the recovered memories which may come later. It quickly becomes a wickedly complex hall of mirrors in which the truth perishes somewhere in the many reflected surfaces. If things like forcible sexual intercourse and all the other forms of victimization can be defended in moral terms, we are a long way from understanding how.

Turner's voice was not the only one shouting to be heard with this unhappy truth, and many abduction researchers and hypno-therapists agree with her overall negative take on the experience, though they may not express it in those same exact terms. Ann Druffel, for instance, has written extensively about methods for resisting alien abduction, one of which involves invoking the name of Jesus immediately after an experience begins.

But it is Turner who remains the most eloquent spokesperson for resistance from among the abductees, and we can only wonder if her voice was silenced by her death from cancer as a deliberate act of the aliens, who were intent on enforcing some form of damage control to counter the "bad press" she was giving them. Such a thing is unknowable of course; the vagaries of when an illness like cancer presents itself may have nothing to do with aliens, even in Turner's case.

Similar frightening accounts have come from other sources. Writer and publisher Timothy Beckley relates the nightmarish stories of a couple of pairs of witnesses who encountered ships and aliens while driving the freeway that doggedly pursued the hapless motorists for many miles. In one case, a married couple named Bob and Jackie Blair told their story to a newspaper reporter in Sauk Centre, Minnesota.

"They had been experiencing unexplainable phenomena for three days," the newspaper report said, "for 900 miles across three states, and when they stopped in Sauk Centre, Minnesota, hardly anyone believed them."

The pursuit had begun in Montana when what the Blairs at first took to be stars in the night sky turned out to be nine small ships and one large one. Things turned hostile quickly when the couple's car was shot with needle-like shavings of silver metal that penetrated the couple's windshield. The shavings ruined the truck's new paint job and when Jackie touched them they caused her fingers to break out in blisters; Bob had a similar blister on his wrist. The reporter says that their fingers glowed from the unknown substance they had touched and Bob exclaimed, "We might be dying right now! We don't know what it is. We have to get to a doctor!"

The incident is dead on creepy as the couple says that a group of attacking "individual things" were "shaped like about eight-inch people with V-shaped heads, wings on their backs," like prehistoric birds. They were said to be exceedingly hostile and went into attack mode several times, cloaking the scene in a dense fog.

"It was like a backwards tornado coming from the mouth of the leader of the ships. It was like a ray that he was sending down with this funnel. He did it five times, than left," Bob said.

This is a classic example of the kind of mental and emotional agony often left behind after a UFO encounter.

Beckley's research has also unearthed a terrifying highway encounter that happened to a young woman named Mickie and her girlfriend, an experience so blatantly bizarre that Beckley compared the story to an LSD trip. At one point in the women's drive across the country, with the UFOs in hot pursuit, a monster "dog" appeared in their backseat, complete with glowing red eyes. Beckley believes this adds considerable weight to the "ultra-terrestrial" concept, meaning that other realities are merging with our own in many close encounter cases, placing the abnormalities outside the realm of wandering spaceships and alien occupants into a totally different conceptual dimension.

My own research has yielded up such unsettling possibilities as the mental co-opting of world leaders in government, religion and economics and the open hostility of the alien presence. In an interview I did with researcher and political activist Michael Brownlee, he argues quite convincingly that if anyone else were to abduct members of our citizenry by the millions or over-fly and disable our nuclear missile sites, we would regard it as an act of war and respond accordingly.

Why is it we give the aliens a free pass in those terms? One answer may be that we are humiliatingly outgunned and outmanned, and the authorities simply can't go public with a situation they can neither control nor influence. However, efforts like the Star Wars Space Defense program, begun under President Ronald Reagan, seem to be a step in the right direction, Brownlee said, and he knows personally people in the defense industry who are continuing to work to develop adequate technology to fight back against the aliens' superior weaponry.

Writer, editor and Emmy Award-winning producer Tim Swartz points out that the meetings between beautiful-looking Nordic blondes and the early contactees cut against the grain of the alien-related popular culture and Cold War paranoia of the 1950s. With potential atomic warfare between the USA and the USSR casting a dark cloud over the era, combined with science fiction movies about hostile aliens such as "War of the Worlds" and "Invasion of the Body Snatchers," the benevolent Nordics seem out of place and too good to be true.

Which they were, according to Swartz, who provides several case histories of negative UFO contact from that same timeframe. In one case, which took place in Caracas, Venezuela, in 1954, two truck drivers found their way blocked by a glowing disc-shaped object about ten feet in diameter and hovering about six feet above the street. They next encountered a hairy dwarf whose yellow, catlike eyes glowed in the headlights of their truck. The creature began to claw at one of the truck drivers with webbed hands, and when the driver fought back with a knife, the blade glanced off the being's shoulder as if the creature were made of steel. After the encounter, a doctor determined that both men were in a state of shock and that neither of them had been drinking. Swartz has also written about similar stories from throughout the world that bolster the arguments for declaring the UFO presence to be a hostile one.

There is also the work of Brad and Sherry Steiger, celebrated authors and longtime veterans of UFO and paranormal research, who have revealed some further contact episodes with a wicked ET force that does literal and irreparable harm to its human victims.

In one story, which took place in 1970, a 40-year-old, healthy farmer near Sao Paulo, Brazil, was stunned and knocked to the ground by a mysterious beam of light from the sky. In tremendous pain, he managed to make his way to the home of his sister.

While the farmer showed no evidence of burns, within a matter of hours the once robust man began to deteriorate right before the eyes of his startled friends and family. Although the man did not complain of pain at any point, his "insides began to show, and the flesh started to look as though it had been cooked for many hours in boiling water. The flesh began to come away from the bones, falling in lumps from his jaws, his chest, his arms, his hands, his fingers. Soon every part of him had reached a state of deterioration beyond imagination. His teeth and his bones stood revealed, utterly bare of flesh. His nose and ears fell off."

Six hours after being struck by the terrible beam of light, the farmer died. He was unable to reach a hospital before he was reduced to a grotesque skeleton, and he passed away attempting to communicate details of his awful experience.

As the reader can see, a lot of the material included here is not for the squeamish, yet one should face the ET threat as bravely as possible and hope that the courage of mere mortals is enough to sustain us in this strange warping of reality as we know it.

The great bard Shakespeare once famously wrote, "The fault, dear Brutus, is not in our stars, but in ourselves." But perhaps, in the case of alien abduction, the fault originates somewhere out there in the stars after all.

AN EXCERPT FROM KARLA TURNER'S "TAKEN" (1994)

Chapter Three, "Polly"

In this excerpt from Dr. Karla Turner's 1994 book, "Taken," an abductee named Polly develops unhealthy sexual obsessions after a lifetime of experiences with the dark ultra-terrestrials.

* * *

POLLY first contacted me in late 1992, before she even finished reading INTO THE FRINGE. "I am on page 176,'" her letter said, "and I had to stop to write you."

A passage discussing alien interest in human sexuality had struck a chord that resonated with some of her possible experiences. In the small town where she lived, Polly said, she couldn't find a good support system because the only UFO study group in the area had no women. She asked if I could put her in touch with other female abductees "for mutually beneficial correspondence." What she needed to discuss was too intimate for sharing with anyone other than another woman with similar experiences.

"I have been involved with the UFO phenomenon apparently all my life, and my children also are or have been involved," she wrote. "My father also has had experiences, but he is very careful whom he talks to about them, as he is respected as a technical person and is active still in [a military organization]."

Polly explained that she needed "a woman abductee buddy" because of the sexual nature of some of the events she had endured. "I have all my life been seriously traumatized, with the symptoms of a victim of long-term incest," she wrote, noting that her obsession with "fantasies of strange sexual abuse involving [unfamiliar] intrusive instruments" began when she was four years old.

And its consequences had deeply affected her adult life. "You stopped me short with your discussion of alien-instigated sexual obsessions," she continued. "I have since my teen years found myself every few years in a totally irrational sexually obsessive relationship, characterized by some intelligence talking to me in my mind, directing my actions, and apparently setting up bizarre coincidences to stage interactions."

For the most part, Polly noted, her personal relationships had not been obsessive. But having learned from experience that she could be externally manipulated in her sexual activities, she no longer sought out such involvements. "I now simply stay out of all relationships of a sexual nature," she told me. "The sexual and 'psychic' energy in [the last relationship] was intense to the point of being ridiculous, totally 'directed' and involved frequent telepathy and transference of feelings. I am in counseling for childhood incest, but there is only so far I can go with it, because I don't have a human incest background."

Polly's letter listed several UFO sightings and alien-encounter incidents in her family's experiences, and most of the details were familiar from my research with other abductees. The list included "interactions with 'Elves'; a creature that seemed to slosh through physical objects as if they were water; the usual zigzagging lights; lights that appeared outside my window every night at about the same time and watched me for several hours; maddening poltergeist activity; and many, many vivid 'abduction' dreams."

"I make no claim for them," Polly wrote, "but I know how they felt, a sense since young childhood that something was in my head to keep track of me, a squealing sound sort of in my head which seems associated with contact, and bedroom visitors which my dog, my son, and I all saw."

Polly had merely listed these events, but as a researcher I was interested in the details. I was also interested in the person who was trying to cope with this phenomenon. Replying to her letter, I asked for more information about her experiences and offered to be a good listener, both as an abductee and a woman. Although I had no recollection of any sexually oriented encounters myself, I had learned much from others who had been through such events. And my husband Casey, whose full account is related in INTO THE FRINGE, had himself experienced a sexual scenario with what appeared to be a hybrid alien female when he was a very young teen. Such events, I knew, were real in terms of their sensations and aftereffects, and any understanding of these scenarios would shed important light on the overall abduction agenda.

I explained these two concerns when I answered Polly's letter, and she agreed to share her information with me as part of my ongoing research. Through letters, phone calls, and taped discussions, I learned much about Polly and the things she and her children had experienced. A tall, fair, striking woman in her mid-forties, Polly's ethnic background is European, primarily Celtic, and Scandinavian. She is an excellent artist, but much of the time in supporting her family she has worked at rather physical jobs. Polly was born in 1946 in New Jersey and grew up in the Southeast. Widowed, she now lives with her children in the Adirondacks.

In addition to the various UFO sightings they had witnessed in this area, it soon became clear that her youngest son, Sam, was also having current alien encounters. In his taped communications and the drawings and reports to Polly which were shared with me, Sam showed unusual maturity and insight for an eleven-year-old.

Everything they told me came strictly from their conscious recollections which, concerning any given event, were very incomplete. Polly relegated some of her experiences to the "vivid dream" category, a common response of many abductees. The statement, "I make no claim for them," meant that she could not objectively verify these events as part of our "usual" reality. Some of them are similar to the virtual-reality scenario (VRS) dream discussed earlier, and some seem to have been simply the surfacing memories of actual events. Nonetheless, to Polly they were "experienced" events, and if they occurred strictly within a mental or psychic framework they still gave her every semblance of reality. The nature of that "reality" was often ambiguous, however, but there were some experiences she had verified as "real" because they had been multiply witnessed or perceived while she knew herself to be in a conscious state of mind.

These began very early in Polly's childhood. "When I was four years old," she told me, "I saw the skinny being who appeared in silhouette against my window shade. It was night, but a bright light, perhaps orangish in color, shone from the other side of the shade. The room was dark except for the illumination outside the shaded window. The being turned to approach me. When I get to this point in the memory, I start shaking my head and saying, 'No, no' and then the memory stops. I tell myself if the memory comes over me again, I will get beyond this point and find out what happens next, but I never do."

This was also the age, probably not coincidentally, at which she began having the sexual fantasies of "intrusive unfamiliar instruments" used on her. Additionally she reported, "About age four, I had a sense of something having been put behind my left ear."

The next event possibly related to alien activity occurred around the age of fourteen: the onset of an obsession with understanding "the workings of the universe." She explained, "It was like I awakened to a sense of cosmic mission and to an apocalyptic sort of sense of human destiny. I felt I must understand the universe. It became a constant undercurrent of striving which persists even now." Given the reports of other abductees, some of which will be presented later, it was interesting that she related this "job and task on earth" to "Armageddon."

When she was in her late twenties, living in a different location, the next event took place. "Outside the cabin in the Blue Ridge Mountains," she said, "very loud stomping, like several men in work boots, suddenly began on our front porch after no sound of approach. We saw shadowy figures accompanying the very loud stomping. But I don't remember it stopping. I recollect we went to sleep in the midst of all this commotion, which of course makes no sense if we were lying only a few yards from prowlers. We awoke in the morning, remembered the stomping and shadowy figures, and went outside to hunt for footprints but found none."

In early 1987, however, Polly had a conscious look at her mysterious intruders. While sick in bed, she said, "I had a couple of bedroom visitations by two black-robed figures. They had large slanted, glowing, lemon-yellow eyes with no pupils, just like lights. The black-robed figures were about four feet tall. They were identical except that one was a little lighter, like charcoal gray instead of black. When they moved they did everything simultaneously to each other. They glided through my son's toy box when they left-the lower parts of their robes just went right through it."

Polly noted that this event occurred before she had ever seen the cover of Whitley Strieber's COMMUNION or any other representation of the typical Gray alien figures.

"Someone asked me if I had asked the figures what they wanted. My response was NO! I didn't want to give them any openers! My feeling was that they had come to take me permanently, and I devoted all my energy to rebuking them."

An extremely unusual series of events commenced in late 1987. "The whole thing started with a dream," Polly explained. "I dreamed I was flying over the Atlantic toward the Mediterranean. A white plane with red markings shaped like a small Concorde was approaching me from the opposite direction, the east.

"Shortly after this dream," Polly continued, "I noticed that I was having conversations in my head in French. This was most apt to happen around 4 p.m. My communicator identified himself as a professor in a Russian university. I had a sense of it being near Kiev. At night he would privately beam out psychic messages toward the West in an effort to expose a situation of psychic warfare which he claimed was being waged between political powers worldwide, and in an effort to help bring about peace between the then-USSR and the West.

"One thing I remember him saying very strongly was *maintenant c'est la guerre, maintenant c'est la guerre*, and he emphasized *maintenant*, telling me that psychic warfare was now being waged, directed to influence people in high positions and others who could serve the purposes of the perpetrators-perhaps obscure people who could nevertheless influence events and public opinion."

Her last contact with Evec was in December 1987 as she drove her son, through a snowstorm, to another town. The driving conditions took all her concentration, so she was startled when the French communication began.

"Evec was saying that he wanted me to join with him in prayer for world peace. So I tried praying in French, and that was a total disaster. I don't remember whose idea it was, but we decided to pray in Latin, and that went much better. I was saying things from the Mass in Latin, clearly seeing the snowy surroundings and driving competently, but just as clearly I began to see, like in some sort of parallel vision, the inside of a (probably Russian Orthodox) cathedral. There was a priest in a dark red robe with some kind of tall, funny hat. The interior was not ornate, but the ceiling was high and there was a lot of rich, polished wood. There was a choir consisting of both men and women.

"I wish I had had a tape recorder in my head. The choir was singing the most magnificent mass I had ever heard. I could clearly distinguish that it was sometimes in eight-part harmony. It was all in Latin, and it was definitely not any mass that I have sung or heard. This went on for a long time, the whole rest of the ride. I don't recollect it ending, but we did arrive at our destination. This was the last time I ever heard from Evec. I had the feeling we had accomplished all we could together. He had not been seek

These two events in 1987, Polly's visitations by the black-robed beings and the recurrent telepathic conversations with Evec, marked the onset of what would prove to be frequent UFO and alien-related activities in her family's lives. It seemed to focus on Polly and her youngest child, Sam.

A few months after Evec's last communication, Sam had an encounter that paralleled Polly's experience with the black-robed beings. At age six, he saw "black figures flying about the room." Although they were similar to the beings Polly had witnessed, Sam described these characters as "smoke-like" with red eyes. They told him, Come with us, we'll take you to a better place.

But Sam wasn't convinced of their good intentions, and even though he was quite young he refused the offer. "No way," he replied, "I'm not going anywhere with you guys!"

After this incident both he and Polly had a number of experiences involving UFO sightings, mainly witnessed from a nearby hill, and a series of the "vivid dream" events that indicated repeated alien encounters.

"We've seen many UFOs with colored lights around them or shooting out from them," she said, reporting that it was "common to see white central lights flash amber, red, and blue."

This was also the onset of several experiences with what Polly and her family referred to as the "Elves." These beings, she said, "would squeak-talk very loud at night" and were extremely frightening to another of her

UFOS – WICKED THIS WAY COMES: THE DARK SIDE OF THE ULTRA-TERRESTRIALS

children who also witnessed some of this activity during the most intense period of activity in 1989 and 1990.

Around this same time, in September 1989, Polly's family also had an experience with a different sort of creature. They perceived it as "sloshing" through solid matter, moving "through physical objects as if they were water." In spite of no clear confrontation with this being, Polly felt that it was "reptilian, huge and loud," making "crashing sounds in the woods like some very large two-legged creature lumbering through the woods in a very wet area. This sound had no approach and no departure," she said, "but there was the definite sense that the perpetrator of all this noise was approaching us. This occurred on a night which included a lot of UFO activity. We witnessed UFOs apparently pursued by fighter-reconnaissance at the air base."

Polly, Sam, and others in her family have had a number of UFO sightings, not only from the hill but also from other parts of the area. In June 1993, for instance, while Sam was traveling in a car driven by a family friend, he watched three UFOs cavort in the sky. "Sam saw three bright UFOs," Polly related. "A bright light suddenly appeared high above and a little ahead of them. It moved quickly downward, then disappeared as suddenly as it had appeared. Then a second appeared suddenly with no gradual approach, to the left of where the first one had, then zoomed across the sky to the right and disappeared." Shortly after this, the car turned onto another street, and Sam watched a third light appear suddenly. It flew a short distance and then went out of sight.

Within a matter of a few weeks, Sam had another sighting, this time of three UFOs together. And the following month, after yet another impressive sighting, Sam wrote me himself about what he'd seen on the night of August 19. "Last night was awesome for UFOs," his account began. "I saw one triangle-shaped one which made a whooshing sound for a long time. It looked like it might have been similar to the triangular one sighted in Belgium in 1988 or 1989. We saw it on TV. The one I saw was flying low....I had heard a whooshing noise first."

Another impressive sighting occurred on August 30, in the same area of the previous sighting. Sam said that this one was a large diamond or triangular shape with blinking lights on the front and rear. "It looked to be really high," he said, "but I could still see it good. I could see solid matter inside the light pattern" as the UFO arced across the sky.

Alien contacts continued to occur, usually recalled the morning after the event as both dreamlike and yet real. "Sam told me of an abduction dream which he found frightening," Polly wrote in December 1992, "and this is unusual for him, as he is the only one of my children who seems to seek them and even to miss them. It included some interesting disclaimers to usual UFO accounts, such as 'there was gravity, I was not floating.' He said the interior was about ten feet by ten feet, rounded on the outside, but he felt inside there were some corners. He said it was 'spinning and wobbling' and throwing him around. He was frightened and recollected not wanting to enter the craft. He also recollected being able to see out a window of the craft part of the time and could see stars. He said he felt it was 'a blessing' that he was able, briefly, to see out."

Sam also said he sensed having had contact at some point with "bad aliens who are red, not gray," tacitly identifying the ones he had otherwise remembered as Grays, the same sort of figure so many other abductees have reported. Even more disturbing for Sam, however, was a dream he reported to Polly on the night of March 3, 1993.

"Sam just took me aside," Polly wrote, "to tell me about a dream he had last night. He said, 'Can I talk to you in private? It's personal.' He has a partial memory of this dream, or else the dream itself was a fragment. He was with some people approaching the entrance to a UFO. He went through an entry way which led to a place that was all white, but he commented, 'You know how scientists say dogs are colorblind to our colors? I felt like maybe I was colorblind to their (ETs) colors and it wasn't really all white.'

"He said he was in a line with other people and the person in front of him was older than he. This young man proceeded into the craft and approached a long, white tube. He put his penis into the tube. After a little while he apparently withdrew it and left by some way other than the entrance. Sam was next. He did the same thing with the tube as the man before him had done, but his memory ends at this point. He felt this had something to do with the aliens wanting sperm. He said there was no sound and he did not see any aliens. He kept asking me for reassurance, saying, 'That was just a dream, right, Mom?'

"He does not read adult level books and I had never mentioned the sexual intrusions to him. It seems that just in the past year his experiences have become less agreeable to him. Previously he was the one of my children who seemed to feel a need and desire for 'them.' That is not completely gone, but certainly some intrusive elements have been introduced. Damn it, Karla, something is sexually molesting my eleven-year-old boy!"

After pondering on the situation a while, Polly commented, "I think the motive is not sperm gathering, but control. What affects the depths of the human psyche more than issues related to our sexuality? It is a perhaps unadmirable fact that sexual identity is probably the deepest, most primitive, most powerful identity concept that a human being has. Violate sexual identity in a situation where the human is made to believe that he/she is totally powerless, and you have gained a measure of control probably unattainable by any other single act."

Like Polly, I was concerned about Sam's discomfort with this scenario, and its implications. I was also fascinated by his statement that he had not seen any aliens in the experience. Later, Sam expanded this thought on a taped conversation he and Polly sent me. "In UFO dreams," he said, "after I've done what they make me do, they don't let me see them. It's like they make me want to do it, even though I don't want to. I see maybe them disguised as humans, or humans hypnotizing me. I'm not sure if they're humans."

Polly also had a number of abduction or UFO dream-events which felt extremely real to her and sometimes included human-looking figures. Many of the details, some of which will be described below, are amazingly similar to cases I've investigated and which other researchers and abductees have consistently reported. She also occasionally found typical marks on her body, although without any memory of getting them, including "IV-type bruises" on the bend of her arm and "bruises in a triangular pattern" on her upper arm.

Polly's abduction dreams became so frequent and realistic in their details as well as in their effects upon her that in 1991 she began keeping a journal of the dreams and of actual UFO sightings, from which the following excerpts are taken.

"August 31, 1991. I was with a group of people in a light colored room, and aliens were testing us for AIDS. I was found to have some strain of it, but they seemed to be communicating to me that it would not kill me or even seriously harm me. I don't know if this was because of something they did. Others had it as well-many of us were in the same situation. I think communication was telepathic.

"One thing that has characterized my UFO dreams has been an intense feeling of Wow, this is really This is the real thing! This is really happening. Typically I am out of doors and I see a UFO or UFOs in the sky. They land or one hovers above me. When I felt the dizzying sense of spiraling upward [in a previous event she had described], that one was different because I was conscious of being in my bed and being spun and sucked upward into a UFO. I think my mind was sucked out of my body."

Questioning the 'reality' of this dream about AIDS, Polly noted that she had in fact been diagnosed with lupus erythematosus, an autoimmune disorder, during her teen years.

"October 19, 1991. I remember a dream of a week or so ago which involved aliens. I recollect exiting a craft with them. I remember flying before we landed. There were other humans on board. Some of us went up front, but on the lower level the underside was clear-not glass but something thick yet perfectly clear. We could see down to a spread-out village below. It was daylight. The landscape below was fairly flat, maybe some low hills off to our left beyond the village. We landed, and I remember that I and others exited the craft with the aliens, whose form was like a very simplified human form-no muscle development evident. I think they may have had on form-fitting suits. They had no hair. I recollect something about some covering which had a seam near where an ear would be, but this is a vague memory. They were quite tall, not the four-foot type."

"October 23, 1991. I dreamed I was holding a baby for the purpose of healing it. He was in a room at the end of a building that was like a nursery. None of the babies' parents were there. I think I dreamed of a lot of stuff happening in this building. I can still mentally see the face of the baby very clearly. I held it on two occasions. It was blond and blue-eyed, a little boy, and could hold himself erect when you picked him up. His eyes were crossed, one worse than the other, and as I held him he started to get a little better. When I held him the second time, he was strong enough that I could prop him on my hip.

UFOS - WICKED THIS WAY COMES: THE DARK SIDE OF THE ULTRA-TERRESTRIALS

"Then when he was wanting to nurse, I had this really weird thought, sort of apart from the dream, like standing off a little watching the dream. I thought, What if he isn't really a baby? What if he is really some midget pervert? I emphasized this last part because it indicates an awareness that we might be interacting with something less human and less innocent than it seemed."

"October 26, 1991. I was in some sort of medical situation in which my head was the object of attention. There were doctors around me. Before my head was the object of attention, I remember sitting up - something about my stomach hurting. I was sitting on something flat, and they were somehow making me travel very fast. I was afraid I would slide off the end and expected them to care, but somehow they did not seem to care. I remember when I sat up I said I could breathe better that way. Then they were going to put long needlelike things in the sides of my head, and I remember thinking in my dream, When the aliens do this it doesn't hurt; it is just pressure. Then I started saying over and over again, I'm in outer space, I'm in outer space, and they put the long needle things in, and I could sort of hear them going in, like a scraping sound, and feel pressure but no pain.

"The next thing I remember, I was like flying from west to east. I approached a four – corners intersection in the country. I felt like it was just west of [the hill where she and her family often witnessed UFO activity]. It was like they somehow landed me there, at that intersection, and the next thing I remember my eyes opened abruptly and I was in my room. When I woke up I kind of felt different than from a regular dream, like there was something more real about that experience." [It became even more realistic when, in the summer of 1993 Polly came upon that very intersection while out driving. It was a remote, unpopulated area west of the hill.]

"November 17,1991. Actual sighting, not a dream. Returning at night from the mountains which lie to the east of us, I saw a distant UFO. It changed color from red to white to red, etc., but was not a plane because it hopped around so much in all directions-quick movements."

"December 21, 1991. Had dream of sighting and being abducted by UFO. I was with some young man on a roadway on a hillside. I think there were big evergreens around, and down the hill a bit was an open field.... We went down to about the middle of the field and looked back up the hill. Soon the

UFOS - WICKED THIS WAY COMES: THE DARK SIDE OF THE ULTRA-TERRESTRIALS

UFO appeared, larger and larger as it approached us. It glided low over the field and landed very close to us. My left arm was linked through the young man's right arm. I remember feeling, This is it-like this time it's really coming close. When it landed right near us, I said to the young man, 'Well, here we go!' Three beings came out of the UFO. They were human-looking, dressed in black or very dark colors, male, and surprisingly, taller than we were. I believe they took hold of us and began taking us to the craft, but it didn't feel real unfriendly. The three were pretty much identical. I don't remember faces. It was like they had one mind."

"January 30, 1992. Had a clear and detailed UFO sighting dream. It was daylight and I was looking east. I saw a UFO which was white and pale blue against blue sky. It hovered in one place for a long time while I and others viewed it. I remember looking at the portholes or windows. Then there was a scene where the UFO beings were among us and were taking all those who loved war and aggressive military attitudes and actions. They were taking even children. I was not among those taken. We were made to leave and we knew that the military-minded would suffer, and we felt really bad for them. I think a lot of the aliens were tall and close to human-looking, but also others were sort of like the Grays but I think lighter. I know some had big eyes."

"February 28, 1992. MAJOR UFO DREAM - felt very real. I was standing with another person or people-may have been first in my car, me driving. I saw them [UFOs] above and got out, pulling over to the left. I think there was one we saw very clearly and two others more distant. There were also planes up there, military looking planes. I remember feeling, This was so realistic. We waved our arms to draw attention, and the clearest one began coming nearer. I was thinking, They are going to take us; how am I going to deal with this? And then it was like the atmosphere of my mind changed. I was suddenly in a state of mind where I could handle this, not go into some kind of fear-shock at the absolute strangeness of it.

"The UFO was sort of grayish, not all lit, and some aliens approached us, also grayish. They were not human looking. I think there were three, but I especially focused on one who was either sort of leaning forward so that his head was more noticeable than any other part of him, or else I just noticed his head the most. I said something to the effect that we were really going with them, and in my altered state of mind I felt I could do it, but I knew I would be subjected to them in the craft. It was like I knew, but in my altered state, well, I can't turn back now, might as well accept it. After that I don't remember anything. I think I felt a little responsible, like I had involved the people with me in this and maybe it was not good for them. I had a slight bloody nose when I woke up, but think it was related to a cold."

"June 23, 1992. [Recounting an actual event that preceded the dream] my son Sam and I felt compelled to go up on the hill at 10:30 p.m. as there was a glow in the sky which we felt must be from the sun, as it is not much after the longest day in this north country. When we got up there we felt intensely peaceful. Everything was very, very still, although there is often a wind up there when there is none anywhere else. There were a few fireflies. Then I saw a larger, brighter flash of light in the grass across the road from where we sat. I said to Sam, 'Nothing is really happening, but I feel like if we stay any longer it will.' I felt that if we continued to sit there with our minds focused, we would interact with some energy there and something would happen. I felt it had already begun to happen, but that we still had the option of breaking it off and leaving."

They returned home, and that night Polly had a UFO dream. "I was walking or otherwise traveling along a road at night," she described. "I first saw lights, then saw UFOs-round, a little bigger than stars, and not as bright as stars. They were up to my right, quite near the tops of the trees. I said, 'Wow! I'm really seeing them!' Then I looked up. There was one overhead which descended closer and closer to me. I could clearly see the round bottom part, like an opening. I said, with a little fear, 'Okay, take me.'

"At this point I felt a feeling of being lifted which was like no feeling I can adequately describe. It was like being sucked by force, a dizzying, blinding, overwhelming force. While it was happening I felt intensely that the experience was absolutely real, and in most dreams it never occurs to me to pass judgment on the reality of anything. I was sort of afraid, totally caught up in it (literally and figuratively), very aware of the sense that it was real, and feeling, Well, I'm in it now, so wherever I am going it is not under my control.' I couldn't see much, but I felt such an incredible feeling of being lifted higher and higher, like it took my mind.

"After the lifting I was aware of being in a white place, but it was not the standard 'round' white room of many UFO reports. I think it was white like white paint, and I recollect a corner, which is also not typical, and some sort of black or dark object. It was like I was seeing only one little part of this place.

"Another thing I recollect was being in some sort of craft and being behind the pilot, who sat on the left side, and noticing his head. It was hairless, apparently with a skull similar to ours, and the skin was white like putty. He turned toward me and appeared to have on some sort of clown mask, although it did not really look like our typical clowns. It had the color orange on it and was otherwise white like plastic. The feeling I got from this pilot was of a detached sort of kindness, not any malevolence but also nothing that could really be called emotion.

"I have some recollection of coming into a base or land while in this craft. It was light, like daylight (whereas I had been abducted in the dark of night). I could see a building, I think with a flat roof, and an outdoor area to my right of the building. I also vaguely recollect at some point desiring to see more clearly and 'them' doing something so that I could, and things came into better focus. In the outdoor area beside the building there were flowers and shrubs and children playing, human children.

"The pilot was still with me when I found myself inside the building. He said they call us something like 'the short round ones' and showed me models of humans between three and four feet tall. These models looked to be made out of hard plastic or something similar and were orange and white. I pointed out to the pilot that I was exactly his height (5' 7"). He was thinner built than a human man, maybe a little lighter weight than I, though I am small-boned. A few other aliens were present, also.

"In this building were some human children. Now that I think about it in my waking state, maybe they call us 'the short round ones' because they have so many of our children. Our children, when healthy, are rounder than they. They appeared thin and lightweight, but it was hard to judge because they were clothed. I don't have a clear recollection of their clothing, I think light-colored jumpsuits.

"I felt I was not the only adult human there but that there were more human children present than human adults. Near me was a little blond-headed boy about three years old. I picked him up and held him, and he really seemed to like that. Then I said, 'Where is your mommy?' and he looked sad and didn't say anything. I got the strong feeling that the pilot

UFOS – WICKED THIS WAY COMES: THE DARK SIDE OF THE ULTRA-TERRESTRIALS

who stood to my left and others of his kind very much disapproved of my asking that question. Then I noticed a little girl, also blonde. I feel she was eleven years old for some reason, though I think she was more the size of an average nine-year-old. I asked her if she was the boy's sister, and she said no. I had the feeling they had no kin people with them. The little girl also seemed sad, and I remember feeling grateful that 'they' hadn't taken my children from me, but I was sad about these children and the many others.

"There was a big window arched at the end to my right. Outside the window was a little play yard. A dark-haired human woman was tending a group of human children. I felt she was no kin to them, except that they were all human. I did not see the other adults whom I felt were there somewhere.

"I recollect that there was a process of returning me, but I don't remember it in any detail now. I felt that the experience within the piloted craft seemed 'staged' somehow for the benefit of my belief system, but the intense lifting feeling felt somehow necessary and real."

"January 24, 1993. Three nights in a row I have had dreams including UFOs, a craft, and beings. The next night in actual awake reality, I watched UFO activity in the sky, two luminous fiery balls a little bigger than basketballs."

One of Polly's most vivid and recent dream-events she reported to me at length in a letter, complete with drawings of the creatures she remembered seeing.

"On the night of June 27 (1993)," she wrote, "I had dreams which included vivid visual impressions of aliens and appearances of very bright, very real-feeling lights. The aliens did not look like what I would have depicted if you had said, 'Draw a typical alien.' The characteristics were a pronounced brow-ridge, convolutions or folds on the forehead and beside the eyes, eyes back under shelter of the brow-ridge, and gray or gray-green skin. They were proportionately tall and thin. There were at least three and I am pretty sure more, standing closer together than I have drawn them. I am not sure about my depictions of nose and mouth, but nose and mouth were somehow represented. I'm also not sure about details of the lower body.

"I remember being utterly fascinated with their brow folds and the folds beside their black eyes, but not looking directly into those eyes. Also with the texture of their fairly tough skin, which was sort of like an artist's kneaded eraser. I have a recollection of having been very close to the one on your left [in drawing], so close that my face was right up by the right-hand side of the face, looking closely at those folds. Then I recollect being back a little further from them seeing the group standing together, but I don't know what happened first.

"I felt as I awakened that what I retained were two fragments of a much more detailed experience, as if I had sort of mentally photographed those two segments to 'bring back' as souvenirs-yes, it was almost as if they posed for these memories! That is why I could get so close to that one without having to become engulfed by his eyes, and it is why they stood so obligingly in that little group!"

Polly and Sam reported these and a number of other experiences for almost a year, many of which seemed to be reflections or memories of fairly current experiences. And once she felt more comfortable with our relationship, she was able to address the sexual issue and share the painful memories from her childhood.

"The area of my psychology which I feel has been most damaged by 'them' or by some very early influence," she confided, "is the area of my sexual concepts. At approximately age four, I became obsessed with sadomasochistic sexual imagery. The images involved a little girl on a flat table similar to a doctor's exam table, but I think it may have been metallic looking, silver metallic, a little grayer than actual silver. I remember being obsessed with these images day in and day out, and I would try to detach from them by saying that the little girl was not me, but yet at the same time I knew it was.

"Sometimes there would be one 'person' doing things to the little girl and sometimes several. There were generally those who observed. I had the sense of both males and females present. Occasionally a female would do a procedure, but more often a male."

There were machines involved, as well as probes and needles. "The intrusions involved what I now understand to be the genital area, but I did not understand at the time, as well as the rectum. Also, I do recollect needles to the navel, and this now makes sense when I read adult women's accounts of intrusions through the navel. My sense of the 'people,' if it ever was clear, is now indistinct. My early medical history does not include anything like this.

"One thing I did which could have been a cry for help and an attempt to resolve this situation was that I drew pictures of these events. I remember especially at five and six drawing the little girl on the table and the 'people' around her with the intrusive machines. I showed these pictures to my mother, but I have no recollection of her reaction except that I don't think she shamed me.

"If I had been molested by adult family members I don't think I would have had images of an exam table and needles associated with machinery, especially at ages three and four. I think these images had to have come from some source outside my own imagination. This early influence imprinted my sexuality with the dynamics of sadomasochism. I feel this imprinting set me up to be victimized and set me up to expect all sexual encounters to involve humiliation by a dominator."

In fact, she said, whenever she found herself in 'power-sex' situations, "There was a voice that would talk to me and say, Everything is right on schedule. Everything is going as planned. But the plan did not prove benevolent toward me!"

The overall discernible effects of all their experiences on Polly and Sam, to this point, are several. Sam has an overly mature outlook for his age, evincing an interest in questions of cosmic importance including reincarnation and the history of the human race. And, after the sperm-taking scenario, he is also, according to Polly, very uncomfortable with the idea of alien intrusions upon his developing sexuality. For Polly, too, the sexual aspects of her life have been altered by these events. She avoids sexual involvements now, in an attempt to regain control over the compulsions that have caused many problems for her in the past.

She has no explanation for the alien intrusions into her family's life, only a strong sense that this involvement has been with her for a very long time. Most of it has been unseen. In addition, or as part of the UFO events, Polly has experienced internal communications from "spirits," although she cannot identify them more specifically.

"They so often enter or I enter them in a sense," she explained, "in a sense in which we each or all allow each other to be there simultaneously. I don't know if this is a UFO thing, but they are multi-dimensionals."

Her experiences comprise many elements: UFO sightings, entity encounters, dream-events, physical effects, spiritual teachings, and a sense of an unknown mission she must perform. In their experiences, Polly and Sam have both felt positive and negative presences, fellowship and fright, which makes it hard to place all of the events into a single framework, the acts of a single group. There is also the question of human involvement, since both of them report encounters with humanoid figures that have not yet been clearly discerned or identified.

The amassed data from reports like Polly's show that the abduction agenda is much too complex for any of the current explanations, both in the events and in their effects on the individuals involved. Certainly on the individual level, the phenomenon is profoundly disturbing and transforming, but it is even more so when the massive numbers of people having abductions is considered. The agenda, given this level of pervasiveness, must involve much more than the transformation of the individual. The entire society is beginning to feel its effects, and there would seem, from the testimony of witnesses like Polly and the other women in this project, to be much more yet to come.

AN EXCERPT FROM KARLA TURNER'S "MASQUERADE OF ANGELS" (1994)

In this excerpt from Karla Turner's last book, co-written with Ted Rice, the authors struggle against those who would call alien abduction a "good experience."

Write the vision, and make it plain upon tables, that he may run that readeth it.
—Habakkuk

WITH this new confirmation, Ted reluctantly accepted the possibility that his disturbing "dream" reflected a real event. And his instinctive response to that was not a happy one. Since it seemed to involve UFOs and their little gray occupants, he decided to tell his friends at the bookstore about the experience. His opportunity came the next Saturday when he was there waiting in his small office for the next client to arrive and listening to a conversation among several of his friends in an adjacent room.

"Did you see the TV special the other night about cattle mutilations up in Arkansas?" one woman asked. "It showed all these dead cows with missing parts. Some had their tails cored out and parts of the jaw cut away. And there was one with the uterus removed by some type of unknown surgical procedure, maybe a laser, that literally cut between the cell layers."

Intrigued, Ted stepped out of his office. "Did they say anything about why these cattle were being mutilated?" he asked.

"No," the woman replied. "They didn't say it was definitely aliens, they gave several possibilities. But we know the ETs are responsible."

"Why would aliens be interested in cows?" Ted asked.

"I'd say they're studying the different species on our planet," a second woman said. "Probably they're looking for ways to improve the nutrition we get from beef. They may even be genetically engineering a new cattle breed to withstand the coming earth changes, so that the human race can be assured of survival."

"We can't prove it's ETs," the first woman added, "but it must be them. Common sense tells you that our government would stop it if it were only thieves. Besides, rustlers would want the whole cow, not just a cored-out rectum."

Everyone laughed, including Ted, and she continued. "I think the ETs do their experiments to help mankind," she said. "Word has gotten around the universe about how wicked the human race is, and how self-destructive, and they want to help us clean it all up."

"I hope you're right," Ted replied, "but I don't understand why the ETs don't just land outright and tell us what they want. Why all the secrecy?"

"Look, Ted," a young man explained, "you know how humans are. If the ETs land, the first thing humans would do is get their guns and start shooting. We're just not spiritually evolved enough to handle a massive close encounter. The whole world would panic, and the ETs know it. That's why they behave in the manner they do. They're here to teach us, not scare us. They know better than to just land."

"Well, they sure as hell scared me," he replied, pouring out the story of his abduction with the neighbors.

His friends reacted with excitement and elation.

"I'm not surprised," one of them remarked. "Some of the things you've told us made me wonder if you weren't having alien contacts. How marvelous! You're obviously a special person, a chosen person."

"I don't know why this happened to me," Ted said. "I don't know anything about ETs, and to tell you the truth, the whole thing scared the living shit out of me. I don't want them coming back to my house, or

UFOS - WICKED THIS WAY COMES: THE DARK SIDE OF THE ULTRA-TERRESTRIALS

kidnapping me and my neighbors again. Why did they pick me?"

"You're trying to make it too complicated, Ted," the first woman said, "but it's really quite simple. You weren't kidnapped, nor were your neighbors. ETs don't kidnap people, they make contact with them. They've probably been helping you a long time, and you just didn't know it. I'm sure your spirit guides allowed the ETs to make contact. They would have warned you if it weren't okay."

"The ETs know you are here in this incarnation on a psychic mission to help humanity," her friend agreed, "and they're assisting you. I think it's very beautiful. Who knows what they may be teaching you?"

"You think that it's my psychic abilities that attracted them to me?" Ted asked. "You think they're going to lead me and teach me things like in the Close Encounters movie? Well, you can think again! I don't care if my abilities do interest them, I don't remember inviting them into my bedroom in the middle of the night to scare the hell out of me. Where are their manners?

"With their technology," he continued, "I do believe they could call before dropping in. You can say whatever you want, but I'm telling you right now that there is something about this whole thing that stinks to high heaven. I don't like it, and I don't want any part of it."

"You're overreacting," she said, "and besides, you can't do anything about it. Your higher self gave permission for it on some level, probably before you were reincarnated. It's all been planned, so you may as well kick back and enjoy it."

"Maybe so," Ted hedged, "but I know one thing. They better start knocking before entering if they want my help. If it was all that wonderful, like you say, why couldn't I sleep at night? I want to know what happened to me from the time we left the field until the time I was brought back home, too, because I don't remember any part of that."

"I'm sure they were just teaching you," the man assured him, "and when the time is right you'll remember."

However, Ted wasn't satisfied by their explanations. Inevitably, whenever they got into further discussions about the aliens and their actions, the talk usually turned argumentative. The others were firm in their belief that the ETs were wonderful and benevolent, but Ted had reservations about any sort of beings whose actions were so intrusive.

It was during this time, not long after the neighborhood incident, that Ted received a surprisingly clear communication from a source he couldn't identify. He'd always assumed that such messages came from the spirit world, but now with an awareness of extraterrestrial involvement he wasn't sure.

In spite of its nebulous source, the message was quite specific, about a book that Ted was directed to write. In past readings that other psychics had done for him, he had repeatedly been told that he would be involved with the production of a book. Some of the readings, all the way back to the 1970s, indicated there would be more than one book. But Ted had never felt the urge to write a book, at least not until this new message.

Now the idea caught his fancy. He felt a compulsion to write about his life and experiences, but being no writer, he was frustrated and uncertain of how to begin. So, as he'd done in the past, Ted put the whole thing in the hands of his spirit guides. He told them that if they really wanted him to write, they would have to provide him with the proper equipment and inspiration.

"I don't even have a typewriter," he told them. "If I'm going to do this book, then I want a word processor."

He let the thought go with that, but later, when a friend of his died and bequeathed Ted a word processor, that challenge to the spirits came back to him. A vivid dream soon followed, in which some unidentifiable entities showed Ted the very book he was supposed to write. The next morning, he told a friend about the dream, convinced that it was important.

"They're serious," he said, "they really must want me to do this book. Not only did they show it to me, they even told me what to call it - THE LIGHT WORKER."

But even though the spirits were insisting and the equipment had been provided, Ted delayed starting on the book. His doubts about the nature of these entities tempered his enthusiasm for the project. Instead of writing, Ted put his energy into the psychic readings at the bookstore, yet he continued to think about UFOs and to discuss them with his friends.

One afternoon, when they had just had one of these conversations at the bookstore, Ted began rummaging through the books alone. A few moments later he glanced up and noticed a woman, small and mature but very attractive and well-mannered, watching him with a smile.

"I was just browsing," she told him, "and I overheard your conversation."

"Oh?" he replied. "Pretty interesting stuff, isn't it?"

"I really feel that you should read this," she continued, handing him a book.

Ted took it and glanced down at the cover. It showed a drawing of a strange being with large, black eyes, and Ted cringed. It wasn't that he felt the being was familiar, but still it sent a chill through his body. The title was COMMUNION.

He looked up to ask the woman about the book, but she was gone. Quickly he searched the bookstore without finding her, so Ted went over to his friends in the back of the room.

"Who was that woman?" he asked.

"We don't know," Beverly replied. "We saw what she did, though. I thought it was someone you knew. I don't think I've ever seen her in here before."

"I've been meaning to tell you to read that book, too," Felicia remarked. "Since you're having ET visitations, you ought to read this. It should help you a lot. Take it home, and when you finish it, there's another one you've got to read, too-TRANSFORMATION."

"Okay," Ted agreed, taking the book with him when he left. Reading COMMUNION triggered some strong emotions in him, and by the time he finished the book he was pretty well convinced that some of his experiences were indeed alien visits. He read TRANSFORMATION as well, and after that Ted opened up and told his bookstore friends about several other of his unusual past events.

"See," his friends responded, "we told you all along that they were alien visitations! You're so lucky, Ted, to have been chosen by them."

Ted didn't feel very lucky, but he tried to accept what his friends said. If most other people did not have such experiences, maybe he was indeed "chosen," although he saw no reason for it. Still, he gave up arguing with his friends about the benevolent nature of the aliens' actions and motives. It would require more knowledge and more experiences, he reasoned, for him to form any opinion of his own.

And occasionally such new events did occur. Once, late in 1989, for instance, when Ted and Bud were driving home from a trip to Florida, they both witnessed UFO activity. It was around three in the morning, as they approached the area near Crystal Springs, Mississippi, traveling along the small, winding roads and trying to stay awake and alert. Bud took the wheel, and Ted climbed into the back seat to take a nap and refresh himself for the next stint of the journey.

As soon as he lay back and closed his eyes, Ted had a psychic flash, a vision of several deer standing by the side of the road.

"Bud, I think you better slow down," he said, raising up again to peer out the front windshield. "With all these trees, it's hard to see the roadside, and I just had a psychic glimpse of some deer ahead. If we come on them too fast, they might dart in front of the car and cause us to have a wreck."

Bud slowed down accordingly, and about three miles further they saw three deer very near the road, refusing to move away. The car went by them slowly, and as he watched the animals, Bud remarked, "I wish I could do things like that. It never ceases to amaze me how you can do such things."

"I don't know how I do it," Ted replied. "It just seems to happen."

"Things like that prove your psychic ability to me," Bud told him. "I don't have any doubt about that. But I still have a problem with the UFO stuff. It isn't that I doubt what you've told me, but I've never seen anything myself. And the stuff you see on TV isn't very convincing. Besides," he continued, "the government says it's all bullshit, it's not real. I just don't know what to believe. Hell, I wish I could have some kind of physical proof and know it for myself."

"I wish I could give you some," Ted laughed, "but I don't know of any. I have no control when they come and go, and I don't even know what it is they do."

He lay back for a nap, but a few minutes later Bud called out, "Ted! Take a look at that!"

Ted sat up again and looked out the window. Descending through the sky straight in front of them was what appeared to be a bright shooting star.

"Pretty damn brilliant," Ted said, "and really clear. But, you know, that shooting star seems to be going slower than the ones I've seen before."

A few minutes later, a second shooting star suddenly shot up from behind the car, flying over and directly in front of them, completely silent.

"That's odd," Ted said, "for that star to follow the same path as the first one, don't you think?"

Then a third star shot overhead maybe three minutes later as Ted and Bud watched in amazement. But they hardly had time to comment on it when a fourth one appeared, flying slowly in the same direction as the others.

"Enough, that's enough!" Bud insisted. "I don't want any more proof! That's all the proof I need. I believe you, Ted, I believe you!"

And that was the end of the shooting stars after that.

A much more dramatic event occurred in the following spring, in April 1990, when Ted was visited by Marie Jackson, the woman who had first brought him into the spiritualist association and who had trained him in his psychic development. Although he was no longer actively involved with the association, he and Marie remained very close friends over the years. But since they lived so far apart, visits were rare, and their first few days together were filled with long talks as they caught up on each other's activities.

A few nights later, well after midnight, Ted was startled from sleep by Marie calling his name from the living room where she slept on a sofa-bed.

"Ted!" she shouted, "get in here! Right now!"

She sounded anxious, so Ted roused up and hurried into the living room. Every light in the front of the house was blazing, and there was Marie pacing nervously, puffing on a cigarette and looking very worried.

"My God, Marie, what on earth happened?" Ted asked.

"I don't know," she replied, shaking her head, "but it's really got me going. This was just too weird."

Ted tried to coax her into sitting down, but she was too agitated.

"I was reading in bed," Marie told him, still pacing, "and I don't feel like I drifted off to sleep. I raised up in the bed and looked around, and suddenly all the walls in the trailer just, just disappeared!"

"Huh?" Ted said in astonishment.

"Listen," Marie went on, "I could see outside. I could see from one end of the trailer to the other, and I could see all the way down into your bedroom. The walls were just gone! I saw you in bed, on the left side facing the wall."

"But how could that happen?" Ted asked, bewildered.

"I don't know," Marie shrugged, "and that's not all. When I looked back around, I saw two of the strangest spirits I've ever seen in my life! They came right through where the wall should be, and they walked up and started trying to take me outside."

"Are you all right now?" Ted asked.

"Yeah," she nodded. "They tried to get me outside, but I really threw a fit then. I'm too stubborn, I wasn't about to go anywhere with them, and I gave them hell. By the time I got through with them, they turned me right back around."

"What did they look like?" Ted wanted to know, and as he listened to Marie's description of the small grayish beings, his heart sank. They sounded just like the little creatures who had taken him and his neighbors to the large UFO in the field.

"They must have been some of your ET friends," Marie finished, lighting another cigarette and glancing around the room nervously, "because they sure weren't any friends of mine, not from this world or any other I've ever known. And I don't want to have anything to do with them."

Beyond plants are animals,

Beyond animals is man,

Beyond man is the universe.

The Big Light, Let the Big Light in!

—Jean Toomer

UFOS – WICKED THIS WAY COMES: THE DARK SIDE OF THE ULTRA-TERRESTRIALS

Even before Marie's frightening encounter at his home, Ted felt that the aliens' interest in him was growing stronger. The display of 'shooting stars' that had confirmed for Bud the reality of UFOs also signaled an upcoming change for Ted. He noticed that after his return from Florida in late 1989, the type of clients coming in for psychic readings was decidedly different. Formerly, most of his clients sought information about personal or mundane subjects. They wanted to know about their love affairs, health problems, or jobs. But many of his new clients had a more serious interest in metaphysical rather than personal questions.

And, although he didn't know what to make of it, Ted also found that in quite a few readings he was beginning to turn up evidence of alien contacts. Such things simply hadn't happened in his psychic work before. Now, however, when Ted sat down to read for a client, several times he received unusual images and sensations about the person. And when he described these feelings, more often than not the person confirmed that some strange situation had indeed occurred which matched Ted's information-and pointed to involvement with UFOs and alien beings.

So many of these cases surfaced, in fact, that someone finally suggested forming a group to meet for UFO-related discussions. Ted and some of his clients soon began gathering on a monthly basis. In the meetings they shared information from books and also from their own unusual experiences. As he got to know these people better, Ted found that some of them had been suffering from many of the same problems he had. Like him, several people in the study group had recurrent sleep disorders, and some of them had also been through the anxiety and mental turmoil so familiar to Ted from his own past.

The group continued on through the next year, evolving a strong sense of support among the members. Ted realized that none of them, however, really knew enough to feel certain about the true nature of the aliens, their plans and actions and motivations. But they discussed all the possibilities and shared a variety of opinions. Belief in the benevolence of the ETs still dominated the group, though, which prompted occasional trips out into the countryside at night, where they sat around talking together, waiting and hoping to see a UFO. Such a sighting never happened, but the group was encouraged by another exciting development that gave them an even greater appreciation of Ted and his special abilities. In their lively discussions, one or another of the members often posed questions for general consideration. No one, including Ted, really expected a solid answer to be forthcoming.

But then he began to have nighttime contacts again, and this time the information he received was clearly related to the questions raised in the study group. The contacts always came while he slept, and upon waking the next morning Ted could remember only the message, not the messenger.

Each time he received new information in this way, Ted shared it with the group, fueling new discussions and new questions. His friends gave serious consideration to the insights communicated by what they felt sure were Ted's friendly ETs. But Ted himself, after years of accepting spirit communications as commonplace, was more puzzled than dazzled by these new contacts.

He was especially bothered by the nebulous nature of his so-called ET visitors. Some of his study-group friends talked about various 'homes' from which the aliens supposedly originated, such as Zeta Reticuli, Orion, and the Pleiades, certain that the ETs were physical entities. If the aliens truly were real, as humans are, Ted wondered why they hid their physical nature from him, communicating only through telepathy or dreamlike, dimly remembered encounters. Until he had more objective confirmation of the reality of UFOs, Ted decided, he couldn't be sure just who was communicating with him.

Such was his state of mind one evening as he sat watching Spielberg's Close Encounters of the Third Kind. He'd seen it before, but this time Ted's attention was caught by a scene in which a small round light was shown flying in and around a UFO. Orange and red, with quick movements, it behaved as if it were somehow controlled by an invisible umbilical cord.

"I wonder what that was all about," he mused, mildly curious, but a few nights later, when part of that movie scene was reenacted right in his own house, his curiosity turned to amazement.

After retiring for the night, Ted awoke from sleep with a sudden start, his heart racing. He looked around the dimly lit room, thinking more uninvited guests were about to arrive. He felt his panic surge as a round sphere slowly floated toward him from across the room near the ceiling. He'd seen it just as it made its entrance through the bedroom wall. About the size of a basketball, it shimmered with a red and orange glow. Ted thought that it would probably look like a ball of fire if it were seen moving rapidly in total darkness.

Ted closed his eyes for a few seconds, hoping that perhaps he was hallucinating or holding an image from a very vivid dream still in his mind. But when he opened his eyes, the ball of light was still there, only now it had moved much nearer. In fact, it was now directly over him, forcing him to look straight up to see it. The light was within arm's reach, and in spite of his almost paralyzing fear, Ted slowly lifted his hands to touch the floating sphere.

To his amazement, a voice commanded him to stop. The voice was somewhat mechanical, and it sounded as if it came from every direction at once. Ted turned to look down the hallway to see if someone had spoken to him from that direction, but it was empty. He thought of jumping from the bed and making a dash down the hallway as he glanced in that direction, but almost as if the ball of light heard his silent thoughts, it spoke again.

"Do not fear,' it said. "I have come only to deliver a message."

Ted lay silent on his bed looking up at this strange device hovering three feet from his face. He could discern large grooves crossing the sphere in several directions. Inside these grooves, spaced a few inches apart, were nickel-sized 'lenses' that made turns to focus in all directions within the bedroom, as well as at Ted's face.

At that moment there was a tremendous inflow of information into Ted's brain. It felt as if someone had pushed the "enter" button on a computer to store pages of information. It literally was that quick and sudden, but Ted was unable to recognize the data at that moment. As he was analyzing what had just happened, the device drifted toward the bedroom door and made its way down the hall.

Ted silently crept out of bed and began to follow it. As he and the light made their way into the living room, it picked up speed quickly and made some ninety-degree turns, demonstrating its independence of his physical and mental control. Then it accelerated rapidly toward the kitchen wall and vanished right through it.

Still in his underwear, Ted ran outside onto the patio and into the yard trying to follow the ball of light. But there was no trace of it in sight.

UFOS - WICKED THIS WAY COMES: THE DARK SIDE OF THE ULTRA-TERRESTRIALS

Ted looked at the clock when he went back inside. It was 3:47 a.m. The entire event had happened in only three to five minutes, Ted knew, but it seemed like a lifetime. With jangled nerves, extreme curiosity, and quite a bit of fear, he sat up the rest of the night. By dawn he was ready for the sleep that he knew he could now get with the rising sun, his old familiar security blanket from many sleepless nights in the past.

He awoke at 11:20 a.m. and took a quick shower. Feeling quite refreshed, he went into the kitchen to make coffee, and glancing up at the kitchen wall, he suddenly was flooded with memories of the entire event the previous night. As he sat sipping hot coffee, he realized that he not only remembered the event this time, but he could also remember the message, and the messenger.

Information which the machine had somehow put into his mind explained that it was a device controlled from a nearby UFO, as humans call them, but the occupants referred to them as their life-support vehicle. These ball-shaped, lighted objects are scanners, he was informed, used to inspect a dwelling before their couriers are sent inside for their mission.

The scanner with its numerous lenses and listening devices allows the controller in the craft to view the entire layout of the dwelling. The controller is able to see where every person is located, how many are in each room, and if they are asleep or awake. Are they dressed or armed in any way? Are there any animals around? Will the contactee need to be manipulated to another room so as not to disturb the others? The object is to complete the mission with as little resistance as possible.

As Ted sat there with his coffee, for the first time since all the UFO business had entered his awareness, he felt really violated, intruded upon, and helpless to stop this invasion of his privacy. He decided to call all of his study group members and share this experience with them, hoping someone would have a suggestion as to how he could stop this outrageous intrusion.

By five p.m. Ted had spoken to five individuals about the nighttime visitation. He detailed the whole event objectively to each one, careful not to overreact or exaggerate the occurrence. Each conversation was openly received until Ted began to bring into focus the negative ramifications, such as invasion of privacy, being spied upon, feelings of helplessness to control the visits, possible danger of radiation, and just plain agitation at the arrogant attitude that it was all right for the ETs to enter at their convenience, not Ted's, with no invitation whatsoever.

After he finished speaking to his friends, Ted was totally frustrated. All of them immediately turned the situation around to show Ted just how privileged he was to be taught this valuable information. No matter what he suggested, his friends countered with some justification that made it all acceptable. They told him he was being ridiculous to even consider that the alien device wasn't one hundred percent benevolent in its nature and intent.

One person came over to inspect the wall where the ball of light entered and exited Ted's house, searching for any evidence of penetration. Another insisted that Ted should try to direct the UFO controllers to his home because he would not show them the lack of respect and consideration which he felt Ted obviously had for the situation. Ted wondered if he was being just plain negative, as his friends accused him, or if they might be walking around with some metaphysical blinders on their eyes.

"Oh, well," Ted reminded himself, "I haven't been injured, just frightened a bit, so maybe something good will come out of all this yet. But one thing I do know. I'm going to play the game like my friends are, that it's all for the good, until I know otherwise, because I'm tired of getting attacked every time I even suggest that there are elements to this that I don't like."

Through the people to which Ted told his story, word got around the Shreveport UFO community about the ball of light. Within ten days, he received three intriguing phone calls from local people who chose to remain anonymous.

One man, who worked for a utility company, told Ted that he, too, had had a strange experience only a few weeks before, with a marble-sized ball of white and yellow light that made a slight buzzing noise. He noticed it hovering over his head while he was up a utility pole at work. It slowly traversed his entire body, softly humming and making almost undetectable clicking noises. The man said he never saw where it came from, but that when he came down the pole, what had seemed like a ten-minute event had actually taken over an hour.

He, too, felt that something had crammed his brain with information that went in too quickly for him to decipher. The thing that disturbed him most, he said, was that in spite of everything he tried to do, he couldn't get the strange device to go away, and that it finally entered his chest, not to be seen again. He wasn't able to tell anyone about this until talking with Ted, and he wanted Ted to reassure him that it was all right and that he wasn't in any danger.

Ted could only share experiences with the man and comfort him with the fact that if anything were really wrong, it probably would have shown up by now. Other than losing a little sleep the first few nights, the man seemed to be okay. Ted talked to him a few weeks later, and the man stressed that nothing else had occurred, and that he felt better after discussing the experience with Ted.

Another caller, a woman, told him about a night three years earlier, in which she and a friend observed a similar device floating around her large, open porch during the wee hours of the morning. The two friends had been out to a local club that evening and arrived back home around 1:30 a.m. They both got ready for bed but then decided to sit on the porch for a while, enjoying the cool summer night, to have one more cigarette before retiring.

As they sat there, an object that looked like a ball of fire darted across the lawn and made a right-angle turn toward them on the porch. It hovered silently in front of them for about ten seconds and then sped away. The women were frightened and locked themselves in the house for the rest of the night. They shared their story with one other friend, who laughed and suggested they stay out of the bars, and that maybe someone had slipped them some LSD in their drinks.

The women insisted that wasn't true, but they realized this was not an experience that just anyone would care to hear. So they vowed not to bring it up again. One of the women told Ted that she was relieved to find someone else who could relate to her experience. As she wished Ted well, she told him that she prayed every night that she would never see the device again because it left her with an uncomfortable and uncanny feeling. Her friend rarely spoke about it. The women had no recollection of any missing time, just jangled nerves.

A nineteen-year-old man from a nearby community also phoned. He insisted that such a ball of light met him one night on the way home from a date. He said it was shortly after midnight when he came face to face with the light after his pickup suddenly stalled on a dark country road. The man got out of the truck to raise the hood, trying to determine why the vehicle died, when to his surprise a glowing, basketball-sized object, just as Ted had seen, suddenly came out of nowhere and hovered within arm's reach.

He said he felt and heard nothing. The ball of light seemed to float near him only a few seconds and then disappeared as if it blinked away. He jumped back into the pickup to grab a flashlight, but he found that the truck was now working again. He drove at a high speed the rest of the two-mile trip home. He had no recall of missing time and claimed he had never seen a UFO but would like to see one, having become extremely interested in the subject since the encounter with the ball of light.

Thinking about his own encounter with the monitoring sphere, Ted realized just how much the strange event had echoed the movie scene in Close Encounters, and he wondered if someone or something had been listening when he had made the remark about it to himself while watching the film. He also realized that if he had witnessed the light display at any time before 1988, he probably would have accepted it as a signal or a manifestation of some spiritual entity.

But now Ted realized that the encounter, imitating the movie scene, was meant to direct his attention to a UFO-based explanation for many of his previous experiences. Was this event, he wondered, meant to give the objective confirmation he'd been asking for? Maybe so, he mused, but that ball of light, in spite of its very real but brief appearance, was still not enough to convince Ted.

UFOS - WICKED THIS WAY COMES: THE DARK SIDE OF THE ULTRA-TERRESTRIALS

ENTERING THE DARK REALMS OF THE ULTRA-TERRESTRIALS
By Scott Corrales

SUBTERRANEAN cities and temples played a major role in pre-European Latin American societies; religious rites of all kinds were held in these underground locations and tradition holds they were used as ambries for the storage of treasure and forgotten lore.

Still other traditions hold that these underground facilities were not built by the civilizations to which historians and archaeologists usually ascribe their provenance, but by ancient "elder races" whose only remains can be found in mysterious megalithic constructions around the world.

Official science pays no mind to this speculation, dismissing it with the same certainty as they would brush aside the factuality of the video game "Tomb Raider" (which follows the exploits of cyber-heroine Lara Croft through a number of underground Andean locations). But can we really be so sure?

The Quest for Lost Chincana

Dr. Raul Rios Centeno of Peru's INDECOPI organization formed part of a six-man team (five researchers and a guide) who braved the dizzying altitude of the Andes to go in search of La Chincana, the subterranean city located beneath the former Inca capital of Cuzco. On July 15, 1998, after undergoing a brief acclimatization period to the 3500 meter elevation of Cuzco, Dr. Rios's team met up with Inez Puente de la Vega, a historian whose knowledge of

Inca culture and command of the Runa-Simi variant of the Quechua language would prove of great help in their expedition.

The group's initial efforts focused on finding a point of access to the fabled Chincana; locals informed them that one of the main entrances to the underground city was precisely beneath the Sacsahuayman archaeological fortress—whose giant stonework is pre-Inca in origin—about a kilometer away from Cuzco.

Other sources hinted at the existence of two other gateways: one in the Koricancha or Palace of the Sun, which was partially demolished during the Colonial period to build the Carmelite Monastery, and still another beneath Cuzco's great cathedral.

Not surprisingly, scholars at the University of San Antonio de Abad and the Andean University, both of them in Cuzco, refused to speak to the explorers about the putative underground city. But as chance would have it, the Rios party managed to gain access to the Andean University's library, where a fascinating piece of information was uncovered.

In 1952, a group of twelve explorers—a mixed group of French and American researchers—managed to gain access through the Sacsahuayman entrance with enough provisions to last for five days as they embarked upon what they termed "the greatest discovery since Machu Picchu."

The team ventured into the Sacsahuayman entrance and nothing further was heard from them until fifteen days later, when French explorer Phillipe Lamontierre emerged from the hole suffering from acute dementia and with visible signs of malnourishment and even the bubonic plague (attributable, says Dr. Rios, to the bats inhabiting the underground spaces).

The broken survivor indicated that his fellow adventurers had died, and some of them had even fallen down unfathomed abysses. Among his belongings was an ear of corn made of solid gold, which was later entrusted to the Cuzco Museum of Archeaology (no indication is given as to whether it is on display or not).

While sobered by the Lamontierre experience, Dr. Rios' group resolutely asked the National Institute of Culture's authorization to enter the depths at their own risk, and requested that the concrete plug covering the entrance be demolished. Officialdom turned a deaf ear to this plea, and the group had to find more devious ways of accomplishing its objectives.

Having given "valuable consideration" to the security guards at Sacsahuayman, the Rios group managed to get into one of the connecting chambers to the underground complex. Equipped with infrared goggles, the group penetrated a chamber that measured scarcely 1.13 meters from the door's stone frame to the rocky floor.

"The stench within the [connecting chamber]," writes Dr. Rios, "was nauseating, as it had been employed as a latrine for some time. For some strange reason, the stonework did not reflect infrared rays. However, with the aid of our friend Jorge Zegarra, we were able to apply a RAD-2 X-ray filter, which provided a radio-opacity of 400 to 600% that of aluminum.

"It was thus that we reached a hallway whose height progressively diminished until reaching a scant 94 centimeters," continues his letter. "And given that our average height is 1.80 meters, we had no choice but to return to our starting point."

The Rios party tried to obtain readings on their Geiger counter without much success, but through the RAD-2 X-ray filter, they managed to secure a number of photos which led them to the conclusion that "a coating of some dense metal"—comparable to lead—existed within the hallways, and that there were cracks in the stonework which indeed allowed for the passage of X-rays. At this point, the guide abandoned the mission out of a very real fear of reprisals by the Culture Institute.

Dr. Rios concludes his letter by saying that the images captured by means of the RAD-2 device were being analyzed by Carlos Garcia and Guillermo LaRosa Richardson of the School of Engineering in Lima, Peru.

The Amazing Story of Juan Moricz

The name of Juan Moricz—a Hungarian nobleman turned Argentinean citizen—stands head and shoulders above all others in these accounts of subterranean lairs in South America.

Indefatigable author and investigator Magdalena del Amo-Freixedo met Moricz in Ecuador and was able to hear from the late miner/explorer's very lips the story of how he came upon a subterranean realm verging on the fantastic.

Moricz stated that when he was a newly-arrived emigre in Argentina, he ran across an old man who told him about the "lost treasure of Atahualpa" and how it had been concealed by his followers in a series of subterranean cities. Fired by this knowledge, young Moricz decided to cross the breadth of Argentina until he reached the Andes and headed northward to where the mighty South American mountain range gives birth to the Amazon's headwaters.

In a scene straight out of Spielberg's "Raiders of the Lost Ark," Moricz came across tribes of fearsome Jívaro headhunters who are openly hostile to all outsiders. But rather than ending up another shrunken head, he discovered that he could make himself understood to the Jívaros by addressing them in his native Magyar! While this alone might strain anyone's suspension of disbelief, the fact remains that Moricz was able to live among the Jívaros long enough to learn their ways and make an important discovery: the jungle natives had peculiar dotted tattoos across their faces, centered on both cheeks, the chin and the nose. One day, he came across two Jívaro sentries guarding a boulder covered in the same design as the natives wore on their faces. Beyond the rock lay a narrow cave, and the explorer knew that he'd come across the access to the alleged lost hoard.

But the Jívaros cautioned him against entering, stating that the "dwellers in the depths" were gods endowed with beams capable of killing intruders and cutting through stone. The natives insisted on having seen the ground split open and produce brilliant balls of light that would rise heavenward.

UFOS – WICKED THIS WAY COMES: THE DARK SIDE OF THE ULTRA-TERRESTRIALS

Moricz decided that he was willing to place his life in jeopardy merely to see this fabled underground realm. He ventured into the cave, and then down some sort of chimney formation, leading to a slanted corridor made of perfectly dressed, angular stone. His wanderings eventually brought him to a chamber that was "perfectly lit by a quartz column" and from which many other hallways radiated.

Following one of them, Moricz came to a hall with a large circular table of polished stone, surrounded by seven stone seats. The walls were so highly polished as to be mirrored. Dubbing it "The Hall of the Seven Elders," the explorer pressed on, entering a series of narrow hallways which were as filthy as the earlier chambers had been clean. By now tired and forlorn from his meandering in this series of forgotten galleries, he was most startled to come across a cascade of greenish-blue water which appeared to be self-luminous. His heart sank upon realizing that it had reached the end of the tunnels.

Suddenly—he told Del Amo-Freixedo—it occurred to him to go under the cascade and see if anything lay beyond. He was rewarded by brilliant sunlight and a sort of "terrace" looking down at the jungle canopy, hundreds of feet below. A narrow ledge led him to a large flat stone and the urge to "dig under it with his bare hands" to move it. Succeeding in this attempt, he reentered a series of ascending and descending passageways which ended in a vast chamber whose size he estimated at five hundred meters long by four hundred meters wide. The contents of this gargantuan hall—piles of gold, skeletons clad in unusual golden armor—appeared to be its source of illumination.

And it is here where Moricz's already incredible story becomes fantastic: at the end of this "treasure chamber" were five creatures clad in metallic garments and having egg-shaped heads with large slanted black eyes. Their hair was held by an emerald-bearing band. "Your boldness has led you to where you are now," one of them reportedly said. "We have allowed you to reach us." The creature then expounded on the catastrophes that had destroyed the surface races and how the entire history of their species was kept in gold-leafed books. He was then told to turn back and return to his people, but not to touch anything. "If you do, you will never return to the surface," they cautioned.

Many experts have written off Moricz's exploits as "tall tales" in the best tradition of Baron Munchausen, and cite his collaboration with Erich Von Daniken on "The Gold of the Gods" as proof of Moricz's nearly bottomless "private stock." It is up to the reader to decide.

The Central American Tunnels Explored

But even if we should choose to dismiss the adventures of Juan Moricz as merely fanciful, it by no means discredits the existence of the subterranean galleries.

In 1985, Spain's eminent UFO researcher, J.J. Benítez, joined the late Andreas Faber Kaiser and brothers Carlos and Ricardo Vílchez in exploring a series of clearly artificial tunnels which were not in the Andes, but in the Central American republic of Costa Rica.

According to the story, a Costa Rican family had learned many years ago that there was an ancient tunnel—located on the top of a nameless hill—which very possibly led to an underground city. The family sold all of its belongings and literally "took to the hills," engaging in amateur excavations which resulted in the discovery of the opening to the tunnel. They found a shaft which dropped almost vertically and constituted the access to a corridor of dressed stone.

Members of the anonymous family group approached investigator Benítez and urged him to take a look. Accompanied by his fellow researchers, Benítez descended by means of rickety ladder and found himself staring at vast cyclopean blocks—carefully dressed and placed with almost geometric succession. At the end of the gallery, a side wall revealed a curious inscription written in an unknown language.

Subsequent linguistic research by Prof. Jesús Conte revealed that the curious inscription in the forgotten Costa Rican tomb was very similar to *ancient Assyrian script* [my italics]. Prof. Conte's painstaking analysis disclosed that the characters stated: "Beware! Impending Disaster!"

No good reason has been offered for the discovery of proto-Assyrian text in a cyclopean gallery fifty meters beneath the earth in Costa Rica, thousands of miles from the Middle East. Benítez speculates that this proto-Assyrian may have indeed been the language spoken on Atlantis and which later survived in the Fertile Crescent. If Benítez's suppositions are on target, the reader can well imagine what impeding disaster was being referred to.

Stories of networks of artificially created tunnels riddling the five continents are certainly nothing new; adventure writers of the 1930s waxed eloquent on the supposed tunnels in Central Asia which linked a number of cave systems to the mystical realm of Agharta, or the tunnels beneath Lhasa's Potala temple linking it to other lamaseries in the Himalayas; the connectivity between the cave systems of the Rocky Mountains is also well-known. But we needn't strap on our headlamps and go spelunking just yet—a fully electrified and technological subterranean "culture" was discovered in 1993 in Northern Italy.

A Number of Mexican Oddities

Mexico offers its own share of subterranean mysteries. Foremost among these is the "sunken palace" of Dzibilchaltún.

In 1941, a group of teenagers bathing in one of the Yucatan Peninsula's many limestone *cenotes* was startled to discover that behind the jungle thickness that surrounded their favorite bathing spot was a wall of dressed stone. They notified the authorities, which in turn advised the Secretariat of Education. Faced with the prospect of cleaning up this twenty square mile area, containing approximately four hundred structures, the Mexican government turned to the Middle American Research Institute at the University of New Orleans, which would in coming years begin exploring the ruins of Dzibilchaltún—the name given by an old Maya shaman, who informed them that the word was not of Mayan origin. However, the lagoon near the ruins had a clearly Mayan denomination: Xlacah, "the old city."

The archaeologists were clearly mystified by this denomination, and suspecting that the old shaman was making reference to some sort of acropolis, requested more information. They were then regaled with the story of how in ages past, a massive palace had once occupied the area—the home of Dzibilchaltún's ruler—and how one day a stranger had appeared at the palace gate, requesting shelter.

The ruler ordered his servants to prepare lodging for the unexpected guest. The following day, in exchange for the *cacique*'s hospitality, the strange traveler produced a large green gem from his satchel and turned it over to the ruler, who soon turned greedy and asked the stranger if his satchel contained even more treasures. When the stranger refused to answer, he was summarily executed by the guards and the satchel was handed to the ruler, who was disappointed to find in it only some travel-stained garments and a large black stone. In rage, the *cacique* hurled the black stone out a window; it struck the ground with a tremendous explosion, causing the palace and its occupants to slide into the newly created hole.

It wasn't until 1961 that archaeologists would brave the depths of Xlacah. Their exploration of the muddy cenote proved that the limestone structure was shaped like a boot and extended to a depth that was hard to fathom. Upon reaching the end of the vertical segment, they found the remains of the "sunken palace's" columns and adorned walls.

Hot Times Under Moscow

There are, of course, individuals who remain skeptical about any notion of subterranean occupancy of our world—that goes beyond provisional shelters and subway stations— indicating the difficulty in providing ventilation, temperature control and sanitation for any permanent underground tenancy, particularly one involving tens of thousands of people.

However, the prestigious "Bulletin of Atomic Scientists" (May/June 1997) presented an extraordinary article involving the existence of multiple subterranean tiers under the city of Moscow. Following the adventures of Vadim Mikhailov and his group "Diggers of the Underground Planet," the BAS article reveals the shadowy underworld of the Russian capital. The Diggers made their way through fallout shelters to a colossal warehouse owned by a Russian marine biology institution, containing among other nightmarish holdings "a room of tanks of formalin, containing various sea monsters."

After well over a decade of urban spelunking, the Diggers have presented the world with a map of the nightmarish that occupies these levels: gypsies, malcontents, dissidents and "professional hermits" have occupied the levels closest to the surface, gaining access through heating vents and sewer systems. On one particular journey deep under the Centrobank building, the Diggers encountered squads of uniformed people lighting their way with powerful halogen lamps. The authorities dismissed the explorers' claims as fanciful, but the BAS article quotes Mikhailov as saying that the authorities in fact have no idea who these armed, masked individuals could be, and insist that the security services themselves do not venture down to those levels.

At even greater depths under the city, Mikhailov's group encountered stranger things, such as mass burial sites from an unknown age, ancient weapons similar to maces; a "secret" railway system built under Stalin and never used by the public; deserted laboratories with outdated equipment and intriguing flasks, and perhaps more interestingly, a bunker able to hold thousands of people beneath the location of a demolished cathedral. According to Mikhailov, the dean of the Cathedral of Christ the Savior approached him with a request to enter the area and remove a strange container that filled even the dean with terror. Under the Skliffasovsky Clinic, the urban spelunkers ran into a strange cult in monkish robes, circumambulating around a stone altar. The monk-like figures ran away upon being seen by the explorers.

The Diggers have since engaged in what could well be considered their most important quest: the resting place of the trove of manuscripts brought from Constantinople to Moscow in the 15th century by Sophia Palaeologus as part of her dowry. This collection of priceless texts is reputedly safeguarded by paranormal forces which have caused misfortunes to those seeking them.

Underground Realms Here and Now

Bruno Tinti, district attorney of the northern Italian city of Ivrea, did not believe at first the reports of a lost and magical city in the foothills of the Piedmont. In a country racked by extremist terrorism, Tinti took no chances: he promptly dispatched a regiment of *Carabineri*, who would later confirm the city's existence. Not far from the town of Baldissero Canavavese, near the city of Turin, a secret entrance leads to the thirty-meter depth where the occult community of Damanhur thrives. A seemingly endless maze of temples, labyrinths and meeting halls, decorated with Ancient Egyptian and esoteric symbols, Damanhur boasts inordinate wealth: the floors and walls of its chambers are covered in marble, gold, mosaics and mirrors worthy of the grandest European palaces.

Founded in 1975 by Oberto Airuldi, the earthmoving activities which led to the creation of the subterranean city were financed by the 300 members of Damanhur's "Council of Elders"—captains of industry and commerce whose activities net them a combined income of over $8 million dollars per annum. Damanhur is a fully independent state, with its own government, constitution and minted coinage. Although its inhabitants resented the intrusion of the police authorities, they are reportedly secretly pleased that word of their hidden city has reached the outside world.

Damanhur consists of five temples linked by a number of passageways; its stonework is so elaborate that it has reminded many of that of the Egyptian great pyramid, and others of the heliolithic ruins on the island of

Malta. The Damanhurians (for want of a better name) have an interesting and progressive social system in which human initiative and freewill are considered of paramount importance, as well as the role of the individual over that of the family. Marriage vows are reconfirmed every three years and, as in most utopian societies, children are raised in common by the community and taught how to solve problems and glean information using both hemispheres of the brain.

The five temples of subterranean Damanhur represent the culmination of the Damanhurians' secret lore. Allegedly, each temple represents one of the four elements (air, water, earth and fire) and the fifth temple is forbidden to outsiders. According to the fortunate few who have been invited to this subterranean empire, the temple of air is completely covered in mirrors and surmounted by a depiction of the universe and the temple of earth contains under its dome the largest stained glass image ever built by man.

Conclusion

The existence of Damanhur points to the human need to build subterranean structures for a variety of esoteric and exoteric reasons. The avowed purpose of this magical city in the Italian piedmont is to preserve man's occult and alchemical knowledge. Can we not assume that earlier human civilizations may have felt a similar impulse on the genetic level to "preserve" the best of their achievements for their descendants many aeons into the future? What if a catastrophe changed the face of Europe, and in a few centuries, skeptics scoffed at the existence of a "Damanhur" and its works? Are we not doing the same with all these other locations that lore and human endeavor have been made known to us? Places like Chincana, the unplumbed tunnels of the Andes, mysterious Moscow, and many others possibly contain the legacies of our forerunners. We are morally bound to find them.

UFOS – WICKED THIS WAY COMES: THE DARK SIDE OF THE ULTRA-TERRESTRIALS

UFOS – WICKED THIS WAY COMES: THE DARK SIDE OF THE ULTRA-TERRESTRIALS

EXTRATERRESTRIALS, ULTRA-TERRESTRIALS, OR DEMONS?
By Brad Steiger

ROBERT, a short-order cook at an all-night diner, was getting off work about four o'clock one morning when he thought he saw three men praying at the side of the road. Because he was extremely tired and didn't want the glare of oncoming traffic in his eyes, he had taken a little traveled country road. Although he was tired to the bone after a grueling night's work, his curiosity got the better of him and he stopped the car to see what was up with the three men kneeling beside the road.

In retrospect, he may have been a bit foolish when he decided to open his car door and step out on the gravel—for that was when he discovered his mistake. The three beings weren't men at all. He didn't know what they were.

The figures he saw that night were short and stood in a triangular pattern, facing the opposite side of the road. The entity at the point of the triangle suddenly raised its arms above its head, and it appeared to be holding some kind of rod in its hands. Robert was startled when he saw blue and white sparks jumping from one of the creature's hands to the other, just above and below the rod.

Robert was now becoming extremely anxious about his safety. He had parked beside the strange trio in a rather remote stretch of country road next to a heavily wooded area just west of the main highway. And now, their strange ritual with the sparkling rod completed, they turned to face him.

The headlights of his car illuminated the three beings so he was able to get a good look at them. They were all about three and a half feet tall with grayish complexions and skin-tight uniforms about the same shade of gray as their faces. They had large, straight mouths without lips, and indistinct noses. Their eyes seemed basically normal in human terms, but they had no eyebrows. The upper portion of their heads was bald, with what appeared to be a roll of fat or a ridge of bone running across the top.

Their bodies were, in Robert's opinion, a bit lopsided. Their chests appeared to swell to an unusual bulge on their right sides, and their arms were of uneven length, the right one longer than the left. Their clothing above the waist—if indeed it was clothing—was skin-tight and gave no evidence of any line separating them from the skin portion of the creatures, which was the same grayish color.

Although he had felt some understandable anxiety at being alone in a remote area with such an eerie trio, Robert said that he felt no real fear of the humanoids until he started walking toward them to meet their advance. Then, suddenly, he strongly sensed that he should stop, turn and run for his car, and get the hell out of there. As he accelerated past the three creatures, he was nearly overcome by a powerful, nauseating odor that seemed to be directed at him by the dark figures, who stood watching him drive away. Later, Robert told me that he was convinced if he had not decided to run when he did that the creatures would have either killed him or done him terrible harm.

It was in 1967 that I first participated as an observer in the hypnotic regression of men and women who claimed to have encountered crew members from UFOs and even to have been abducted by them. Later, from 1972 to 1994, I myself conducted dozens of hypnotic regression sessions with UFO contactees or abductees who recalled having been given some kind of medical examination by alien beings. In some instances, the experiencers still bore peculiar punctures and markings in their flesh.

Among the hundreds of abductees, contactees, and other witnesses of alleged extraterrestrial activity whom I have interviewed, there has been a general consensus among the percipients:

* The UFOnauts stood between four and half to five feet tall and were dressed in one-piece, very tight-fitting clothing, usually gray or greenish-gray in color.

UFOS – WICKED THIS WAY COMES: THE DARK SIDE OF THE ULTRA-TERRESTRIALS

* Their skin color was most often reported as being gray or greenish-gray, and they seemed devoid of body hair of any kind.

* Their heads were round, large, disproportionately oversized by our human standards. In a few reports, pointed ears were mentioned, but usually the witnesses commented that the aliens had no external ears of any kind.

* Their facial features were dominated by large, lidless, staring eyes, very often with slit catlike or reptilian pupils. They had no discernible lips, and where one might expect to see a nose, the witnesses cited only nostrils, nearly flush against the smooth texture of the face. On a few occasions, witnesses reported very flat noses or in some cases, tiny "stubs."

Since my early investigation into the UFO enigma in the late 1960s, it has seemed apparent to me that if humankind is indeed interacting with an extraterrestrial species, then those UFOnauts, the "Grays" as they are currently nicknamed, may be representatives of technologically superior reptilian or amphibian humanoids. Furthermore, it also seems evident that these Serpent People have been interacting with Earth for millions of years—either appearing in cycles of programmed visitations or steadily monitoring our species' technological and societal development from underground or undersea bases.

It also seems evident to me that at some point in their many centuries long interaction, some ultra-terrestrial entities began to exploit humankind in foul, lascivious, and wicked ways. Whether they be extraterrestrial or multidimensional in origin, they have become known to those unfortunate humans with whom they have interacted as evil, cruel, and demonic beings.

Susan Koebler, a young attorney from the Ft. Worth, Texas, area, stated in her report to me that it is her habit to take a hot bath after concluding the day's work schedule. She lights a number of aromatic candles and places them around the tub to add to the therapeutic fragrance emitted by the powders and oils that she sprinkles into the steaming water.

"I stretch out in the tub, adjusting the water until it is as hot as I can comfortably stand it, then I sip a glass of white wine and listen to some New Age type music," Susan said. "This ritual not only completely relaxes me, but

UFOS – WICKED THIS WAY COMES: THE DARK SIDE OF THE ULTRA-TERRESTRIALS

I sometimes slip into a meditative state and really clear my consciousness of all the uglies and nasties that might have beset me at the office that day."

On this particular evening in late October of 1997, Susan found herself entering a very strange "mental place." As she was driving home to her apartment, she thought that she had sighted a strange light in the evening sky and she wondered if she had experienced a UFO sighting. She had never had an interest in stories of extraterrestrials or outer space exploration, but she was open to the subject.

As she slipped into the tub of warm water, she began to feel herself drifting into an altered state of consciousness in which she saw herself with a group of other young women in a forest. "I was linking arms with other girls and dancing under a full moon," she recalled. "It was so real, so detailed."

After at least half an hour relaxing in this visionary experience, Susan emerged reluctantly from the tub, dried herself, and draped a robe loosely about her body. "I was still feeling extremely relaxed," she said, "so I walked into the bedroom and lay down on my stomach across the bed, my feet sticking out over the sides. I had lain there, nearly asleep, when I felt someone grab my ankles and start to turn me over on my back!"

Susan screamed her surprise, shock, and rage, feeling certain that someone had forced his way into her apartment and was now attempting to force himself upon her. But the scream became a stunned kind of gasp of horror when she saw that there was no one there.

"Yet someone, *something*, invisible, but of tremendous strength, was trying to spread my legs apart," Susan stated. "I fought against the thing with all my will. The struggle must have continued for several minutes. Every muscle in my thighs and lower back was burning with the pain of the constant tension—yet I would not yield and permit my genitals to be exposed in such a vulnerable manner."

At last the pressure ceased, and Susan lay gasping on the bed. "Then, suddenly, he was there—solid, visible, repulsive," Susan said. "His eyes were cat or snakelike with the pupils thin slits against yellow-gold retinas. His skin appeared smooth, kind of grayish-green in color. And his teeth! They were rotted, brownish stumps in what almost appeared to be set in double-rows in purplish jaws. And this thing was very large and very muscular."

Susan stated that she could never be certain if the grotesque creature actually spoke aloud or if she perceived his thoughts telepathically. However the communication was accomplished, the effect was the same. *"You will want me. You will desire me,"* the monster told her.

Susan lay on the bed before the creature, sprawled out as if she were some kind of sacrificial offering to the dragon-like beast.

"The ugly thing smiled and reached out a hand with long fingernails to caress my hair, still soaked from the tub," Susan said. "The monstrous gargoyle was changing its tactics. It was moving away from attempted rape to seduction. But those putrid brown teeth jutting from its jaws in its pathetic attempt at a smile made a travesty of gentleness and compassion. It was only after one thing from me—and by now it was very apparent that the creature was very definitely male."

And then, Susan wrote, there was something about the monster's eyes that had suddenly become very compelling, very hypnotic.

"There was something in those reptilian eyes that wanted to make me stop resisting its sexual advances," Susan said. "I found myself staring into their depths, and it suddenly seemed as though I had been mistaken. My uninvited guest was really not so bad. In fact, he was really quite handsome and virile."

Susan will forever be thankful that she realized what the creature was doing to her, that it was seducing her with an almost irresistible hypnotic power.

"I cried out for my guardian angel to help me," she said. "I started to cry out for all things holy and of the Light to drive away this creature of darkness."

Susan concluded her report by stating that she is thankful to her guardian angel and all benevolent entities who rallied around her that terrible evening to drive away whatever the grotesque monster was that materialized in her apartment and tried to force itself upon her.

UFOS – WICKED THIS WAY COMES: THE DARK SIDE OF THE ULTRA-TERRESTRIALS

Quite likely the entity that appeared to Susan Koebler was a type of ultra-terrestrial entity that has sought to sexually molest human beings ever since our species became "fair" and appeared capable of providing a warm, fleshly body for a spirit being to possess for minutes, weeks, months—or permanently. In my over 50 years of researching the strange, the unusual, and the unexplained, I have come to understand that as much as our materialistic and scientific age might wish it could relegate such supernatural sexual molesters to a much less sophisticated past—somewhere around the Dark or Middle Ages—these ultra-terrestrial demons have not relinquished their grip on the human psyche. According to a good many men and women, such sexual offenders from other dimensions are as much a nasty nuisance in the shadow world of our supermarket and space-age culture as they were in the superstition-saturated and sexually tortured Middle Ages.

While those ultra-dimensional beings that seek to possess and enjoy sexually the physical bodies of mortals are terrible and demeaning enough, even worse are those fiends who invade the psyches of men and women and command them to maim, mutilate, or murder their victims. Perhaps the most monstrous of all the frightening creatures that issue forth out of the dark claim those tortured individuals who heed fiendish commands to kill. The media proclaim in each day's newspaper headlines and news broadcasts that these disciples of murder and mayhem are very real. And so are the demons who scream at them relentlessly to do their awful bidding and kill without mercy.

Here is what Dr. Morton Kelsey, an Episcopal priest and a noted Notre Dame professor of theology, had to say: "Most people in the modern world consider themselves too sophisticated and too intelligent to be concerned with demons. But in thirty years of study, I have seen the effect of demons upon humans."

The Rev. James LeBar, an exorcist for the Archdiocese of New York, commented in September 2000 that there had been a "large explosion" of exorcisms in recent years. In New York alone, he said, the number had accelerated from none in 1990 to a total of 300 in the last ten years. Rev. LeBar said that men and women have diminished self-respect for themselves and decreased reverence for spirituality, for other human beings, and for life in general.

All right, you protest, Rev. LeBar is a priest, an exorcist. His theological training has conditioned him to believe in demons. Then take into serious consideration the comments of Dr. Ralph Allison, senior psychiatrist at the California state prison in San Luis Obispo: "My conclusion after thirty years of observing over one thousand disturbed patients is that some of them act in a bizarre fashion due to possession by spirits. The spirit may be that of a human being who died. Or it may be a spirit entity that has never been a human being and sometimes identifies itself as a demon, an agent of evil." A good definition of an ultra-terrestrial entity with evil intent toward humans.

In a recent report released by the American Psychological Evaluation Corporation, Dr. Andrew Blankley, a sociologist, issued alarming statements about the rise in contemporary sacrificial cults, warning that society at large might expect a "serious menace" to come. According to Dr. Blankley, human sacrifice constitutes an alarming trend in new religious cults: "Desperate people are seeking dramatic revelation and simplistic answers to complex social problems. They are attracted to fringe groups who provide the ritualistic irrationality that they crave. In the last ten years, fringe rituals often include the sacrifice of a human being."

Dr. Al Carlisle of the Utah State Prison System has estimated that between 40,000 and 60,000 humans are killed through ritual homicides in the United States every year. In the Las Vegas area alone, Dr. Carlisle asserts, as many as 600 people may die in demon-inspired ceremonies each year.

Mutilated bodies of hitchhikers and transients are being found in forested regions, beside lonely desert roads, and alongside river banks—their hearts and lungs removed, strips of flesh slashed from their bodies.

Devil-worshipping rites are being held in our state and national parks. Human blood is mixed with beer and drunk by all participants. Human bone fragments, teeth, and pieces of flesh are discovered in the ashes of campfires.

The terrible power which drives and compels those obsessed with sacrificial murders is something so much more insidiously evil and complex than can be created by the distortion of creeds, ecclesiasticisms, or belief structures. The monstrous voices that command men and women to kill others are not those of mortals. Those who have fallen under the deadly spell of the possessing ultra- terrestrial-multidimensional entities claim to have been controlled by something outside of themselves—usually personified as Satan or one of his demons.

However one wishes to identify these Parasites of the Spirit, they have the ability to sense and to seize the moments of vulnerability in the strongest of men and women. They possess the uncanny power of knowing the precise moments when even the most righteous can be tempted, when even the most devout can be led astray, when the most disciplined moralist may be seduced.

Here is only a sampler of men and women who were possessed by multidimensional demons and commanded to kill:

* On January 5, 1990, authorities searching an Ohio farm commune found the slain bodies of a family of five—all victims of human sacrifice. Jeffrey Lunden, a self-declared prophet of a new religion, had decreed the sacrifices necessary to persuade the "forces" to present the cult with a magical golden sword.

* Daniel Rakowitz couldn't quite understand whether or not the voices said that he was actually Jesus reborn, but he knew that they were insistent that he was a messiah. The voices also told him to form a new satanic religion to be named the Church of 966, thereby discarding the old and familiar 666 label. To insure his messiah-ship, in September of 1989, he sacrificed his girl friend.

* The voices told Herbert Mullin that California was about to be destroyed by a cataclysmic earthquake and a giant tidal wave unless he immediately began sacrificing human life to Satan. The voices nullified Mullin's squeamishness by declaring that the sacrificial victims would actually be grateful for being given the opportunity to serve the greater good of California. Before he was stopped on February 13, 1972, Mullins had sacrificed thirteen victims and, in his mind, become the Savior of California.

* While other households in the Queens District of New York watched the Thanksgiving Day parade on November 22, 1990, Joseph Bergamini

honored the satanic promise that he was immortal by stabbing and killing his mother and wounding his father.

* As a teenager, Mark David Chapman had experienced a vision of Jesus which led him to become an advocate for the common man. When the visions later revealed the popular idol John Lennon was no longer a working-class hero, but a prosperous businessman, the voices decreed that the former Beatle must die on the night of December 8, 1980.

* Inspired by the vampire movie "Lost Boys," Tim Erickson and other Minnesota teenagers decided to form a vampire cult in March 1987. They murdered a drifter and drank his blood.

* July 1991, Jaime Rodriguez was convicted and sentenced to life for beheading a teenage runaway as a sacrifice to Satan. He also severed one of her fingers to wear as a charm around his neck. Augustin Pena, a fellow Satanist, kept the girl's head in his refrigerator.

* December 2000, prosecutors charged a man in Great Falls, Montana, with killing a 10-year-old boy, butchering him, eating his flesh in specially prepared dishes, then feeding the remains to his unsuspecting neighbors. A psychiatric evaluation indicated such demonic fantasies about cannibalism and the taste of human flesh. Encrypted writings found in the suspect's home revealed a list of recipes involving the bodies of small children.

The list of assaults by demonic ultra-terrestrial /multidimensional beings on the U.S. Presidency is a frightening one:

* When John Wilkes Booth, the assassin of Abraham Lincoln, was but an infant in his crib, his mother, Asia Booth, had a horrid vision of her son being one day transformed into a monster with a grotesque hand that would commit a terrible deed.
* On the morning of July 2, 1881, Charles Guiteau could no longer resist the demon voices that commanded him to kill President James Garfield. The President clung to life through the agony of a long summer before yielding to the assassin's bullet in his back. Guiteau was relieved that he had fulfilled his mission. He went to the gallows confident that the demon he hailed as "Lordy" would take care of him in the afterlife.

UFOS – WICKED THIS WAY COMES: THE DARK SIDE OF THE ULTRA-TERRESTRIALS

* Lee Harvey Oswald was obsessed with his fears that "devil-men" would usurp all earthly governments. The death of JFK would serve as a kind of sacrifice to keep them at bay.

* Sirhan Sirhan's legal defense in his trial for the murder of Robert Kennedy strongly considered arguing that he had been possessed by the fanatical spirit of a dead Arab nationalist.

* Squeaky Fromme, one of Charles Manson's family, received mental instructions from her imprisoned master to murder President Gerald Ford on August 5, 1975.

* John Hinckley was literally possessed with the impulse that the assassination of Ronald Reagan would somehow impress the actress, Jody Foster.

* On January 11, 1990, the Secret Service arrested John S. Daughetee, a medical school dropout, who was acting under the orders of his "voices" when he robbed eight banks to finance his assassination attempts on Presidents Reagan and Bush.

On September 19, 2000, the *Chicago Sun-Times* reported that the Archdiocese of Chicago had appointed a full-time exorcist for the first time in its 160-year history.

In the November 28, 2000 issue of the *New York Times*, an article by John W. Fountain ("Exorcists and Exorcisms Proliferate Across U.S.") quoted Rev. Bob Larson, an evangelical preacher and author who heads an exorcism ministry in Denver, as saying that he had 40 "exorcism teams" across the nation. "Our goal is that no one should ever be more than a day's drive from a city where you can find an exorcist," said Rev. Larson.

If, as some theologians and scholars predict, there is soon to take place a major conflict between the Forces of Light and the Forces of Darkness, one would be well-advised to be wary of those seductive creatures of the shadows, the multidimensional/ultra-terrestrials who have for centuries sought to confuse us humans into believing that their counterfeit illumination is truly a Guiding Light.

CONTROVERSIAL DEATHS OF UFO INVESTIGATORS, RESEARCHERS AND AUTHORS
By Peter Robbins
© 2013 Peter Robbins

(Originally presented as a paper for the Roswell UFO Conference in July 2007, this article is not so much about the dark side of aliens as it is about the dark side of us humans working within the cover-up.)

* * *

PART of the myth and legend which has accompanied UFOlogy for decades is that certain people who've immersed themselves in the work, and perhaps gotten too close to the truth, or *a* significant truth about UFOs, have been murdered to keep them quiet.

These allegations have attached themselves equally to civilian investigators as well as to specific individuals in government. Such claims are usually difficult if not impossible to prove beyond a reasonable doubt and are often heavily influenced by the beliefs or agendas of the researchers making the claims.

I don't consider myself a conspiracist, but my studies have shown me that history is littered with conspiracies. And while the term itself has become something of a buzz-word for loopy or paranoid in contemporary society, Webster defines the word conspiracy simply as "a secret plan," which is hardly some rare or complex phenomenon.

UFOS – WICKED THIS WAY COMES: THE DARK SIDE OF THE ULTRA-TERRESTRIALS

Believing In Things Unproven

Speaking for myself, I remain unconvinced that Lee Harvey Oswald acted alone in the assassination of President Kennedy and resent the stock rationale regularly put forward by proponents of the lone gunman theory, that when an important or significant person dies under questionable circumstances, or in some cases of seemingly natural causes, a certain segment of the public will always refuse to accept it as such. They – me in this case – have a deep need to believe that the departed could not possibly have died of natural causes, or in a freak accident, or at the hands of a single, mentally unstable personality. There is in fact real wisdom attached to this point of view, but there are exceptions that prove the rule as well. Lee Harvey Oswald's killer, Jack Ruby, died of cancer in a Dallas jail while awaiting trial on murder charges. While people die of cancer every day, it would not surprise me to learn that Ruby's cancer had been, well, "introduced" into his system to shut him up for good. That's what I believe, but I can't prove it.

I know people who feel that taking literally *any* conspiracy seriously is akin to believing in the tooth fairy. This kind of overly simplistic thinking is not just ignorant, it is insulting and can even be dangerous. Even former President Bush has used the term "conspiracy theory" to belittle or dismiss notions that everything has not been completely on the up and up in his administration. At the same time there are those of us who've become so accustomed to our government lying to or deceiving us that we (understandably) suspect them of complicity anytime history looks at us cross-eyed. The truth likely lies somewhere between these two extremes. Today we're going to take a look at the lives, and deaths, of eleven people, nine of them men, two of them women, who made significant contributions to UFOlogy or were otherwise seriously involved with the subject. Some of these studies are fairly brief, others more in depth and the final one particularly so. I've done my best to remain as objective as possible in each case, but some of these profiles are noticeably more personal than others. I met one of these individuals years ago, corresponded briefly with another, and considered four of them friends, three of them good friends. The information in this paper has been drawn from thirty six different print sources, some supporting Internet research, and personal knowledge of four of the individuals, and of the circumstances surrounding their deaths. To help us understand why these eleven might have been targeted for extinction, and to better allow you to come to your own best conclusions, it's important to have some appreciation for the lives they lived and the contributions they made.

Morris Ketchum Jessup

Our first subject was a popular UFO writer of the 1950s, Morris Ketchum Jessup, better known as M.K. Jessup. It's alleged that he was murdered and that the murder was made to appear as a suicide, or that he was brainwashed into taking his own life, the reason being that he was getting too close to the truth about UFOs. Jessup's books on the subject, "The Case For the UFO," "The Expanding Case For the UFO, and "UFOs and the Bible" are considered classics and are still among the most readable and thoughtful contributions to the otherwise often simplistic, mystical or paranoid flying saucer literature of the era. "The Case For the UFO" became a national bestseller in 1955 and remains one the most comprehensive and rational collection of case studies of the time.

Dr. Jessup's credits were outstanding and varied. He began his career as an instructor in astronomy and mathematics at Drake University and the University of Michigan, where he also studied for and received his Doctorate in Astrophysics. The university then hired him to supervise the building and operation of the Southern Hemisphere's (then) largest refracting telescope. Jessup's passion for and scholarship in the twin fields of archeology and anthropology led him to carry out significant independent research at Maya and Incan ruins in Central America and Peru, then to become an acknowledged expert on the megalithic stoneworks of Peru, Easter Island

UFOS - WICKED THIS WAY COMES: THE DARK SIDE OF THE ULTRA-TERRESTRIALS

and Syria, among other locations. He then became interested in the subject of UFOs.

In 1956 Jessup was preparing to travel to Mexico to survey meteorite craters and to continue his research into ancient extraterrestrial visitations, but upon learning that this author of UFO books was to be part of the expedition, the University of Michigan, the project's main sponsor, withdrew its support and the venture quickly died. Aware that his UFO-related writing that year would bring in very little income, Jessup decided to publish his own books and sell them through the mail. But nothing came of this plan and he did not publish any more books. Two years later the writer separated from his wife and moved from Florida back to his home state of Indiana, where he worked as an editor and pursued his growing interest in psychic phenomena. On an October 1958 visit to New York City he met with zoologist Ivan Sanderson, author of "Invisible Residents" and "Uninvited Visitors," among other titles. Sanderson found him in a gloomy state. Jessup complained that a series of strange events which he hesitated to discuss had pulled him "into a complete world of unreality" (Sanderson, 1968). During this time the two manuscripts which Jessup sent to his publisher were rejected as not being up to par.

The writer left New York soon after, but apparently did not return to Indiana. Two weeks later, when his publisher tried to contact him, he was nowhere to be found. The following month he was located in Florida, where he explained he was recovering from a serious auto accident. Jessup's depression continued to deepen and in April 1959 he wrote a letter to his friend, the radio host Long John Nebel. Sanderson characterized it as a "straight suicide note." On April 20, the fifty nine- year-old Jessup drove from his Florida home to a quiet spot in nearby Dade County Park where he made good on the contents of the note, specifically, by wiring a hose to the exhaust pipe of his car and feeding the other end through a small opening in the window. He died of carbon-monoxide poisoning not long after being found at about 6:30 that evening.

I'd heard years ago that there were things about this suicide that didn't add up. For example, that the space above the car window admitting the hose had been stuffed with wet rags to keep the carbon-monoxide in, and that subsequent investigation found no container in the car that could have held the water necessary to wet the rags. I have not been able to confirm this allegation through any source. Richard Ogden, a UFO researcher in Seattle, claimed the suicide was a "frame up" and that Jessup had been sent a tape recording that contained "self-destructive instructions," but this was never substantiated either. In fact, there was no autopsy, contrary to Florida state law, but not much else I've been able to establish as non-standard or menacing.

Jessup's close friend, John P. Bessor, maintained that Jessup was very disappointed and discouraged over losing his battle to make UFOs respectable among scientists. Ivan Sanderson's wife Sabina saw the suicide note which Jessup had sent to her husband and recalled that it "makes it clear that he chose suicide as the only possible alternative to an insupportable future, and did so after careful consideration. Certainly the mysterious 'they' had nothing to do with it." I have to agree with Sabina Sanderson. Given everything I've learned about Morris Jessup's life and the circumstances which led to his freefall into profound depression, I have to conclude that this pioneering UFO author and investigator was not killed by anyone other than himself.

Media Personality Dorothy Kilgallen

Dorothy Kilgallen was an extremely well-connected media personality and highly syndicated newspaper columnist from the 1940s through the mid-60s. While best known to millions of Americans as a long-time panelist on the TV show "What's My Line?," she was also a serious investigative reporter who maintained a highly critical attitude toward the official explanations offered for both the JFK assassination and for UFOs. Kilgallen was found dead in her bed in 1965 and many still feel that she was murdered because of what she might reveal about one or both of these explosive subjects.

UFOS - WICKED THIS WAY COMES: THE DARK SIDE OF THE ULTRA-TERRESTRIALS

For years Kilgallen's "Journal American" column, "Voice of Broadway," alternated between celebrity gossip, hard news and exclusives. In May 1947, a month before Kenneth Arnold's sighting and about six weeks prior to Roswell, she reported the crash of an unidentified flying object near Spitsbergen, Norway. Rational concern that the wreck might represent advanced Russian technology was undercut by the Norwegian Air Force Colonel who chaired the Board of Inquiry and is alleged to have said, "... Some time ago a misunderstanding was caused by saying that the disc probably was of Soviet origin. *It has–this we wish to state emphatically–not been built by any country on earth.* The materials used in its construction are completely unknown to all experts having participated in the investigation."

Eight years later, Kilgallen published an article entitled "'Flying Saucer' Wreckage Assures Britons of Reality." It appeared on May 23, 1955, in London's International News Service and was then picked up by numerous papers, including "The Los Angeles Examiner." To quote: "I can report today on a story which is positively spooky, not to mention chilling. British scientists and airmen, after examining the wreckage of one mysterious flying ship, are convinced these strange aerial objects are not optical illusions, but are flying saucers that originate on another planet. The source of my information is a British official of cabinet rank who prefers to remain unidentified. 'We believe, on the basis of our inquiry thus far, that the saucers were staffed by small men—probably under four feet tall. It's frightening, but there's no denying the flying saucers come from another planet.' The official quoted scientists as saying a flying ship of this type could not possibly have been constructed on Earth. The British government, I learned, is withholding an official report on the 'flying saucer' examination at the time, possibly because it does not wish to frighten the public."

While Kilgallen never made her source of this extraordinary news story public, key investigators have speculated that the account originated with Lord Mountbatten. One of them was Gordon Creighton, a former diplomat and British Army intelligence officer. He was also editor of Britain's "Flying Saucer Review." After reading her column, Creighton "...wrote to Dorothy Kilgellen at once, seeking further information, but never got a reply from her, and she died a few years later. We may take it as certain that she had been effectively removed." Additional support for this account can be deduced from a statement issued at about this time by Britain's Air Chief

Marshall Lord Dowding, who said in part, "I am convinced that these objects do exist and that they are not manufactured by any nation on Earth." While no investigator has been able to confirm the authenticity or source of Kilgallen's published account, Timothy Good writes in "Above Top Secret," "Why should Dorothy Kilgallen risk her reputation as one of the USA's star journalists by propagating an untrue story? ... To the best of my knowledge (she) never denied the story. Furthermore, a number of similar stories from reliable sources have surfaced over the years, not all of which can be discounted, however absurd they may sound."

Marilyn Monroe And JFK

I had hesitated to bring Marilyn Monroe into this story for obvious reasons. I mean, really. But given the well-documented friendship between the actress and the columnist, and the prevalence of this account in the literature, I could not ignore it. It stems from a CIA document of at least questionable provenance which related a conversation recorded via phone tap between Kilgallen and her close friend and Hollywood insider, Howard Rothberg, who at one point states that Marilyn "had secrets to tell," one of which was that the president had confided to his then-lover that he'd visited "a secret air base to inspect things from outer space," the extraterrestrial implication being obvious. Kilgallen responded that she'd heard in the mid-1950s that there was a secret effort by the US and the UK governments to identify the origins of a crashed craft in New Mexico. Again, while this document has not been authenticated to my satisfaction, it did bear the date August 3, 1962, which would have been three days before Miss Monroe's death.

Following the assassination of President Kennedy, Kilgallen was one of the few national news reporters not to go along with the lone gunman theory, and, to the best of my knowledge, the only one to interview Lee Harvey Oswald's killer, Jack Ruby. This interview and other factors convinced the reporter that the president's killing was the result of a conspiracy about which she laid out her thoughts in a series of columns, even publishing the text of Ruby's classified testimony before the Warren Commission. Unfortunately, she was very public about the fact she was saving her best material for a book—one that was never written.

On November 8, 1965, Dorothy Kilgallen was found dead in her bed with a book propped up in her lap. It was known, however, that she had already finished reading the book. More, her reading glasses, which would have been necessary to read the book, were never found.

Kilgallen's hairdresser, who was also a close friend and confidant, pointed out that she was wearing a blouse over her nightgown which she would never have done. She was also found wearing her false eyelashes, which she always took off before going to bed. And she was not found in her normal bedroom; she was in the master bedroom, which she had not slept in for years.

Additionally, Mark Lane, the pioneering JFK assassination researcher who wrote "Plausible Denial," also believed she had been murdered and that the CIA might have been involved. Not surprisingly, the extensive file she had built on the incriminating aspects of the Kennedy assassination was missing from her files and never found. Personally, I'm convinced that Miss Kilgallen was in fact murdered, but more likely for what she intended to publish about the assassination rather than her knowledge of or interest in UFOs, though who can say for sure? By the way, the most knowledgeable investigator on this story that I know is my friend and colleague Nick Redfern.

The Sad Case Of Dr. James E. McDonald

Dr. James E. McDonald was an atmospheric physicist of great intelligence who had the courage to attempt bringing the subject of UFOs to the serious attention of both the American public and establishment science, much to the detriment of both his professional and personal life. His lectures and writings on UFOs ring with passion, intelligence and anger and are still very much worth reading. It's alleged that this member of the National Academy of Sciences, the American Meteorological Society and the Institute of Atmospheric Physics was murdered, and that his murder was made to look like suicide.

James McDonald was born in Minnesota in 1920, earned a B.A. at the University of Omaha, an M.S. from M.I.T., and his Ph.D. at Iowa State University. McDonald's investigative specialty was cloud physics, but a wide ranging curiosity led him into other areas of scientific study as well. On a drive through Arizona in January 1954, he had a UFO sighting with three friends. McDonald reported the sighting to the Air Force and searched for a conventional explanation of what the four had seen, but could find none. The event was not an earth-shaking one for him, but it did add the subject to his list of interests. He began an investigation of sightings in Arizona in 1958 and quietly became affiliated with the now defunct National Investigations Committee on Aerial Phenomena (NICAP) that same year. As he became more involved in the field, he grew to feel that neither the Air Force's Project Blue Book nor the scientific community were paying proper attention to the phenomenon.

His curiosity grew as a result of the 1966 Michigan sightings, which made him all the more interested in conducting his own UFO study. As a result, he applied for and secured a small grant from the Office of Naval Research to review the Blue Book material kept at Wright-Patterson AFB in Ohio. The ONI felt that certain kinds of clouds might account for some UFO reports and radar trackings, and being a cloud expert, McDonald was a logical choice for this effort.

During his visit to the base he was able to read the CIA's 1952 Robertson Panel report and was astonished to learn that their efforts were being directed toward a cover-up and debunking effort. A request for a photocopy was denied by the agency, which informed him that it had been reclassified shortly after he'd read it. While the reclassification proved to be temporary, his Wright-Patterson research established that the Air Force's UFO investigation was half-hearted at best.

Now increasingly convinced that legitimate UFO sightings were evidence of extraterrestrial visits, Dr. McDonald met with Blue Book consultant Dr. J. Allen Hynek that summer, whom he attacked for continuing to toe the official line. Hynek explained that he'd grown to feel much the same as McDonald and was about to reverse his public position, but McDonald chided him for not having done so in 1953. Hynek associate Jacques Vallee was impressed with the newcomer's resolve and later wrote that "It is clear that an entire era has come to an end. This man has many contacts, many ideas, and he is afraid of nothing." From this point on, almost all of McDonald's professional efforts were devoted to UFO investigations and to convincing scientists, politicians, journalists and other opinion makers of the seriousness of the subject.

UFOS – WICKED THIS WAY COMES: THE DARK SIDE OF THE ULTRA-TERRESTRIALS

Shortly thereafter James McDonald went public with his extraterrestrial hypothesis. By this time the Air Force had identified the scientist as an enemy and an internal memo issued at about this time discussed the need to "fireproof" him, Air Force slang for discrediting someone. His one-man crusade included the interviewing of hundreds of UFO witnesses, continued research on more classic cases and lectures to the American Meteorological Society and as many other scientific and professional associations as he could get invitations from. He wrote brilliant criticisms of Blue Book's failings and of Harvard's UFO debunking astronomer Donald K. Menzel. In 1967 he was even invited to speak before the UN's Outer Space Affairs Group by Secretary General U Thant. The scientist's criticism of Dr. Edward U. Condon, outspoken skeptic and the Director of the University of Colorado's ongoing UFO study, succeeded primarily in making the academics furious with him for exposing their highly flawed scientific methodology. In 1968, McDonald joined Hynek, Carl Sagan and other scientists in addressing the House Science and Astronautics Committee. His particularly blunt, no-nonsense comments read in part, "(My) position is that UFOs are entirely real and we do not know what they are, because we've laughed them out of court. The possibility that they are extraterrestrial devices, that we are dealing with surveillance from some advanced technology, is a possibility I take very seriously."

But it was Menzel who regularly received McDonald's harshest criticisms, even calling into question the astronomer's competence. His remarks before the American Society of Newspaper Publishers that year included this remark about the astronomer: "When it comes to analyzing UFO reports, he seems to calmly cast aside well-known principles almost with abandon, in an all-out effort to be sure that no UFO report survives his attack." And attack Menzel did at every opportunity, and with as much vengeance as Edward Condon, who'd grown to hate McDonald.

They were soon joined by upcoming debunker Phil Klass, whose knowledge of atmospheric physics was dwarfed by the scientist's. Klass soon abandoned his ball lightening and plasma UFO theories for the many and varied accusations of hoax that would become a career hallmark of his skewed methodology. But Klass, an editor and writer for "Aviation Week" magazine, was nothing if not tenacious. He struck back in increasingly effective ways, petitioning the Navy's Office of Intelligence, which had given McDonald another small grant to pursue research in Australia, to drop their support for what many considered crackpot research. The ONI did withdraw the grant and Klass's attacks caused McDonald to suffer additional embarrassment and lost support through a series of broadsides which questioned his logic, knowledge and even honesty. Each new attack served to erode his credibility further.

McDonald continued his one-man crusade throughout 1969 and into 1970, but it was not difficult for those close to him to see that he was paying an increasingly high price for his efforts. He had isolated himself from his more conservative colleagues and his opinions about UFOs were now being used against him more and more effectively.

In March 1971 his expertise in cloud and atmospheric physics resulted in a request to testify before the House Committee on Appropriations. The subject was the proposed production of a supersonic transport, or SST (commercially realized some years later as the Concorde), and the potential level of harm that its exhaust represented to the atmosphere. McDonald testified insightfully for two days, but congressmen who did not understand the science involved, or just disagreed with him, responded with pure ridicule. After all, why should they believe anything this physicist said? Didn't he believe that "there are little green men flying around the sky"? Now nationally humiliated, McDonald returned home to a marriage that was quickly disintegrating and to an academic community that wanted no part of him. His testimony before the House Committee on Appropriations would be his last public appearance.

In fact, his singular attention to UFOs had put terrific stress on his marriage, and Betsy McDonald was feeling increasingly neglected. She genuinely appreciated that the SST controversy had only increased her husband's state of depression, and as a result was willing to wait until a better time to discuss their deteriorating relationship. But McDonald insisted that they do so upon his return. The fact was that Betsy had become involved with another man and wanted a divorce. McDonald more than appreciated the situation which he had set in motion, but it was too late for the couple to reconcile their differences and his depression became full blown. Almost immediately he began to work out a plan for suicide, but not without considering the financial security of his family, this in the form of the value of his personal papers and extensive archive. He decided that he would take his life on March 26, but the date came and went as he continued to organize his files and complete one final paper. However, early on the morning of April 9th, he found himself alone in the house, composed a brief note to Betsy, then shot himself in the head with his handgun. But the bullet missed his brain and all but destroyed his optic nerve. Now blind, he was briefly committed to the psychiatric ward of Tucson's Veteran's Administration Medical Center. Betsy and their daughters rallied to his side to help him adjust to his blindness; she putting her plans for divorce on hold as well.

Over the next few months, Dr. McDonald began to recover and got back to the business of life and work at the Institute for Atmospheric Physics, even at times with real enthusiasm. A minimal amount of vision had returned, too, but his wife was not fooled, and she grew increasingly concerned that he was working hard to deceive those around him and was still intent on ending his life. Time proved her to be correct.

On Tuesday, June 13th, he left the Institute on his own and hailed a cab, asking the driver to take him to a pawn shop in town. With just enough vision returned to pose as a seemingly sighted man, he purchased a used Spanish 38. caliber revolver and some ammunition, then asked the cabbie to drive him to an isolated intersection in the desert. From here he apparently made his way on foot to a bridge that was about a mile from the intersection. Somewhere between eight and ten hours later, a family out hiking near Tucson came upon his body under the bridge. The revolver was found to the left of his head, a brief suicide note in his pocket.

Speculation that the scientist's death might have been the result of foul play was immediate within a segment of the UFO research community. I think that Dr. McDonald was driven to suicide by the collective forces arrayed against him.

Perhaps in a more perfect world the likes of Condon, Menzel and Klass might have been indictable as co-conspirators in his death, but all the facts point to McDonald himself as the man who pulled the trigger. If you'd like to learn more about this outstanding contributor to serious UFO studies, get yourself a copy of Ann Druffel's definitive biography "Firestorm." Ann is one of our finest UFO scholars and was a close associate of Dr. McDonald's. I cannot recommend this book too highly.

Frank Edwards

Frank Edwards was a popular broadcaster and author, and a longtime public proponent of the extraterrestrial hypothesis of UFOs. He is said to have died of a coronary, but there were those who felt he'd been murdered for bringing so much serious attention to the subject of UFOs.

Edwards certainly qualified for the title of pioneer radio broadcaster. He began his career as a radio announcer in 1924, was a White House correspondent from 1949 to 1954, and was cited as one of the nation's top three broadcasters along with Edward R. Morrow and Lowell Thomas in a 1953 poll. By the 1960s, his best-known radio show, "Strangest of All," was syndicated on hundreds of radio stations around the country. Many of the stories he related on the air went on to become the subjects of his newspaper column that was syndicated in about three hundred American newspapers.

Edwards was also a successful author with seven books to his credit, four of which dealt with inexplicable phenomena: "Strangest of All," "Stranger Than Science," "Strange People" and "Strange World." But it was not until the mid-1960s that he really hit his stride as an internationally best-selling author with the publication of his dual UFO exposés, "UFOs – Serious Business" in 1966 and "UFOs – Here and Now" in 1967. Both books were translated into numerous languages and cemented his position as the best-known and most outspoken radio personality in America regularly addressing the subject of UFOs. Edwards first became interested in UFOs in the late 1940s. In 1953 he got hold of an advance copy of Major Donald Keyhoe's "The Flying Saucers Are Real," and while its author had no previous books to his credit, he was a respected and decorated retired

UFOS – WICKED THIS WAY COMES: THE DARK SIDE OF THE ULTRA-TERRESTRIALS

Marine Corps combat pilot. The book was arguably the most popular yet published on the subject, and Edwards succeeded in scooping the competition by becoming the first broadcaster to report Keyhoe's shocking conclusions: that the objects were extraterrestrial craft, and that Air Force officials were aware, but refused to acknowledge it. Edwards' report made the wire services and the broadcaster was hooked on the subject. He and Keyhoe became fast friends and the Major was a regular guest on his radio shows after that.

Mr. Edwards was a member of the Board of Governors of NICAP (along with former CIA Director Roscoe Hillencotter) from 1957 until his death. His ongoing, on-air discussions about flying saucers and other unidentified flying objects were both unflinching and hard-hitting, and given the widely syndicated reach of his show, millions of listeners grew to take his conclusions seriously, as did certain Washington insiders.

I've read differing accounts of Edwards' final months. Some of them maintained that he was in failing health, others that he was never ill. Whatever the truth was, he passed away a few minutes before midnight on June 23rd, 1967.

In New York City, an event called the Conference of Scientific Ufologists had been scheduled to begin the next morning, taking advantage of the fact that it was the 20th anniversary of the Kenneth Arnold sightings. The organizer chose to begin his remarks with an announcement of the sad news and by some accounts the audience of more than one thousand gasped as one.

This slight misunderstanding – that the famed broadcaster had died *on* the anniversary itself, fed an instant suspicion among many that the coincidence had been just *too* coincidental. But there were other factors that fed their concern, and I'm not sure what to make of them. Edwards' obituary in the "New York Times" read that his death was "apparently" due to a heart attack, which didn't help matters any, but a more disturbing claim was made public by radio personality and Edwards protégé Long John Nebel, who went on to take up the UFO cause on his long running syndicated radio show.

Nebel related that just prior to the conference, famed UFO researcher and author Gray Barker showed him two unsigned letters he'd received stating that Frank Edwards would die during the convention. Barker also phoned him, again, just prior to the conference, to say, "John, something happened a few minutes ago that really shook me up. I got a phone call from a man who said that Edwards would not live to see the end of the convention. That's all he said before he hung up."

Gray Barker was one of the golden age of flying saucers' most colorful figures, and while a dedicated chronicler of the phenomena's early days, was not above playing a bit fast and loose with the facts. His landmark 1956 paranoid classic, "They Knew Too Much About Flying Saucers" (great title!) attests to this tendency, but John Nebel on the other hand was known for his straightforwardness and dedication to the subject, and if he went on record that he's seen these letters and received that call, I have to take him seriously. As such, this is a case where we have to credit extraordinary multiple coincidences as the cause of ongoing murder rumors, or admit that Frank Edwards may really have been the victim of foul play, to which I'd have to agree.

Dr. J. Allen Hynek

For twenty years Dr. J. Allen Hynek was the best known and most influential figure in international UFOlogy, bar none. Given his importance, some in the field felt his death might not have been natural.

Briefly, Allen Hynek was born in Chicago in 1910 and received both his Bachelor of Science and Ph.D. from the University of Chicago. A teaching position at Ohio State followed and in 1956 he was hired by the Smithsonian's Astrophysical Observatory at Harvard to track the earth satellites that the United States planned to begin launching in the near future. His affiliation with the Air Force began in 1960 as a consultant with Project Stargazer, which was involved in launching telescopes on balloons into the upper atmosphere. That year he also joined the faculty of Northwestern University as professor of astronomy.

But his involvement in UFO studies actually began in 1948 when the Air Force invited him to begin looking into sighting reports. Initially skeptical, Hynek contributed to the public's less-than-serious perception of the phenomena, creating the now-famous musings that "swamp gas" was an explanation for the unknown aerial objects. He went on to work with the

UFOS – WICKED THIS WAY COMES: THE DARK SIDE OF THE ULTRA-TERRESTRIALS

University of Colorado on its huge, misleading report on UFOs, but by this time was becoming dismayed by the service's inept and unscientific handling of the subject. And while he did not get along very well with Dr. James McDonald, he was impressed and respectful of the physicist's passionate UFO investigation and attempt to bring UFOs into the scientific mainstream. Hynek's book, "The UFO Experience: A Scientific Inquiry," was published in 1972, the year after McDonald's suicide. The book accused the Air Force of conducting their UFO investigations with indifference and incompetence and gave voice to his growing view that some UFOs were extraterrestrial in origin.

"The UFO Experience" was actually well received by many in the scientific community. In 1973 he founded The Center For UFO Studies. It was renamed the J. Allen Hynek Center For UFO Studies following his death. His second book, "The Edge of Reality" (written with Jacques Vallee) came out in 1975, while his third book, "The Hynek UFO Report," was published in 1977. That year The Center, which is located in Chicago, enjoyed a jump in attention after the astronomer had assisted in helping to promote Steven Speilberg's "Close Encounters of the Third Kind." His cameo appearance toward the end of the film is still memorable and made him into something of a pop culture figure and he went on to became a regular speaker at UFO conferences.

I met Dr. Hynek in 1984, interestingly on the same day I met my future co-author (of "Left At East Gate") Larry Warren. We had all come to Westchester County, New York, that day to learn more about huge triangular craft that were inundating the area at the time. Not long after we met, Dr. Hynek was diagnosed with a brain tumor, and while his name appeared as the first of three authors on 1987's "Night Siege," which is about New York's Hudson Valley UFO sightings, the book was fully written by investigators Phil Imbrogno and Bob Pratt. By the time the contract had been signed, Allen Hynek was too ill to participate. He died on April 27th, 1987, in Scottsdale, Arizona. Nothing I have learned about this singular contributor to the field of scientific UFO studies indicates or leads me to believe he was sitting on any explosive or potentially embarrassing information which might have made him a target of interest of the Air Force, the intelligence community, or any other governmental agency. Unless or until I learn anything to the contrary I have to conclude that he died of natural causes.

UFOS – WICKED THIS WAY COMES: THE DARK SIDE OF THE ULTRA-TERRESTRIALS

Pete Mazzola

<u>Pete Mazzola</u> was a charismatic, intense and extremely courageous UFO investigator who also happened to be a tough, no-nonsense New York City Police Detective. Water damage to some of my files has left me without a photo of him. In the 1970s, Pete founded a research group called the Scientific Bureau of Investigation, better known as the SBI, whose membership was primarily composed of police officers. Pete served as its National Director until his death, which occurred just two months after Allen Hynek's, also from the effects of a brain tumor. And much as in the case of Dr, Hynek, his death was followed by speculation that the tumor was artificially introduced to quiet Mazzola's growing, authoritative presence on the UFO scene. He was also a mentor or mine, and a good friend to me and my family.

Pete was born in Brooklyn and grew up in a traditional Italian American family. In private conversations with me and with my colleague Antonio Huneeus, he related a UFO experience that he remembered from childhood that had occurred in Brooklyn's Prospect Park. He never chose to go into great detail about it, but it led both Antonio and I to feel that he might have been an abductee. From what I've learned in the intervening years, especially in my work with Budd Hopkins, I'm fairly convinced that that was the case. If so, it may have formed the basis for his lifelong interest in the subject. But whether this had been the case or not, he would have a UFO experience when he was in the Army that would change his life.

Mazzola had joined the New York City Police Department as soon as he was age eligible, but becoming a cop had to be put on hold until he had completed his military service. Pete volunteered for the Army and saw combat in Vietnam, and it was there that the reality of UFOs assumed—or reassumed—a central place in his life. Following his honorable discharge, he returned home and served the city of New York as a Manhattan-based foot patrolman before becoming eligible for the highly coveted gold detective's shield. Being a cop in a big city is challenging and dangerous work, and in the course of being on the job he was both shot and stabbed. The detective sergeant was decorated for his bravery and his other accomplishments on a number of occasions, much of his service concentrated on working with troubled juveniles. He took particular pride in being one of a handful of police officers selected by the department for special training in regressive hypnosis for criminal investigation. His skills in this area helped in the solving of a number of crimes, and were instrumental in helping to break the particularly high profile case of a young violinist who was murdered on the roof of Lincoln Center's Metropolitan Opera House.

On his own time he continued to research and study UFO cases with the same scrutiny and professionalism he'd acquired in his training at the city's John Jay Police Academy and networked with fellow police officers around the country who were likewise caught up in the subject. He also began to apply his skill as a forensic regressive hypnotist to working with individuals who claimed to have had alien contact and abduction experiences.

As time passed, Pete became known in the field and began to do radio interviews and appear on TV shows. He was always a good sport about being "the UFO cop," and took the good natured kidding and occasionally stupid kidding of his fellow officers with a grain of salt. But his record as a detective remained solid and he was granted permission to process the audiocassettes of the UFO-related hypnotic sessions he conducted through John Jay's Voice Stress Analysis facilities. Access to this highly accurate technology allowed him to quantify the stress in the voices of his subjects so as to better evaluate their accounts. He was the first person to conduct regressive hypnotic sessions with my late sister Helen, who would later go on to work with Budd Hopkins. He hypnotized me as well so that I might re-experience the UFO sighting we'd had as kids. It was remarkable to be fourteen years old again and to relive every detail of that amazing afternoon.

Now, an unexpected side effect of the Air Force's termination of Project Blue Book in 1969 was that individuals who'd have traditionally filed sighting reports with the Air Force began to call them in to their local police departments. They in turn had no official agency to pass such reports on to, and in the early seventies Pete established a twenty-four hour hotline for just this purpose. The reports were soon coming in droves with Detective Mazzola following up on them as his schedule allowed. By the time we were introduced in the late 1970s, Pete had quietly built the SBI into a well organized non-profit scientific and educational foundation whose monthly bulletin was always filled with data on vintage and late breaking cases. When Pete learned that I had a degree in fine arts and was a painting instructor at The School of Visual Arts, he appointed me to be the SBI Bulletin's Art Director. But being the micromanager he was, he never actually allowed me to do any art direction. It was nice having my name on the masthead though. In 1984 the Bulletin became the first American UFO publication to take a look at Britain's Rendlesham Forest UFO incident, this several years prior to my becoming involved in the case.

The SBI sponsored several New York-based conferences, one of which was the first conference I was ever invited to speak at. Other speakers included Budd Hopkins, Larry Fawcett and Barry Greenwood, the authors of "Clear Intent," as well as Larry Warren and my sister Helen.

As best I recall, Mazzola sustained seven serious injuries during his more than twenty years of service—knife, gun and beating—and ultimately decided to retire from the force when he was forty or forty-one years old, much to the relief and happiness of his wife Elaine and their two children. Many of Pete's friends were pleased as well because we knew this would allow him to devote himself fulltime to his primary interest. But then, the unexpected happened. Pete had been asked to speak before a research group in the Midwest—it was to be his first following his retirement—and he was met by his sponsor at the airport. As they were driven to his motel prior to the talk, a car on the opposite side of the divided highway went out of control and jumped the divider. Pete had not buckled his seatbelt and the head-on crash between the two vehicles shot him through the windscreen and caused him to suffer multiple internal injuries and break more than half of the bones in his body. For the next year he refused to see all but his immediate family and doctors, and while the physical injuries healed over the next months, he remained weak and continued to suffer from problems that did not seem the result of the auto accident. A cat scan was finally ordered and revealed the last thing that his doctors had considered or been looking for: an inoperable brain tumor. Pete never returned to the UFO research he was so passionate about and died on June 10th, 1987. He was only forty-two years old.

I have no idea if the cancer that took him from us was natural or induced, but given the freak nature of the terrible accident that served to hide its spread, and the all-too-common plague that is cancer in modern society, we were all certain, Pete included, that it was just that—a freak accident which could not have been intentionally engineered under any circumstances, which is never fair, but does remain an equal opportunity killer. I don't know if there was any history of this or any other type of cancer in his family, and have had to make my peace with the fact we will never have a hard answer to its origin. I still miss him though, and the first edition of "Left At East Gate" was in part dedicated to him.

Dr. Karla Turner

Dr. Karla Turner was a friend of mine and a colleague I had tremendous respect and admiration for. Her petite presence—I think she was all of five feet tall—would not have led you to think she was the aggressive, courageous and rock solid investigator that she was. Karla was a respected psychologist, who specialized in working with abductees, and the author of numerous papers and three books, "Taken: Inside the Human-Alien Abduction Agenda," "Masquerade of Angels" and "Into the Fringe." Her death from cancer in 1997 caused many who knew her or followed her work to speculate that she'd been murdered by the government, the power elite, and given her decidedly anti-"goodness and light" abduction views, by the aliens themselves.

Dr. Turner's interest in the alien abduction phenomenon was not the result of her intellectual curiosity or compassion, though she had plenty of each to spare. She was a lifelong abductee herself and did not see the experience as a transcendent or positive one. Quoting Turner, "I'm convinced that deception is the key to understanding the entire phenomenon. At every level, we are deceived and so we (1) do not know where to put our trust and loyalty, if anywhere, and (2) do not know what actions we ourselves should take to alter our relations with ETs. Most of what we see and remember (even in the first level of hypnotic recall) is not 'true' or objectively accurate. ... So we really do not know what the ETs are doing with us. And if they deliberately deceive us this way, how on Earth can we trust anything they tell us?"

Dr. Turner worked tirelessly for years, spoke at many conferences and remained outspoken about the deceptive aspects of the presences behind the phenomenon. When she was diagnosed with the cancer that killed her, her response was to continue working to the fullest extent she was able. I was very moved that the last UFO lecture she was strong enough to attend was one that Larry and I gave in the summer of 1997. I think she was in her early forties when she passed but am not positive of this. While it was wonderful to see her again, the event was heavily tinged with sadness as it was all but obvious that we would not be seeing her again. As best I recall, she passed away a few short months later. Again we face the question of whether the pathogens that killed her were natural or not, and once again I have no idea of where the truth lies. Karla herself was actually more concerned about the specter of alien retribution for statements she'd made in print. Again, I can only speculate. One thing is for certain though, Dr. Turner never backed down in her unbending belief that the non-human presences behind the UFO abduction phenomenon were not doing so in the interests of humanity, and if they had a least favorite researcher, it might well have been Karla.

Jim Keith

Jim Keith was an investigative writer who wrote about UFOs, but was better known for his conspiracy related books. His published titles included "Saucers of the Illuminati," "Mind Control/World Control," "Casebook on the Men in Black," "Casebook on Alternative 3," "OK Bomb" and "Black Helicopters I" and "II." Given his dedication to exposing conspiracies of all sorts, his death following a fall from a stage in which he broke his knee was naturally suspect.

Jim was truly a consparicist's consparicist. He spoke at numerous conferences about numerous conspiracies and contributed many articles to journals and magazines. Keith did not subscribe to the extraterrestrial theory of UFOs and viewed the phenomena as human in origin. He felt that the craft involved were entirely the product of highly classified governmental programs employing advanced technology and maintained that those responsible were involved in an ongoing, concerted effort to advance the extraterrestrial hypothesis as a form of cover story for their nefarious activities.

In September 1999, Jim took some time off to attend Burning Man, a huge, weeklong arts festival held annually in Black Rock, Nevada. An accidental fall from the stage there resulted in a painful broken knee and he was taken from the venue to Washoe Hospital in Reno for emergency surgery. During the operation, it's understood that a blood clot was released and entered his lung, which was the official cause of his death. It's particularly tempting to yell murder when someone so dedicated to conspiratorial thinking, and to bringing government abuses and cover-ups to the attention of the public, dies under such freaky circumstances, and I don't think any of us have any problem wondering why. But if the cause of death was as reported, a blood clot that had traveled to the lung, it is a legitimate one that, while tragic, is not unknown in many types of surgical procedures. If this was not the cause of his death, as some still maintain, I doubt if we will ever learn what in fact it was. I didn't know Jim Keith, but several years prior to his death we did exchange emails on a subject of mutual interest, and even if I didn't share some of his beliefs, I admired his efforts in attempting to unravel some of the more complex and ominous issues of our time.

Graham Birdsall

Graham Birdsall was a founder and the Editor-In-Chief of England's "UFO Magazine," arguably the best newsstand UFO publication ever to appear in print in the English language. He was also a superb conference organizer and national, then international, spokesman for responsible UFO research everywhere. He died of the effects of a cerebral aneurism in 2003, igniting speculation that he'd been murdered to silence his growing influence and outstanding work.

UFOs aside for the moment, Graham was one of my all time favorite people. I think my friend and colleague Nick Redfern would agree; he was even closer to Graham than I was. Birdsall was a big bear of a guy who grabbed life with both hands and really lived it. A native of Yorkshire England, where he lived his whole life, his intelligence, passion, generosity and great sense of humor literally drew people to him in droves. He was also a natural leader and a true friend to American and international UFOlogy, bringing many of us from our homes around the world to England as speakers over the years. He was also a regular presence and featured speaker at such American venues as the Laughlin International UFO Congress where he was always accompanied by his wife Christine and daughter Helen. He was a riveting public speaker who could address a thousand-plus audience with the ease and intimacy you'd expect to hear in someone's living room.

Graham began his UFO-related life as an independent researcher. In the early 1980s, he and his brother Mark, along with their friend Tony Dodd, a police constable, author and first-rate investigator as well, established a newsletter called "Quest UFO Magazine." "Quest" grew from a hand-mimeographed and stapled several-page newsletter into an internationally distributed publication whose production values were second to none and, in violation of almost every previously known law of UFO publications, was a remarkably successfully business venture to boot.

For more than twenty years "UFO Magazine" and the Leeds-based Quest International Organization went on to sponsor some of the best-organized and most interesting UFO conferences, lectures and events ever staged anywhere. Graham's curiosity was boundless and he was obsessive in following up leads on the stories he published, securing witness testimony, chasing down the details of whatever case he was involved in investigating, then getting it all into print in issue after issue—and on schedule. He also possessed the refreshing trait of actually correcting errors that might have gone into print.

But given his strong personal ethics and unbending opinions, the man was no stranger to controversy and never shirked a good fight. He had his share of fallings-out with colleagues over the years, but once convinced of a case's inherent validity (or lack thereof), never hesitated to champion, or attack, or call it as he saw it. His keen business sense made him a highly respected and influential member of the Leeds business community, no mean feat in a city regarded as a major financial capitol of Europe, especially where your business is UFOs.

Not long after the SCI FI Channel aired their twenty hour long miniseries "Taken," I'd arranged an introduction for Graham with another good friend of UFOlogy, Larry Landsman, SCI FI's Director of Special Projects. The two hit it off famously, and had Graham lived, he would have spent October of 2003 traveling around India as the SCI FI Channel's goodwill ambassador promoting the upcoming broadcast of "Taken" on Indian television—with Hindi subtitles of course. But that was not to be.

In mid-September, Graham collapsed at work and was rushed to the hospital for emergency surgery to relieve pressure on his brain. He passed away at age forty-nine on September 19th, 2003 as a result of complications following a cerebral aneurism, and when he died, "UFO Magazine" died with him. And this brings us to the understandable and unnerving speculation that he had been murdered.

The fact is that Graham Birdsall's death was devastating, not just to his family and friends, but to British UFOlogy as a whole. He was not just *a* significant presence in the field, he was *the* most important presence in the field—a veritable linchpin whose magazine featured the latest cases and best known researchers and whose conferences gave them, along with their leading international colleagues, a world class venue to present their findings in, and always to packed houses and overflow audiences.

No one else even came close, and no one since has stepped forward with the necessary organizing skills, personal charisma and connections to pick up where he left off. I have to admit, that if *I* had wanted to destabilize British UFOlogy, the only person I would have bothered to target would have been Graham Birdsall, so why do I think that he was *not* murdered?

The last night I spent with Graham was Christmas Eve 2002, and after Christine and Helen had gone to bed we stayed up late into the night talking, drinking, trading stories, analyzing a documentary we'd just seen, and smoking cigarettes, both of us admonishing each other that we really had to quit. Graham was not quite a chain smoker, but he was close to it.

He was a type A workaholic who carried around about fifty more pounds than was good for him. His diet was, to put it mildly, not health-oriented, he laughed at exercise, and came from a family where none of the men—his father and uncles—had lived to see their fiftieth birthdays. Taking all of these factors into account, I think that his death, while truly tragic, was the result of natural causes. I still think about him often, remain in regular contact with his family, and doubt that we'll see his likes again.

UFOS – WICKED THIS WAY COMES: THE DARK SIDE OF THE ULTRA-TERRESTRIALS

Dr. John Mack

Dr. John Mack was a distinguished American psychiatrist whose unique credentials made him someone we in the abduction research community could point to with pride. He was best known for his research into how extraordinary experiences can affect personal, societal and global transformation, and his random death as the victim of a traffic accident was immediately and understandably suspect by many who worked with him or who followed his work. Learning that this irreplaceable individual "just happened" to be mowed down by a drunken driver as he crossed a street did not sit well with any of us.

If scientists had tried to piece together an alien abduction researcher—hardly the most revered field of professional study out there—with establishment credentials which would have demanded respect from even the most hardcore skeptic, Dr. Mack would have been the product of their efforts. Born in 1929 into a socially prominent New York family, Mack received his undergraduate degree from Oberlin College and his medical degree from Harvard (Cum Laude) where he served a Professor of Psychiatry for many years. His academic and humanitarian accomplishments were many and varied. In 1983 for example, he was invited to testify before Congress on the psychological impact of nuclear arms on children.

Aside from maintaining a busy private practice and keeping up with his teaching responsibilities, John became a specialist in teenage suicide, which he wrote extensively about earlier in his career. I first heard of him in this capacity several years before we met when I was working as a crisis intervention volunteer.

Dr. Mack went on to found Boston's Center for Psychology and Social Change, the Program for Extraordinary Experience Research (better known as PEER, and renamed the John Mack Institute following his death), and was also the founder of the Psychiatric Wing of Cambridge Hospital in Boston. He was also the author of several books, including "Abduction," "Passport to the Cosmos" and "A Prince of Our Disorder," a psychological biography of T.E. Lawrence (Lawrence of Arabia) for which he received the Pulitzer Prize. Extraordinary credentials indeed.

UFOS – WICKED THIS WAY COMES: THE DARK SIDE OF THE ULTRA-TERRESTRIALS

John Mack's interest in UFO abductions was sparked by a meeting with Budd Hopkins in 1992. As he told me with a smile, he at first thought that Budd might be delusional, but once he had had an opportunity to familiarize himself with some of Budd's scrupulously collected and evaluated data, and meet with some of the people who claimed to have had such experiences, his views on the subject shifted one hundred and eighty degrees. That same year he served as a co-chair of the Abduction Study Conference held at MIT. I met him in my capacity as Budd's assistant and liked him from the start. John was amazingly well read and well traveled and possessed a wonderfully self-effacing sense of humor. In my opinion, my BFA placed me several light years beneath his doctorate, clinical work and numerous academic achievements, but the fact was I had considerably more experience in abduction studies and working with abductees than he, and he always treated me as a respected colleague, irregularly seeking my opinion on questions surrounding the phenomenon.

Given the controversial nature of this research, especially among academics, and John's increasingly high visibility in the field, Harvard Medical School appointed a committee of peers in 1994 to review his clinical care and treatment of people who had shared their alien encounters with him. It was the first time that the distinguished college had censured a faculty member since Timothy Leary had been called on the carpet for his controversial support of LSD use in the 1960s.

After a grueling fourteen-month investigation, during which the psychiatrist was called on to meet with the committee with his lawyer present, the Dean of Harvard's Medical School, quote, "reaffirmed Dr. Mack's academic freedom to study what he wishes and to state his opinions without impediment." This decision was greeted with wide support by many of his colleagues at Harvard.

In 1993 or early 1994, John asked me to proofread his manuscript for "Abduction," and when I discovered an error which would have proved embarrassing to him had it gone into print, he was truly appreciative, inscribing my copy "To our number one sleuth."

Over the years, we had quite a number of disagreements as to the nature of the abduction phenomenon, but they never got in the way of our friendship or our professional relationship. When I could, I attended his lectures, always with great interest, and shortly after "Left At East Gate" was published, he invited me to lecture on it to the staff and guests of the Psychiatric wing of Cambridge Hospital with special emphasis on managing stress in UFO studies. It was one of the sharpest audiences I've ever addressed, and the questions they put forward after the talk were incisive, respectful and sincere.

This brings us to September 27, 2004. John had traveled to England to speak at a T.E. Lawrence Society Symposium in Oxford. His afternoon presentation had been so warmly received that he was asked to stay and present an additional talk later in the day. He was returning "home" that evening (he was staying with friends in London), and as he stepped into a crosswalk on Totteridge Road, was struck and killed instantly by an intoxicated truck driver whose license had been suspended several times previously for drunken driving. I've not had it confirmed, but John *may* have looked the wrong way as he stepped into traffic, an unfortunate trait that many of us American, right-side of the road drivers share.

On October 7, 2005, the driver, Raymond Czechowski, pled guilty of "careless driving while under the influence of alcohol." Dr. Mack's family (he left two sons, three grandchildren and an ex-wife) submitted a statement to the court that read in part, "Although this was a tragic event for our family, we feel that Mr. Czechowski's behavior was neither malicious nor intentional, and we have no ill will toward him since we learned the circumstances of the collision. We all believe John Mack would not want Mr. Czechowski to go to jail. As for ourselves, our grief will not be lessened by knowing that he is incarcerated."

Presiding Judge Linda Stern appreciated the family's statement and generous sentiments, but disagreed, noting that, "a message must be sent. You shouldn't drive with alcohol in your blood." At the time of the accident Mr. Czechowski's blood/alcohol level had been recorded at ninety-seven mgs of alcohol in one hundred ml's of blood.

The legal limit in the UK is eighty mg's. Czechowski was sentenced to fifteen months in prison and had his driver's license suspended for three years. With good behavior he served only about six of his fifteen-month sentence. I'm afraid that I'm not nearly as generous of spirit as John's family were, and felt and continue to feel that the punishment in this case came woefully short of fitting the crime.

UFOS – WICKED THIS WAY COMES: THE DARK SIDE OF THE ULTRA-TERRESTRIALS

As in Graham Birdsall's death, this is a case that almost screams for a world-class villain to blame the tragedy on, and in a way there's nothing I would have liked more than to have uncovered an appropriately evil conspiracy to blame for taking such an important person from us. But this was not the case. It was just a drunken driver doing what drunken drivers do. And given the specifics of the accident, of his coming around the corner at exactly the moment he did, I do not believe that even the most practiced covert ops team could have carried it off and made it seem like the accident that it was. Like it or not, senseless loss is a part of life, and likely a more common aspect of it than is diabolical premeditation. I can only count myself fortunate to have counted him as a colleague and a friend.

In Conclusion

Some of the implications of what UFOs represent are so potentially disturbing, and so disruptive to society as we know it, that I have no doubts that there are those who are capable of just about anything in their efforts to keep the subject from us, and to keep it in its place as an idiot child of history, politics and the media. For those individuals who have shown the desire and predisposition to become involved and remain involved in responsible research, a certain amount of stress and anxiety will be a given. But it is important work, and when approached in a scientific, methodical and principled way, may represent a far greater contribution to society than most of the sleepwalkers who populate the world are capable of imagining. Even in the extreme cases of those who've been taken from us before their time, it's the quality of the lives they lived and the contributions they made that we should remain focused on, no matter what the circumstances of their deaths. So here's to them, and to those who continue to do that work. They didn't allow their lives to be governed by fear and neither should we.

* * * * *

References:

1. *The UFO Encyclopedia*, 1st and 2nd editions, Clark, Jerome, Omnigraphics, Detroit, 1992 and 1998
2. *The UFO Encyclopedia*, Sachs, Margret, Perigee (Putnam), 1980

3. *The UFO Controversy in America,* Jacobs, David, U. of Indiana, 1975

4. *The Philadelphia Experiment,* Moore, William & Berlitz, Charles, Grosset & Dunlap, 1979

5. Other Mysterious Deaths: Lest We Forget, Schellhorn, G. Cope, UFO Universe Magazine, 1997

6. *Firestorm: Dr. James E. McDonald's Fight for UFO Science,* Druffel, Ann, Wildflower Press, Columbus, NC, 2003

7. *Majic Eyes Only,* Wood, Ryan, Wood Enterprises, 2005

8. *UFOs, JFK and Elvis,* Belzer, Richard, Ballantine Books, 1999

9. *Above Top Secret,* Good, Timothy, Sedgewick & Jackson, London,

10. *The Flying Saucer Story,* Le Poer Trench, Brinsley, Spearman, 1967

11. *Liquidation of the UFO Investigators,* Binder, Otto, Saga's Special UFO Report, Vol 11, 1971

12. *Taken,* Turner, Karla, Keltworks Press, 1994

13. *UFOs and the National Security State,* Dolan, Richard, Hampton Roads Publishing Co., Charlottesville, VA, 2002

UFOS – WICKED THIS WAY COMES: THE DARK SIDE OF THE ULTRA-TERRESTRIALS

UFOS - WICKED THIS WAY COMES: THE DARK SIDE OF THE ULTRA-TERRESTRIALS

CALLING DOWN THE ULTRA-TERRESTRIAL SPIRITS
By Tim R. Swartz

THE modern UFO phenomenon is both strange and puzzling. Pop culture sees UFOs as interplanetary spacecraft piloted by humanoid creatures that are hell-bent on shoving bizarre devices up the rectums of unfortunate abductees. However, if one were to conduct even a little research beyond exploitative "reality" TV shows, it becomes quickly apparent that there is an entire universe of weird stuff that surrounds UFOs. In one way or another, practically everything that is associated with the supernatural, or paranormal, can also be connected to UFOs. Because of this, the "simple" explanation that UFOs are physical spaceships from other planets needs to be given a more thorough examination.

Beginning in the early 1950s, individuals such as George Adamski, Truman Bethurum, and Orfeo Angelucci came forward with claims that they had actually met with extraterrestrials. These friendly beings from other worlds were coming to planet Earth because of their concern with our recent development of atomic weapons. The contactees were told that not only would atomic bombs make a mess of our world, but they also would also somehow affect the entire cosmos. For many, this was the proof that they had been seeking about the authenticity of UFOs. Not only were UFOs real, but they were piloted by people from other planets.

The implications were both startling and revolutionary. We were not alone in this vast universe. There were other intelligent creatures out there that took an interest in humanity and seemed genuinely concerned with our ultimate physical and spiritual well-being. Even though, for the most part, the UFO contactee movement was met with ridicule, it did manage to plant a seed as to the possibility that there was life elsewhere in the universe. As the years went by, this seed sprouted into a conviction that is generally accepted today as a reality.

Contact with "extraterrestrial intelligences" is nothing new, however. Long before people became convinced that UFOs were interplanetary spaceships, there were religious visionaries, spiritual mediums and psychic channelers who claimed that they were receiving messages from alleged non-earthly sources.

Emanuel Swedenborg

Emanuel Swedenborg (1688-1772) was a Swedish philosopher and scientist who began his career as an engineer and was the publisher of Sweden's first scientific journal, Daedalus Hyperboreus. Swedenborg devoted himself to geometry, chemistry and metallurgy, as well as studies of anatomy and physiology. In the 1730s, Swedenborg became increasingly interested in spiritual matters and was determined to find a theory which would explain how matter relates to spirit. Swedenborg's desire to understand the order and purpose of creation first led him to investigate the structure of matter and the process of creation itself.

In 1744, at the age of 56, Swedenborg began to have a series of strange dreams and visions. Even though Swedenborg had a lifelong interest in philosophy and theology, he found some of his visions to be highly disturbing. According to Swedenborg's writings, his spiritual awakening opened his eyes so that he could freely visit heaven and hell and talk with angels, demons and other spirits.

In his book, "***Life On Other Planets***," Swedenborg states that he was visited by spirits of beings who lived on other planets in our solar system. He wrote that all the life forms he visited in this solar system and beyond were humanoid in appearance, but they are not having a carbon-based, physical experience in a three dimensional world in the way that we are. They have social and family structures, and they are all well aware of the reality that there is only one God. Moreover, they know that they will live on after their present "bodies" perish. Swedenborg says that every planet and every moon has a spiritual life form on it. The reason for this, he said, is that the universe is the seminary of Heaven. Every planet and moon is a place of learning and growth for the entire spiritual community at large.

Swedenborg cautions that he could not see the actual planet to determine if it was inhabited or not; he was only aware of spirits that were associated with that planet.

From the Planet Mars

Catherine-Elise Muller of Geneva, Switzerland, was a late-19th century spirit medium. Muller discovered spiritualism in 1891 and quickly showed a talent for automatic writing. After joining a spiritualist development circle when she was 30, Muller began to show evidence of mediumistic abilities. In 1892, Muller began to hold her own séances, claiming that the author Victor Hugo was her spirit control.

Muller's most amazing claim occurred in November, 1894, when she stated that her spirit had been transported to the planet Mars. Not only did she describe the Martian plants and animals in detail, she also provided examples of the Martian language. She later reported visits to Venus and Uranus and provided samples of the different languages spoken there.

Like other alleged Ultra-terrestrial communications at that time, Muller's space people did not need flying saucers to physically travel across the vast distances of space. They were perfectly content to use telepathy to establish contact with residents of planet Earth.

Muller's spirit communications with the residents of Mars were detailed in the 1901 book "***From India to the Planet Mars: A Study of a Case of Somnambulism***," by Theodore Flournoy.

An interesting side note to this section: Muller claimed that her spirit guide was the French author Victor Hugo, who helped her travel to Mars and beyond. What is not widely known is that, while in political exile on the Channel Island of Jersey in 1853-1855, Hugo participated in well over one hundred table-tapping séances. During these séances, Hugo communicated with an alleged alien from Jupiter named Tyatafia and with the inhabitants of Mercury. The Mercurians were half-physical, half-spirit, and floated in the atmosphere of their planet like living rays of light.

The spirits asserted that all physical planets in the universe were places of punishment, inhabited by souls who had lived wrongly and now had to undergo a purgatorial existence. On the other hand, there are worlds of reward, ethereal non-physical globes of living light. These worlds were home to the souls of those who had lived lives

deserving of reward. The spirits also asserted that all advantaged entities in our universe are under a strict moral imperative to help all less advantaged entities.

Hugo deeply believed in the reality of these communications, predicting that the transcripts of the séances would become "one of the Bibles of the Future."

Greetings From AFFA

There was a time when the U.S. military and intelligence services were openly interested in solving the UFO puzzle. Even if the original subject of the investigation seemed to be less than credible, there was a willingness to at least conduct an investigation. In 1959, Major Robert Friend, acting chief of Project Blue Book, was approached by two Navy commanders and several CIA intelligence officers who told him of their incredible experience with a woman from South Berwick, Maine, named Frances Swan. According to the officers, Mrs. Swan would go into a trance and write out answers to questions posed to her. The answers were supposedly coming from an entity from space named "AFFA." AFFA said he and his men were part of an inter-solar-system police force investigating atomic tests on Earth.

Questions directed to AFFA, like "What is the length of the Uranus day?" and "What is the distance between Jupiter and the sun at Jupiter's apogee?" were correctly answered. Their story became even more fantastic when it was revealed that when the officers returned to Washington DC, one of them went into a trance and began writing out messages from AFFA.

According to Jay Gourley in his 1979 article, "The Day the Navy Established 'Contact'," the messages said that AFFA and his patrol team members were four extraterrestrials, officers in the OEEV, which meant Universal Association of Planets, assigned to EU or Euenza (Project Earth).

Among the more interesting interchanges later reported to Major Friend were the following:

Q. It's very interesting that we are talking with someone that we can't see, but can we have proof of your existence?

A. What kind of proof do you want?

Q. Can we see you or your craft?

A. When do you want to see?

Q. Now.

A. Go to the window.

All the intelligence people went to the window, where they were shocked to see a UFO that was saucer-shaped and brighter around the perimeter than in the center. The confusion that followed ended the communication with AFFA.

The woman at the center of this controversial incident, Frances Swan, talked of "the good ones," spacemen patrolling the solar system to protect us from dangerous geological faults, and of "the bad ones" who want to colonize this planet. She believed that her communication was a prelude to "the second coming of Jesus."

Major Friend, intrigued at this point, flew to Washington DC to see for himself. On July 9, 1959, in a secret Washington office, along with the Navy commanders and CIA agents, Major Friend watched as the Navy commander went into a trance and began writing.

"There was no doubt about that in my mind," said Friend. "I could see his pulse quicken. I could see his Adam's apple moving up and down rapidly. His handwriting was entirely different from his normal handwriting. The muscles in his torso did not appear to be strained, but the muscles in his arms were obviously stressed – as were the muscles around his neck – especially in his neck.

"I tried to ask some questions, but he did not respond to me. Others asked questions. He responded to only one man.

"I asked the one man that the Navy officer was responding to, to ask AFFA if he would arrange a flyby.

"The officer's arm jerkily wrote out, 'The time is not right.'

"I was convinced that there was something there. It didn't make much difference whether they were in contact with people from outer space or with someone right here on Earth. There was something there that we should have found out more about."

Friend returned to Wright-Patterson AFB and prepared a memo to his commanding general. The general said that he would take charge of further evaluation personally.

Unfortunately, Major Friend heard nothing more about the incredible communication with OEEV or its Earth project commander AFFA. After he retired, Major Friend did find out that Mrs. Swan had agreed to keep her participation with the Navy and CIA a secret. Nevertheless, the mystery remains of just what unknown forces were involved with the strange affair.

Spacemen of the Ouija

Depending on who you talk to, the Ouija board is considered either an entertaining toy or a portal into the fiery depths of Hell. Many a teenager has spent sleepless nights playing with the Ouija hoping for a good laugh, or a good scare. Either way, the Ouija board usually does not disappoint. For those who don't have apparent psychic abilities, the Ouija board offers a quick and easy way to try and contact the unknown realms that exist where our world ends and our imagination begins.

The Ouija board is often used in an attempt to contact those who have left the physical world behind and now, hopefully, continue to live on in the reality of spirit. At times, however, it is not one's great Aunt Maude that comes a calling through the board, but something even more bizarre.

From the website About.paranormal.com, author Stephen Wagner relates the story of Peter S., who was living in Saint Thomas' Mount in India. In 1964, Peter's visiting Aunt and Uncle Theo were operating the Ouija board when a "spirit" who called itself "Ithan" came onto the board. Ithan claimed to be from the planet Venus and informed the group that the popular singer Jim Reeves had just died in a plane crash. Ithan went on to say that the plane wreckage had not yet been found and it would be a couple of days before the news was made public.

UFOS - WICKED THIS WAY COMES: THE DARK SIDE OF THE ULTRA-TERRESTRIALS

Five months later, in December, 1964, Theo's brother-in-law Oscar from Calcutta came for a visit. While they were chatting about family matters, the story about the Venusian named Ithan came up. Oscar told his relatives that a few months back his family had also been fooling around with a Ouija board when it was taken over by a spirit that claimed to be from Venus. During the communication, they were also told that Jim Reeves had just died in a plane crash.

Equally shocking for everyone involved, this spirit also said its name was Ithan.

Peter S. ends his story in 1973 after his family had moved to Melbourne, Australia. As they were watching the TV show "A Current Affair," the announcer interviewed a Sydney clairvoyant, who claimed to be in regular psychic contact with a being from Venus, whose name was - Ithanus!

Beyond the Human Mind and Spirit

UFOs confound us with a number of different mysteries. First we have the mystery of UFOs themselves, unknown, seemingly solid objects that fly around our skies with impunity. Next, there are the UFO occupants that seem to come in as many unusual shapes and sizes as the vehicles they allegedly pilot. And last are the strange after-effects that are suffered by some people who have had contact of one form or another with a UFO.

The reactions that some people have after a UFO encounter indicate a connection between the eyewitness and the phenomena that may go beyond the physical and into the realms of the mind and even the spirit. The question we have to ask is: why would visitors from other planets induce paranormal or mystic responses from human observers? Perhaps we are making some broad assumptions about the true nature of UFOs. Or maybe we are asking the wrong questions altogether.

One of the most striking innovations within contemporary North American Spiritualism is the adoption of extraterrestrials as spirit guides by some contemporary Spiritualists. This comes from Jennifer E. Portera in her article "Spiritualists, Aliens and UFOs: Extraterrestrials as Spirit Guides." Portera says that "Extraterrestrials have come to represent for many Spiritualists the successful achievement of the ultimate Spiritualist goal: the union between spirituality and science. Extraterrestrials are seen as spiritually superior to us because their science exceeds our own; their 'science' is perceived superior because it incorporates recognition of spiritual 'truth.' Consequently, within the North American Spiritualist context, the adoption of extraterrestrials as spirit guides can be seen both as a 'rationalization' of Spiritualist belief through a strong idealization of 'science,' and as a critique of orthodox science for ignoring the 'spiritual' realm. For several of the Spiritualists with whom I worked, extraterrestrials have consequently become excellent choices for spirit guides."

Jerome Clark and Loren Coleman, in their book "The Unidentified," state as their "First Law of Para-UFOlogy" that the UFO mystery is primarily subjective and symbolic. While they admit that the phenomenon is not without objective aspects, they maintain that such manifestations are only "subsidiary" displays "whose cause can be traced to certain extrasensory functions of the brain." Their "Second Law of Para-UFOlogy" says that the objective manifestations associated with UFOs are "psychokinetically-generated by-products of those unconscious processes which shape a culture's vision of the Otherworld. Existing only temporarily, they are at best only quasi-physical."

There are numerous theories regarding the UFOs' place of origin and their true identity. Every investigator has their personal favorite location, whether physical or ethereal. Generally, these arguments are distilled to the central issue of whether the UFO intelligences are essentially physical beings from some other physical planet, or nonphysical beings from an invisible realm in our own world. Conceivably both theories may be correct.

Rendezvous With The Unknown

Author Regan Lee says that the psychic aspect of UFOs seems to be too often ignored or dismissed by many researchers who perceive it as a "New Age-y" element that is an embarrassment to "serious" UFO researchers. However, Lee suggests that there is a psychic thread within the UFO experience, and it is dishonest to ignore it since UFO lore is full of stories of people who have had psychic or telepathic experiences within the context of their UFO encounter.

UFOS - WICKED THIS WAY COMES: THE DARK SIDE OF THE ULTRA-TERRESTRIALS

Gail Mangas of Toledo, Ohio, had no interest in UFOs or the paranormal. She was a divorced mother of two children and a waitress for a local restaurant, with little time to do anything else except care for her family – that is until she had a rendezvous with the unknown.

One night, as she drove home from work, Gail noticed a strange light in the sky that seemed to be following her car. The light was reddish in color and about the size of a half-dollar held at arm's length. When Gail was about a mile from her home, along a particularly deserted stretch of road, the light suddenly zoomed out of the sky and positioned itself directly in front of the car.

"I was absolutely terrified," she remembered. "The object blocked the road so I had to stop or risk running into it. Its light was so bright that I had to shield my eyes with my hand."

Before Gail had a chance to react, the weird light disappeared just as suddenly as it had appeared. Shaken, Gail drove the rest of the way home without further incident. She might have forgotten about her unusual experience if it wasn't for what occurred to her afterwards.

"That was the point where my life changed completely," she said. "I became interested in science and math and read everything I could get my hands on. This was so unlike me; I had barely graduated from high school and now I was reading books that were written for scientists. And the really weird thing was that I understood them."

Gail also noticed that along with her increased intelligence she had also developed the power to heal and to tell what others were thinking.

"It was as if the UFO awakened some part of me that had laid dormant all of my life," she said. "I can't explain it, but I know deep inside that I have been chosen somehow."

Gail also said that she has the feeling that some other intelligence is guiding her to develop both mentally and spiritually. She feels that she has some mission to fulfill for mankind in the future.

"I don't know what my mission will be – I only know that I am not the only one to be contacted this way. There are thousands, maybe millions of others on this planet that are being prepared for something truly great in the future."

UFOS - WICKED THIS WAY COMES: THE DARK SIDE OF THE ULTRA-TERRESTRIALS

Enhanced Evolution

Gail Mangas's experience is not unique. Throughout history there have been others who have touched the unknown and returned changed somehow. Perhaps we are experiencing a sort of enhanced evolution, intended to carry humankind quickly beyond this point in our development when our passions often outweigh our intelligence. Jacques Vallee, in his book "Dimensions," writes that the UFO phenomenon is one of the ways through which an alien form of intelligence of incredible complexity is communicating with us symbolically, and that the paranormal phenomena associated with UFOs are one of the manifestations of a "spiritual control system for human consciousness."

Perhaps somewhere there is an intelligence that can see our potential as an enlightened species and has made it their mission to see us through these difficult times by awakening our hidden, spiritual capabilities. We may have an important role to play on the universal stage. Maybe UFOs, and the Ultra-terrestrials, are here to show us the hidden meaning between the lines of our lives.

Write for our FREE catalog:

Global Communications

P.O. Box 753

New Brunswick, NJ 08903

www.conspiracyjournal.com

mrufo8@hotmail.com

UFOS – WICKED THIS WAY COMES: THE DARK SIDE OF THE ULTRA-TERRESTRIALS

OVER 90 TITLES AVAILABLE ON KINDLE AND NOOK. BOOKS CAN BE DOWNLOADED FROM ANY PC.

SURVEY THE HEIGHTS AND DEPTHS OF MYSTERIOUS MOUNT SHASTA AS YOU READ THE BOOK THAT ALTERED SHIRLEY MACLAINE'S LIFE AND CHARTED THE SPIRITUAL PATHS OF THOUSANDS OF DEVOTED BELIEVERS OVER THE COURSE OF A CENTURY

"DWELLER ON TWO PLANETS" BY PHYLOS REMAINS AT THE HEART OF THE NEW AGE MOVEMENT

Now read our **UPDATED NEW EDITION** – Edited And Grammatically Revised For Easier Comprehension For The Modern Reader By Sean Casteel With New Material Added By Nick Redfern, Timothy Green Beckley And Paul Dale Roberts

The original **DWELLER ON TWO PLANETS** is said to be one of the most important texts of the 19th Century. For over a hundred years it has been passed around among those seeking the true Spiritual Path to life. Many have said it has impacted them greatly. Actress Shirley MacLaine had little interest in the occult when she was browsing in a Hong Kong bookstore only to have this work literally fall into her hands. It led to many changes in her life and a metaphysical best seller of her own, *Out On A Limb*.

Young author/channel Frederick S. Oliver spins a tale so compelling and so spiritually uplifting that it is doubtful that it was written by him alone as a human being. The reader will immediately see that such a wealth of detail about Atlantis and the spiritual reality could not be conjured from the imagination of an eighteen year old while working as a simple fence mender for his father who raised cattle near their home along the base of the mysterious and legendary Mount Shasta in Northern California.

Oliver foreshadows much of what would come after him, like the feminist movement of the 20th Century, the coming of UFOs with their external multicolored revolving lights and the interiors of the craft lit by some unseen light source, details verified repeatedly by modern day alien abductees and UFO contactees. In fact, many of the illustrations in this book of cigar-shaped craft look remarkably like the ships said to have been photographed by George Adamski and others decades later. Oliver, while in the channeling state, held in the thrall of an Atlantian and ancient Tibetan soul, also predicts television and cell phones in a time that predated even rudimentary radio.

Says Sean Casteel, who updated this major work into modern grammar and phraseology:

"The moral dynamics of the story will hold you spellbound, as the sins of one man's incarnation in Atlantis are repaid in his life as a gold miner in the American West. The story of the latter's initiation into a deeply secret gathering of spiritual adepts and how it leads to adventures in other dimensions will open your eyes to mysteries you never knew existed. . .This book is truly a message from the other side, and contains within it countless solutions to the many enigmas we contemplate today, and will restore your faith in the coming of a New Age promised land."

In addition to the "modernized text" you will join researchers Nick Redfern, Tim Beckley and Paul David Roberts as they reveal the many mystical secrets of Mount Shasta, widely regarded as a transformational vortex. Learn of inner earth entrances, the man who lives forever, the existence of Bigfoot on Mount Shasta, and ghost stories that will thrill you.

The book is fully illustrated and graphically designed by "Adman" William Kern. Printed in large format, it will captivate and entice the reader and provoke much thought.

Order The Secrets Of Mount Shasta
and A Dweller On Two Planets for $22.00 + 5.00 S/H.

WANT TO LEARN MORE?
If you missed our earlier work
MYSTERIES OF MOUNT SHASTA: HOME OF THE UNDERGROUND DWELLERS AND ANCIENTS GODS simply add $20.00 to your order.
Both books will impact you greatly!
TIMOTHY G. BECKLEY, BOX 753, NEW BRUNSWICK, NJ 08903

UFOS - WICKED THIS WAY COMES: THE DARK SIDE OF THE ULTRA-TERRESTRIALS

www.ingramcontent.com/pod-product-compliance
Lightning Source LLC
Chambersburg PA
CBHW081915170426
43200CB00014B/2737